W9-CPE-381

WOMEN'S COMIC VISIONS

Humor in Life and Letters Series

A complete listing of the books in this series can be found at the back of this volume.

WOMEN'S COMIC VISIONS

edited and introduced by
June Sochen

Wayne State University Press Detroit

Manufactured in the United States of America.
95 94 93 92 91 5 4 3 2 1

Library of Congress Cataloging-in-Publication Data

Women's comic visions / edited and introduced by June Sochen.
p. cm. — (Humor in life and letters)
ISBN 0-8143-2307-3 (alk. paper). — ISBN 0-8143-2308-1 (pbk. : alk. paper)
1. American wit and humor—Women authors—History and criticism. 2. Women and literature—United States. 3. Women comedians—United States. I. Sochen, June, 1937– . II. Series.
PS430.W6 1991
306.4′81—dc20 90-21070

The book was designed by Mary Primeau.

To the memory of my father, Sam Sochen
(1905–1990), who always appreciated laughter

Contents

Introduction

June Sochen

If the way women have been treated as givers and receivers of humor was not so sad and absurd, it would be funny. After all, can any reasonable person in the late twentieth century take Schopenhauer, Bergson, and Freud seriously, those heavy thinkers of the last century, when they declared that women had no sense of humor? Their further pontifications that women's feeble attempts at comedy were pathetic are best ignored, surely not to be treated seriously or even humorously. Because their views reflected the dominant thinking of the period, they went largely unchallenged. Their weighty reputations in philosophy and psychology gave them the authority to speak on any and all subjects. It is an unfortunate example of their continued power that many discussions of contemporary women's humor, by women, begin with lengthy and erudite refutations of the nineteenth-century writings.

One of the most powerful new perspectives on knowledge in the 1970s and 1980s is the cultural one; members of various academic disciplines now view all ideas, all knowledge, as shaped by the cultural environment in which the ideas are created. Literary scholars, historians, and anthropologists (often leaders in this field) have become increasingly aware of the power of context in analyzing any text, be it a novel, a stage performance, or a political debate. When they analyze the writings of Freud, for example, they recognize his origins in his time and place; the male viewpoint that dominated his education, his family, and his Vienna provide a different angle from which to study his ideas. While every age has its rebels, its critics of the prevailing ideology, Freud emerges as a creative synthesizer of the old (ideas about women) with the new (his invention of the unconscious and psychoanalysis).

It takes a great deal of imagination and integrity to challenge majority opinion. George Bernard Shaw, Henrik Ibsen, and John Stuart Mill, among others, had those qualities, and it is no accident that one of the major idea systems that they attacked was the one regarding women's nature and status in society. They redefined woman's creative power to include the ability to write a poem, acquire an education, and, yes, maybe even imagine a funny story. The nineteenth-century rebels were able to imagine rational, independent women and, by extension, women who were capable of every kind of human enterprise, including being funny.

However, because the conservative point of view dominated, and the rebellious one, albeit a powerful one, was looked at suspiciously by all lovers of the status quo, it took a very long time to overthrow the long-held notions about women's alleged lack of capacity to laugh and to create laughter. It is only in recent years, thanks to the women's movement, that women scholars have taken charge of their scholarship and have laid to rest many male assumptions about women's role in human events. Surely one of the areas of knowledge that was crying out for attention was women and humor. The alleged literature in the field, prior to the women's entry, as already suggested, was consistently of one voice, negative and disbelieving, or, more often, simply ignoring women's contributions in the field.

Women scholars of humor have had the mighty task of retrieving examples of women humorists in earlier centuries; simultaneously, they have had to assess how these women humorists had been received in their own day and, in the case of those women who had been successful in their time, figure out why they have been forgotten by subsequent generations. It is in this regard that the awareness of cultural hegemony comes into play. Contemporary audiences have never heard or read popular domestic humorists of the last century; they have never heard of Frances Whitcher or Marietta Holley. Because the male interpreters of acceptable and respectable literature ignored the popular writings of women domestic humorists, their writings went out of print and eventually out of living memory.

Thanks to the cultural perspective and the supportive environment of the contemporary women's movement, women scholars can replace their anger, exasperation, and frustration with explanations, understandings, and the ammunition to rewrite the past, resurrect the forgotten women humorists, and redress the balance. It is the feminism born of the contemporary reform movement that gives women scholars the framework, the philosophy, and the will to understand how scholarship has been largely in the hands of WASMs (my term: White Anglo-Saxon Males) until recently and that they have controlled the canon of "respectable" literature that has been taught to every succeeding generation of students; in turn, the male scholars have given publishers the cue about which authors to publish and reprint. Mark Twain became a major nineteenth-century example of American humor, surely a worthy choice, but Marietta Holley, another good humorist, was excluded and thereby vanished into obscurity.

The long absence of domestic humorists from our anthologies and college courses points to another long-held cultural value in America: the denigration of domestic activities, practitioners, and products. Women as the primary agents in the domestic realm, a realm decidedly inferior to the public arena—the business world, the government, and the public museums and concert halls—have been undervalued; so have their efforts. Therefore, it is entirely logical and consistent to underrate the writings of domestic humorists. Men avoid the kitchen and the nursery, the cleaning and the cooking in the home, as much as they can. Their work is surely superior. Humor associated with politics, business, and other male pursuits ranks higher in the hierarchy of humor than women's domestic humor. Twain makes fun of politicians and current events; Whitcher jokes about gossipy women and the annoyances of homemaking. Guess whose humor is preserved?

Feminist scholars are actively recovering the literature of women's domestic humor. Researchers Jane Curry and Linda Morris, for example, have recovered and restored the marvelous writings of Frances Miriam Whitcher (1814–1852) and Marietta Holley (1836–1926). Other even less known, and less successful, women humorists are presently being discovered. Holley, we learn, was very successful in her day. She wrote twenty-one books based on the observations of her feminist heroine, Samantha Allen. Readers eagerly looked foward to Samantha's funny thoughts on husbands, politicians, and women's issues. But she was more of an exception than the rule. And this fact points to another observation regarding the cultural view of women and their work. The best-selling women writers of the nineteenth-century, and there were very many, wrote romantic and melodramatic tales, often morally uplifting stories. They devoted their considerable talents to writing fiction that reflected the dominant values of the time rather than create witty, farcical, or satiric commentaries on American life. Knowing what the culture expected of them, women responded accordingly. Those interested in writing—and many did so to earn a living (note Hawthorne's exasperated remarks about his competition, the female scribblers)—knew of their audiences' tastes and preconceptions, and they wrote for them.

Indeed, the literary humor genre, though overwhelmingly a male province, is a minor field of literature. There have never been many practitioners of written humor. Mark Twain's comic performances, his live presentations, were probably his greatest accomplishments, at least to his contemporaries. This fact suggests another dimension to this most complex subject: humor thrives in an oral setting, in a performance mode, not as written and read material. People laugh aloud in an audience of laughers far more readily than in the solitary setting of their living room. And performance, especially in the nineteenth-century, occurred in a public place, clearly the male territory, not the female one.

Women's place was decidedly in the home, not the lecture hall, the burlesque stage, or the saloon. The setting for humor is a very important factor, and American culture offered no public settings for women's humor then. The context, the convivial environment, was—and still is—essential for the production and expression of humor. Women's humor, and men's humor, is often verbal and visual, not literary and silent. If this line of thinking is valid, then would it not be reasonable to assume that women's funny conversations, in the confines of their kitchens and parlors, and directed to their families and neighbors, have always existed but have been lost to subsequent generations? This thesis would also suggest that folklorists and anthropoligists may be better equipped to retrieve the funny stories and humorous tales that grandmothers told their daughters and granddaughters than literary critics or historians. Indeed, the emerging literature in this field suggests that that very phenomenon is occurring. The oral tradition has also been elevated to a status of respectability in scholarly circles only recently. Traditional fields of knowledge such as literature and history have been slow to recognize the importance of the spoken word as text worthy of investigation. By pursuing this more novel path, women's humorous tradition may be reinstated, resuscitated, and reentered into the field of humor.

Men could be satirists and physical comics. Preferably, women were neither, but if they ventured into this culturally forbidden land, they should only display restrained wit—sly humor, perhaps, but not raucous, screaming, demonstrative stuff. In the twentieth century, however, women have defied this cultural taboo and become throwers, as well as receivers, of pies in the face; they have slipped on bananas on television, and they even, in the intimate setting of the cabaret and nightclub, tell dirty jokes. Earlier in the century, black women performers shared their witty observations about life and love with their black audiences. Recently, in the not-so-intimate setting of a concert hall, Bette Midler has strutted across the stage and boldly challenged cultural mores about women and humor. Even more recently, feminist-lesbian Kate Clinton has entertained and enlightened largely women's audiences with her outrageous humor.

It is in performance, primarily in the twentieth-century, that women's humor has entered the public arena for all to see. It can no longer be hidden. Though gaining access to a public forum is difficult, it is not as difficult as getting your writings published by the few established New England publishers who determined what literature was. In dingy basements, public parks, cut-rate recording studios, and segregated nightclubs, black and white women sang bawdy songs, wryly joked about the woman's dilemma, and by their gestures and costumes broke all of the rules regarding proper women's behavior. They also demonstrated, by their words and actions, that Freud and his cohorts knew nothing about women's comic, antic, and anarchic possibilities. And audiences enthusiastically embraced these women comic performers and ensured their continued performances.

The power of cultural attitudes is great but not omnipotent. There are always brave souls challenging from the margins and, when the opportunity arises, within the mainstream. I don't think it is accidental that many great women comic performers in this century are minority women. Black and Jewish women are overrepresented in statistical terms; they far exceed their numbers in the population. But perhaps they have a double advantage: as women and as members of a discriminated-against minority, they understand the strengths and foibles of their oppressors. Part of the necessary equipment of a humorist is an astute understanding of human nature, the weaknesses of all of us. As outsiders looking in, women—black and Jewish women particularly—became sensitive commentators on American life. As survivors, they laughed rather than cried at their observations; as generous women, they shared their humor with others so that they, too, could laugh and not cry.

The humorous angle of life, of course, is a special one and though we all have the capacity to laugh, we do not all, in equal quality, have the ability to make others laugh. It is a special talent to interpret both everyday life and extraordinary moments with humor and a gentle or savage eye. Our culture surely does not encourage, raise, or train women to express themselves aggressively or cruelly. Within the wide spectrum of humorous expressions, these unattractive characteristics appear more often in male form. But again, with the awakening of feminism, the increase in women's education, the improvement in communication, and this culture's love of the unusual, the unique, and the audacious, vulgarity, crudity, and cruelty have become acceptable comic forms for women.

Of the two types of humor, written and oral, I would assume that women have been active practitioners of both, though probably more of them have been oral comics than writers. Earlier in this century, when the *New Yorker* magazine became the premier magazine of wit, Dorothy Parker was widely viewed as the sole exemplar of women's wit, the token woman literary humorist. Her fast tongue, faster than any gun in the West, was reputed to be so lethal and accurate that no one went to the washroom during the long lunches at the Algonquin. Contemporary domestic humorists, who were considerably gentler in their material and tone, also existed, though their reputations never reached the heights of Parker's. Erma Bombeck, the best-known writer of domestic humor today, is enormously popular and effective. Domestic humor has never died; it has had a continuous audience, and today it can be read daily in the newspapers.

Verbal humor was performed humor, comedy on the burlesque, vaudeville, and nightclub stages, settings not congenial to women. As I will discuss in my essay later in this volume, cultural attitudes, as well as circumstances, had to be changed before women comic performers could participate in slapstick or bawdy humor. Situation comedy, in a sense, could be interpreted as domestic humor in performance. Bombeck writes about domestic situations which Lucille Ball humorized in a visual and verbal medium. The movies, radio, and television have transformed the comic environment and have given women opportunities they lacked in earlier times and in other formats. In the last two decades, thanks to the women's liberation movement, open discussions of sexuality, higher education for women, and economic opportunities for more women have transformed all discussions of women's humor. Not only is it acknowledged that women have a sense of humor, but its multiple expressions seem entirely natural.

Rarely does one volume bring together the theoretical and the practical, the literary and the performing. *Women's Comic Visions* proposes to do just that. Philosophers and psychiatrists have theorized about humor while contemporary feminists and social commentators have undertaken analyses of women and humor. The theoreticians rarely act out their theories, while the practitioners rarely know the theories. Each operates independently of the other. Most collections are also confined to literary humor, with no attention given to women performers in the popular media of this century. *Women's Comic Visions* begins the new exploration. It brings Moms Mabley, Bette Midler, and Lucille Ball into the forefront as able performers of verbal comedy. It discusses women cartoonists like Helen Hokinson and Nicole Hollander, as well as domestic humorists such as Jean Kerr and Erma Bombeck.

All of the contributions, originally commissioned for this volume (with the exception of Nancy Walker's "Nineteenth-Century Women's Humor" and Zita Dresner's revised "Domestic Comic Writers"), use American cultural examples and personalities. They all base their judgments on products of America's ambivalent set of attitudes and values toward women and humor. The rhetoric of equality and democracy was, until recently, not applied to women's lives, while the reticent views on women's sexuality and the humorous potential in this material is only currently being explored. There are common threads that unite the three sections of this book: the multiple roles that humor plays in women's lives, the shared experiences of women in this culture, the shared grievances, and the shared discoveries. The staid and the bawdy women comics have also shared a marvelous sense of the absurd in their surroundings and their lives; with male comics, they have recognized the value of humor in offering relief, escape, solidarity, and amusement to all of us.

This collection of original essays brings together the latest thinking and research of an interdisciplinary group of scholars; literary critics, psychologists, historians, and folklorists all participate. Interestingly, their viewpoints and their evidence often overlap. Sometimes, each arrives at the same conclusion as the others by way of a different path; but often they cross disciplinary borders to explore the material and the perspectives of all disciplines that discussed the rarely treated subject of women and humor. One of the recent discoveries of women scholars in all fields has been that interdisciplinary knowledge is de rigueur; the very field of women's studies both demands and invites such a perspective.

Women's Comic Visions enters a relatively new domain. Women have been ignored by most "experts" on humor until recently, and the whole field of American humor still occupies a modest space in the larger field of American literature. With the active support and interaction of a contemporary women's movement and an enlarged sorority of women scholars, women humorists will become regular members in the club of American culture studies.

PART ONE

Theories of Women's Humor

Humoring the Sentence: Women's Dialogic Comedy

Judy Little

For several thousand years, any woman who became literate and who ventured to write learned to "humor" the sentence which she borrowed from a culture and language very largely designed and dominated by her father, her husband, or her sons and brothers. She humored the sentence; that is, she had to get along with it, be nice to it, and give in to it enough so that she could make it give in to her at least some of the time. In doing this, women have also humored the sentence in another way—they have carnivalized it. Those women writers who have a sense of a woman's peripheral yet invested position within a male-dominated culture have given their sentences the license of carnival, a license to overturn, to mimic, and to "deconstruct." Especially in the sentences of women who write comedy, there is a double-voiced tension or "dialogic imagination," to use Mikhail Bakhtin's term, which immerses the piece in a subtle rebellious mockery.

A woman's discourse usually carries with it some hint of the language and worldview of the patriarchal structures in which she lives. There is, as Gilbert and Gubar emphasize, quoting Emily Dickinson, an "infection in the sentence."[1] But one might also say that the infection from the male language and culture produces antibodies; there is a "dialogic" tension, often comic, between the two "voices" that contend in the same sentence. In his examination of Dostoyevski's fiction, Bakhtin describes and illustrates extensively just how a character's own voice (as it muses in first-person or in third-person indirect discourse) will include phrases and sentences that show someone else's worldview and style. In texts and in life, an individual shares a language with others, with an entire culture. "The word in language is half someone else's," Bakhtin notes in *The Dialogic Imagination.* In the literary text, the voice of a character and the voice perhaps of someone with whom that character has recently been talking will collide and evaluate each other within the ongoing thoughts of the musing character. The juxtaposition of the two voices may result in ridicule of one of the voices and of the ideology it brings along, speech diversity being "an indispensable prerequisite for comic style." Indeed, parody can be used as "an exposé to destroy" the language of another.[2]

The comic style of many women writers shows some of these dialogic qualities, or deconstructive qualities, to use Derrida's more drastic term. Luce Irigaray, for instance, in *Speculum of the Other Woman,* inserts entire phrases (sometimes without quotation marks or italics) from Plato and later male philosophers into her own ongoing, teasing exposé of the oppressive effect these ideas have had on women. This dialogic, often harshly comic style is a major feature of the writing of certain French feminists like Irigaray and Hélène Cixous, those writers of an *écriture féminine.* Sandra Gilbert, in her introduction to the English translation of *The Newly Born Woman* by Hélène Cixous and Catherine Clément, asserts that some American writers, such as Susan Griffin, also employ a style similar to that of the French feminists, a style that tries to reverse the usual ideologies and strategies of discourse; Gilbert calls this style a "creative hysteria."[3] The style is essentially dialogic; it deconstructs or exposes the ideologies of authority and power, often by juxtaposing the male voice of solemn formality and the female voice of buoyant hysteria. Such double-voiced discourse relativizes the social and political hierarchies implicit in the teased (male-enunciated) ideology, and the result is a "carnivalization" of dialogue, as Bakhtin calls it in *Problems of Dostoevsky's Poetics.*[4]

In order to carnivalize the voice of authority and power, the rebel comic voice must use that authoritative voice, must parody or mimic it. As Derrida describes the process, a deconstructive discourse "borrows from a heritage the resources necessary for the deconstruction of that heritage itself."[5] What is the heritage that is most likely to be comically violated when women writers carnivalize their discourse? It is the heritage of a discourse of power and control, of law and taboo. Although some have disagreed with the details of Michel Foucault's analysis of Western culture's understanding of sex, women, and power, his overall argument is respected and convincing. He argues in *The History of Sexuality* that a culture's perception of sexual behavior, sexual "perversion," the bodies of women, and the laws that regulate sex and the family are all a matter of ideology rather than scientific fact. Our understanding of these aspects of our culture constitutes a "deployment," a "technology of sex." Modern psychoanalysis is not so much a science as an ideology, one way (among others that could have been used) of deploying the political options for controlling sexual activities.[6] The modern West has deployed a notion of power and law that has also defined a counterpart in the "hysterization of women's bodies." That is, women's bodies have been defined in terms of the uterus, fertility, and the supposed intrinsic pathology that is part of this delicate, female function. In the "creative hysteria" of women's discourse, then, it is not surprising that a comic tension frequently emerges between the (male) heritage of power and a rebellious "hysteria" that carnivalizes or mocks both itself and the phrases borrowed from a language of power.

This comic verbal tension requires a distinct self-reflective voice, a speaking or internally musing voice which can be the medium for the dialogic mimicry and parody within it. Bakhtin emphasizes this voice as a necessary medium, and he even argues that poetry and actual dialogue (as in the drama or in the dialogue passages of a narrative) are seldom fully internally "dialogic."[7] There needs to be a sense of *one* voice, but a conflicted voice in which more than one style and ideology contend. Such a voice may not be typical of realistic drama, but in some experimental plays by women juxtaposed styles occur occasionally within a voice, and the result is a carnivalized discourse. A strong dialogic comedy is also present in some of the poetry by women authors. Nevertheless, prose fiction does seem to be the richest source of women's comic discourse. Most of the following discussion deals with prose, although I want to begin with a few examples from drama and poetry.

In most dramatic literature, in texts written for performance, the major arena of tension (and of comedy) exists *between* the characters, between the bodies moving about as well as between the voices of the characters. A single character's self-reflective, internally dialogic discourse is not a necessary part of the dramatic medium, though such discourse is sometimes present. In the plays of writers such as Megan Terry and Maureen Duffy, a single voice or speech may include within it the parodied voice of (male) authority; that is, the speech is a dialogic, carnivalized discourse. Near the beginning of Terry's play *Calm Down Mother,* for instance, "Woman One" declares that she is Margaret Fuller and that she accepts the universe. The only other persons in the play are asked to respond as follows:

> TWO WOMEN (*assuming superior postures*): You had better. You had better. Carlyle said that you had better. You had better. You had better. You bet your butter. Carlyle said that you had better.[8]

This unison speech is dialogic in that Carlyle's authoritative advice (and controlling put-down) is repeated and distorted ("You bet your butter") so much that this "heritage" of power withers under the rebellious mockery that questions it. The same dialogic, conflicted speech also serves to question the assertion of "Woman One"—does she, can she, really accept the universe?

In performance, the "superior postures" (which in the performance that I saw also included "superior" facial expressions) reinforce the dialogic discourse with what we can call a *dialogic body language.* The bodies of women—of women who have not generally in our civilization spoken the words of law and power such as "You had better accept"—here assume the shoulders-back, chin-in power posture along with the power language of male authority. In so doing, the actors carnivalize both the language and the posture, and indeed the ideology of power itself. A dialogic body language will obviously be a major contributor to the impact of a performance, and to the impact of women's comic drama where verbal discourse is only one element of the medium.

There is, for instance, a vividly dialogic "body" in Maureen Duffy's *Rites.* A group of women in a public restroom beat and kill someone whom they take to be a male intruder—someone "spying" on them. After they have killed the person, who was dressed as a man, they realize it was a woman. This shocking, physical "deconstruction" of the intruder is an appropriate and powerfully symbolic climax to the play. The play's increasingly strident and comic discourse has been full of tension between the cultural presence of male authority and the desperate hysteria of the oppressed and suspicious women. The women in the play represent several classes (there are the lavatory attendants, office girls, two widows in their sixties, two younger women with a boy toddler), but all of them are in a sense "dressed" in the male-designed culture that has trivialized their lives. All of these women are disguised as men; that is, they speak the roles men have imposed on them. The dialogue and the individual discourse show the effects of the "hysterization" of women's lives. No matter what their class, these women have been preoccupied with playing the part of the womb, the fertile, comforting, unseen nourishers of men.

From time to time, various characters in Duffy's play mimic certain cultural scripts that have confined them: horoscopes, advice columns, recipes.[9] The character's voice mocks the cliché of the cultural script even while it repeats it, thus generating a kind of hysteria of resistance. And the resistance culminates in the ritual killing, a parody of a Dionysian fertility rite. In Duffy's *Rites,* however, there is little implication of rebirth and renewal. Although the women have attacked, in comic discourse and brutal action, the male-clothed culture that oppresses them, their own comic, dialogic speech still submits to that culture's clichés about women even while mocking the clichés.

A similar dialogic discourse in which submission and protest scrape against each other in violent comedy is present in poetry being written by women. In Margaret Atwood's poem "The Landlady," the writer's voice describes a sort of archetypal interior landlady whose "raw voice" is part of a "squabble going on below," and who "presides" over the writer's attempts to read, write, or dream of escaping. The landlady's power (she "presides," slams doors, stands and blocks the way) seems to exceed that of the writer. The landlady and her language imply a cultural or psychological inhibition or imprisonment, especially an imprisonment *within* womanhood, within the hysterization of women's concerns. In the writer's humorous, dialogic struggle with her, the landlady still rules the house and is "solid as bacon."[10]

Although a dialogic mingling of two languages in one voice is not a constant feature of Sylvia Plath's poetry, some of her most powerful work does have such a voice. Clearly, when the voice in "Daddy" says she "adores a Fascist," the languages of hysteria and power are colliding: "Every woman adores a Fascist, / The boot in the face, the brute / Brute heart of a brute like you."[11] Here the culture that "deployed" this sexuality of sentimental hysteria on the one hand and brute boots on the other is mocked by one voice that mimics an acceptance of such a destructive relationship.

Even more prominent is the dialogic voice in "Lady Lazarus." The speaker, like an accomplished performer of guerrilla theater, praises her own ability to capture her audience (that is, her oppressors, who have, of course, "captured" and abused her as a Jew, woman, sideshow freak). She mocks the language of power as she says, "O my enemy"—a king's phrase, the words of the guilty King Ahab when Elijah confronted him.[12] She mimics the language of the impresario or master of ceremonies ("The big strip tease. / Gentlemen, ladies") and the language of the learned "Doktor" whose "opus" she is, whose "great concern" she carnivalizes. Like a pedagogue of popular psychology, she analyzes and trivializes her own capacity for death and resurrection ("Dying / is an art, like everything else"). Yet the same voice throughout absorbs into its own zany hysteria these abusive power images and power languages. In the last line, Lady Lazarus declares, "And I eat men like air." She does. Literally, she does; she eats their "letters"; with her airy words she eats their airy words, their language. With its comic dialogic discourse, her language of creative hysteria has been eating the power languages of the men all along.

A much less aggressive and more domestic Lady Lazarus tries to resurrect her inspiration in Susan Griffin's prose poem "This Is the Story of the Day in the Life of a Woman Trying." Here the dialogic oppositions within the narrator's voice are not directly between male control and a resistant female hysteria. Instead, some rather literary storytelling phrases drift in and out of the worried mother's language of domestic oral colloquialism. All in one day, she is trying to write, trying to take care of a sick child, trying to line up a teaching job, hoping to line up a lover, trying to get a baby-sitter, and finally (climaxing this very brief piece) wondering about her daughter's refusal to eat. The initial sentences show both languages emerging and subsiding as the narrator's more literary consciousness maintains a pestering dialogue with her domestic and personal worries:

> This is the story of the day in the life of
> a woman trying to be a writer and her child got sick.
> And in the midst of writing this story someone called
> her on the telephone. And, of course, despite her
> original hostile reaction to the ring of the
> telephone, she got interested in the conversation
> which was about teaching writing in a women's prison,
> for no pay of course. . . .[13]

The first four words are rather formal; they announce a story. But the sentence comes to a comic and painful halt at the colloquial "got sick." Inspiration sticks at the domestic crisis. Soon a very literary and latinate diction ("despite her original hostile reaction") jerks the story back to a remote, objective narrator, yet the "got interested" and the rambling syntax (of a very long sentence which I did not quote in full) draw us again into the nervous language of the irritated mother. The repeated, frustrated "of course" emphasizes the obvious distractions and drawbacks (becoming interested but expecting no pay), as the language veers far away from the writerly, controlled diction and back to the run-on worries. The dialogic comedy in Griffin's portrait of an artist as mother protests the painful and limiting domestication of the woman's ambition and calling.

An earlier writer whose sentences tease and humor the language of her literary inheritance is Virginia Woolf. She was one of the first writers to recognize that a woman with literary aspirations could well find herself in conflict, as a woman, with the largely male-designed literary culture. Defining a certain distance from that culture, she announced in "Modern Fiction" that a free writer must look for a style and novelistic form that would have none of the authoritative formalities, "no plot, no comedy, no tragedy, no love interest or catastrophe in the accepted style."[14] Her own style, along with that of other writers who used various forms of "stream of consciousness," is heavily dialogic; that is, a given consciousness almost always mingles his or her own language with the language and ideology of others as these languages merge or conflict with the musing consciousness. In the consciousness of Woolf's characters and narrators, these dialogic mergings are often comic, and they very frequently highlight the conventions of authority (literary, social, sexual) and a resisting freedom.

All of Woolf's novels make use of dialogic comedy. Centuries of English discourse flow through the mind of the narrator and supposed "biographer" of Orlando. The vital, long-lived Orlando, whose flexible gender alters from male to female near the beginning of the eighteenth century, maintains an evaluative dialogue with the languages and ideologies of her past and present. As she continually adjusts her clothes, behavior, and language to the gender decorum of the era, almost every sentence is dialogic. Near the end of the novel, the female Orlando at age thirty-six (but the "biography" began with Orlando as an Elizabethan boy of sixteen) drives her car toward her ancestral estate. While she tries to understand and sum up her varied experiences, she and the narrator play havoc with the usual authority structures that hold a literary work together. Many of Orlando's earlier "selves" (male, female, young, older) pop into the meditation with a single phrase or question. Every three or four sentences, the narrator, with comic irrelevance, also pops in with a parenthesis that tells us the obvious: "here another self came in."[15] While Orlando, in dialogic comedy, struggles with a "self" that is not confined to the conventional gender structures of power or hysterization, the narrator struggles with the conventions of "biography" and seems ready to concede that the biographer's authority is illusory.

Even in her first experimental novel, *Jacob's Room,* Woolf had developed a dialogic narrator who seems humorously puzzled and playful about the entire business of writing. It is as though the narrator tries, but fails, to take seriously a very serious, even tragic, story about a quite British young man who quits himself well in all the classic passages of male initiation, including the university, love, a tour of Italy and Greece, and death in the Great War. The narrator feigns ignorance of her fictional character and implies sometimes that she, as a female narrator, finds a young man's culture rather foreign and amusing. The third-person discourse, edging into Jacob's own consciousness, moves comically back and forth, for instance, between the serious young man's attempt to appreciate the Italian landscape and the narrator's tourist discourse about how "scenic" it all is:

> These Italian carriages get damnably hot with the afternoon sun on them, and the chances are that before the engine has pulled to the top of the gorge the clanking chain will have broken. Up, up, up, it goes, like a train on a scenic railway. Every peak is covered with sharp trees, and amazing white villages are crowded on ledges. There is always a white tower on the very summit, flat red-frilled roofs, and a sheer drop beneath. It is not a country in which one walks after tea.[16]

Several languages are in subtle comic conflict here, and they thoroughly disintegrate any pretensions the action may have to the status of a manful, Byronic pilgrimage. Jacob's youthful male language condemns the temperature and weighs the odds on the vehicle's achieving the summit. The (female) narrator enters with the voice of someone reading a children's story ("Up, up, up") and thus trivializes Jacob's quest. Her metaphor of the scenic railway and her urgent superlatives ("every peak," "amazing," "always") comically overstate the exclamatory response of the impressed tourist. Yet (the narrator shifts out of the tourist's language and into a fastidious reserve) no civilized British person, especially a British gentlewoman, would deign to walk in such rugged country after tea.

The comedy in the passage is dialogic in that several styles and ideologies collide in it. The contending ideologies tease and question several gender issues. Among these are the relationship of the doting mother (as Jacob's mother certainly is) to the son now going "Up, up, up" in Italy and in life; the relationship of the conventional tourist to the even more conventional and restricted Englishwoman presiding at tea; the relationship of a woman author and narrator to the powerful traditions of a male-designed culture (the tour, classic education, war) in which she lives and aspires to write. Although Woolf's dialogic comedy is more lyric and subtle, it probes the same basic conflicts that Foucault identified, conflicts that the comic sentences of Terry, Plath, and Griffin probe: the domestication of women and the established power of the male culture that has defined this "technology" of the sexes.

Many women novelists since Woolf have made effective comedy from a double-voiced discourse that teases the conventions of gender and power. Among these are Jean Rhys, Barbara Pym, and Christine Brooke-Rose, three writers who are not at all alike in the way they use dialogic comedy and for this reason will illustrate the flexibility of the double-voiced style.

The first-person narrators of Jean Rhys's novels persistently mock themselves (and all self-pitying outsiders and all self-congratulating insiders) with phrases they have picked up through the same desperate promiscuity with which they have picked up men. The comedy is bitter, and the Rhys heroine is bitter. The dialogic discourse feeds into the down-and-out woman's consciousness the malicious phrases of those (usually white British males) whose familiarity with power makes them insensitive to those who lack it. In *Good Morning, Midnight,* Sasha Jansen, after losing her job as a clerk in a Paris dress shop while "Mr. Blank" was inspecting it, repeats to herself the ancient sentimentality that somehow the suffering of *some* people contributes to a sense of fortunate well-being in others. She mimics the language of all the powerful Mr. Blanks: "We can't all be happy, we can't all be rich, we can't all be lucky—and it would be so much less fun if we were. Isn't that so, Mr. Blank? There must be the dark background to show up the bright colors."[17] The repetitions ("we can't all") mimic the rhetorical urgency and authority of a sermon or lesson, and after the repetitions collide with Sasha's smirking question, her discourse takes on the lofty tone of pedantic, philosophic illustration as she offers the poised analogy of dark background and bright colors. Sasha's dialogic, self-mocking hysteria sometimes resembles that of Plath's Lady Lazarus, except that the language of the Rhys heroine never "eats" that of her oppressor; instead, her style (and her life) is consumed by the languages and machinations of power.

At the end of Barbara Pym's *Excellent Women,* Mildred Lathrop, like Sasha, unenthusiastically argues herself into submitting to the way things are (as she perceives them), and her language is hilariously dialogic. Her words argue against themselves, like Sasha's, but the never-married Mildred, an "excellent woman" and pillar of church jumble sales, has long ago made some civilized concessions to her male-dominated society. As a result, her submission is more coy, ironic, and quiet—unlike Sasha's desperate, protesting surrender.

Gradually developing a tentative interest in Everard Bone, who is a rather stiff and self-centered anthropologist, Mildred responds to his dinner invitation and lets herself be coaxed into proofreading his manuscript. She seems to think that this will lead to something else (in a later novel of Pym's, we find that Mildred does marry Everard), and her thoughts ponder the future in understated comic horror. Bone suggests that when the proofreading becomes boring she can work on the book's index for "a nice change." Then it is as though his words (and his ideology about men and women) begin to infect her thoughts. She muses, "And before long I should be certain to find myself at his sink peeling potatoes and washing up; that would be a nice change when both proofreading and indexing began to pall. Was any man worth this burden? Probably not."[18] From proofing to indexing to peeling potatoes, Mildred seems to place her language and life at the disposal of Everard's language and life. Taking him at *his* word, her own sentence still protests with dialogic irony his definition of a "nice change." Both he and she apparently perceive a legitimacy in his authority (and his freedom to be creative) and an inevitability in the hysterization of her life. Yet Pym's distancing dialogic language preserves a sense of larger, open possibilities, even though her delicately and comically self-limiting characters (both the men and the women in her novels) usually are unadventurous and fail to take advantage of these larger possibilities.

By contrast, the characters in Brooke-Rose's comic experimental novel, *Amalgamemnon,* aggressively venture into larger possibilities. They seem confident of redefining the world with their language. They are eager to perpetrate revolutions, terrorist plots, dragon-slaying crusades, and a new "technology" of the sexes, simply by exploiting the carnivalizing power of language. The "frame" of this novel is the ongoing meditation of Mira, a professor who expects to lose her job very soon. The humanities, and hence scholars like herself, are becoming "redundant," she realizes. She invents several alter egos, some male and some female, and launches into sketchy narratives which run into each other as she imagines the future. Indeed, the entire text is written in future tense, with an occasional conditional voice thrown in.

The language of *Amalgamemnon* is dialogic in the extreme and comic in every phrase. Most of the language, and most of the overlapping narratives, are Mira's comic attempts to "deconstruct," as she says, the stifling language and ideology of men, especially of her several lovers.[19] Whether he is Willy (at the beginning of the novel) or Wally (near the end), the man in her life seems to her an "Amalgamemnon," an amalgamation of all the macho heroes, or Agamemnons, of history. In this pun, male heroism and Mira's judgment of male heroism collide dialogically in the same word. The Agamemnon in her life tends to ignore her intellectual interests. She enjoys reading and teaching Western classics, yet her own discourse is in constant comic dialogue with the phrases of male writers and the put-down phrases of her lover. Resenting that her relationship with Willy involves so much pretense, she notes, "Mimecstasy and mimagreement will always go together, like sexcommunication". Fake ecstasy and mimed agreement yield only a deceitful sex life and a relationship that resembles excommunication—outsiderhood and alienation.

The slipping and sliding comic discourse, as Mira considers possible futures, is a continual and liberating reminder of certain assumptions that Foucault and Derrida emphasize: cultural (and gender) institutions are in large part language, deployment, strategy. The language of authority preserves the social and psychological deployment of the male's power. As Mira begins to write her own story, and as her creative syllables begin to invade even the hero's name, her own sentimental hero, Willy, begins to lose his territory. He had anticipated that when she lost her job she would be dependent on him—"wholly mine," as he says, and at last "only a woman". But Mira's comically double-voiced language trespasses on the verbal preserve of the authoritative male. She experiments with a punning phrase that dialogically adopts the authority of mathematics and the godlike diction of fiat. "Let sex equal why", she says, examining the "why" of the X and Y chromosomes and questioning the usual gender myths; perhaps she envisions a new world, "ex almost nihilo", divinely creating it from nothing, merely by her authoritative word. Mira's carnivalizing of both the language of power and the language of submissive or strident hysteria constantly deconstructs these verbal and ideological gestures.

The dialogic comedy of Brooke-Rose's novel is a radical use of the double-voiced discourse which Bakhtin identified as integral to comic style, but the other writers I have considered here also play with the ideologies of style and exploit the opportunities for comic collision when these ideologies are juxtaposed. When these writers humor the sentence, they make it unsay, or partly unsay, what it seems to say. In so doing, these women expose the ambivalent structures of language and its implied worldview. Power is revealed as a linguistic posture (and a bodily posture in the case of drama), while gender categories unravel in the linguistic stripping. Whether we hear the reserved subtleties of Barbara Pym or the extravagant conflicts in the language of Sylvia Plath, whether the dialogic voice belongs to drama, poetry, or fiction, the result is a powerful comedy of a highly political nature. It is comedy that speaks a woman's voice even in a male culture and playfully overturns that culture in a deconstructive dialogue.

Notes

1. Sandra M. Gilbert and Susan Gubar, *The Madwoman in the Attic: The Woman Writer and the Nineteenth-Century Imagination* (New Haven: Yale University Press, 1979), 45–53.
2. Mikhail Bakhtin, *The Dialogic Imagination,* trans. Caryl Emerson and Michael Holquist, ed. Michael Holquist (Austin: University of Texas Press, 1981), 41–47, 293, 311, 364.
3. Sandra M. Gilbert, Introduction, *The Newly Born Woman,* by Hélène Cixous and Catherine Clément, trans. Betsy Wing (Minneapolis: University of Minnesota Press, 1986), xv.
4. Mikhail Bakhtin, *Problems of Dostoevsky's Poetics,* ed. and trans. Caryl Emerson (Minneapolis: University of Minnesota Press, 1984), 167.
5. Jacques Derrida, "Structure, Sign, and Play in the Discourse of the Human Sciences," in *The Languages of Criticism and the Sciences of Man,* ed. Richard Macksey and Eugenio Donato (Baltimore: Johns Hopkins University Press, 1970), 252.
6. Michel Foucault, *The History of Sexuality,* trans. Robert Hurley (New York: Vintage Books, 1980), 77–155.
7. Bakhtin, *Dialogic Imagination,* 285–97. Bakhtin does find

occasional dialogic discourse in Pushkin's *Eugene Onegin;* see *Dialogic Imagination,* 46–47.

8. Megan Terry, "Calm Down Mother: A Transformation for Three Women," in *Plays By and About Women,* ed. Victoria Sullivan and James Hatch (New York: Random House, Vintage, 1974), 279.
9. Maureen Duffy, "Rites," in *Plays By and About Women,* 345–77.
10. Margaret Atwood, "The Landlady," in *The Animals in That Country* (Boston: Little, Brown, 1968), 14–15.
11. Sylvia Plath, "Daddy," in *Ariel* (New York: Harper and Row, 1965), 49–51.
12. Sylvia Plath, "Lady Lazarus," in *Ariel,* 6–9. (And see 1 Kings 21:20 for the encounter between Ahab and Elijah.)
13. Susan Griffin, "This Is the Story of the Day in the Life of a Woman Trying," from *Like the Iris of an Eye* (Harper and Row, 1976); rpt. in *In Her Own Image: Women Working in the Arts,* ed. Elaine Hedges and Ingrid Wendt (Old Westbury, N.Y.: Feminist Press, 1980), 127.
14. Virginia Woolf, "Modern Fiction" (1919), in *Collected Essays* (London: Hogarth Press, 1966–67), 2:106.
15. Virginia Woolf, *Orlando* (New York: Harcourt Brace Jovanovich, 1956), 310–12. For a detailed discussion of comic discourse in *Orlando,* see my "(En)gendering Laughter: Woolf's *Orlando* as Contraband in the Age of Joyce," *Women's Studies* 16 (1988).
16. Virginia Woolf, *Jacob's Room* (London: Hogarth Press, 1945), 134.
17. Jean Rhys, *Good Morning, Midnight* (New York: Norton, 1986), 29.
18. Barbara Pym, *Excellent Women* (New York: Harper and Row, 1980), 255.
19. Christine Brooke-Rose, *Amalgamemnon* (Manchester: Carcanet, 1984), 14–15, 136, 82, 55.

Social Cognition, Gender Roles, and Women's Humor

Alice Sheppard

Women's humor is a topic in psychology that, when dealt with at all, appears elusive and enigmatic. It is rarely conceptualized at the theoretical level, and few attempts have been made to investigate differences between women's and men's humor.[1] A major reason for this neglect stems from psychologists' perpetuation of male-defined topics and tacit acceptance of male-derived standards. Women's humor is thus bypassed in the same way as various aspects of women's personality and experience have been.

Social psychologists interested in the influence of social values and beliefs on behavior have only recently sanctioned gender issues as a major focus. The impetus for change comes from the women's movement, which challenged the overgeneralization of male models, fallacies regarding female behavior, and the neglect of issues of special concern to women.[2] Feminist researchers called for a systematic evaluation of premises and methodology, reaching into such areas as personality, life-span development, and social behavior. These, in turn, set the stage for reconsidering psychological theories of humor.[3]

Correlatively, there has been a shift within social psychology, which has sought to redefine itself as "the study of the social mind."[4] By the 1960s, the concept of social cognition gained wide acceptance, encouraging recognition that belief systems are transitory and promoting the doctrine of cultural relativism.[5] Cognitive theorists argued that ideas shape the categories of social experience itself, thus paving the way for a revision in social theory, including an emphasis on gender-based cognitions. Institutions and ideology, the foundations of social knowledge, are interpreted as fabrications tied to a historical past. Once established, they serve to maintain patterns of social interaction and systems of collective meanings. In *The Social Construction of Reality,* Berger and Luckmann illustrate the meaning of social knowledge in a prototypic case, writing: "I know that 'woman talk' is irrelevant to me as a man, that 'idle speculation' is irrelevant to me as a man of action, and so forth."[6] Their statement additionally reveals the dualism of gender role within social frameworks. Social differentiation into male and female gender roles is integral to most societies. Within a social group, division of functions has been the genesis of roles, these roles evolving as behavior codes.[7] When various subgroups or classes are assigned roles, it gives rise to dominant/subordinate relations. Status, an attribute of role derived from the hierarchical organization of social groups, is elevated when applied to men's productions, which explains why women aspiring to "male" social roles may be admired merely for aspiring to high-status behaviors.

Behavior, cognition, and language underlie social reality, and each is affected by gender. Gender's influence on language is subtle and pervasive, embedded in the fabric of communication and thought. Philosopher Carolyn Korsmeyer termed the result a "hidden joke," when linguists claim adjectives as generically human or believe that linguistic forms for men and women are equivalent. Rather, she observed that frequently "the feminine counterpart of a masculine expression carries a different connotation," which she elaborated as follows: "Under certain conditions, female-designating terms connote something humorous or cute, trivial or ridiculous, where male-designating terms do not."[8]

Language is a constituent of humor, since most humor, if not explicitly verbal, relies on a knowledge of verbal concepts. Additional linguistic effects arise from the identification of male versus female characters or when the writer or performer is female. Deeply ingrained preconceptions and stereotypes affect comprehension, and feminists have been quick to note the difficulty most people have in figuring out riddles dealing with the surgeon's son or the two Indians.[9]

Classical theorists of humor, such as Thomas Hobbs and Henri Bergson, recognized the social foundations of humor. Hobbs's superiority theory made an interpersonal claim that we laugh by implicit comparison of others with ourselves. In Bergson's view, humor serves as a means of social group control; persons whose behavior differs from the norm are ridiculed, whether too avant-garde or passé. Neither specified women in his formulations, assuming a universalized human model typical of their day. It is now recognized that inherent social factors impeded the ability of Hobbs's seventeenth-century woman to feel superior to male compatriots. Bergson's turn-of-the-century female deviant appeared ridiculed more when she aspired to move beyond "woman's sphere," again revealing the social context.

The fact that males have dominated society and social thinking for so long is reflected in male-oriented and sexist humor, such as the cartoons found in *Playboy* or common office jokes. The very existence of misogynistic and sexist humor reveals an underlying imbalance in the humor field.[10] It also provides a foundation for intergroup conflict, primarily in men's humor directed toward women. As summarized by feminist psychologist Lee Marlowe, "Male sexual humor and demeaning characterizations of women maintain boundaries between women and men: men laugh at women; women must laugh at themselves.[11]

Social stereotypes are rampant within humor, from the stock characters of the comedy stage to jokes directed at ethnic, religious, and gender groups. Stereotypes, or generalizations about the members of a particular social group or social category, originate as part truths or may be totally unfounded. They tend to be self-perpetuating; once they are adopted, we "remember and interpret past events in the target's life history in ways that bolster and support these current stereotyped beliefs."[12]

Among gender stereotypes in historical American humor is the belief that women are fundamentally incompetent, of which a contemporary remnant is the woman driver. Similarly, the lady doctors, lady teachers, and other women professionals of the nineteenth century were assumed to be so devoid of womanhood that they could not get a man! Logic, foresight, and ability were not to be found in one's wife or mother-in-law.[13]

Another stereotype is woman's emotionality, often used to justify women's exclusion from professions and politics. Woman was deemed unfit for civic responsibility, as she was unable to overcome her emotional reaction to situations. In this form, emotion dislodges logic, preventing women from making rational decisions or discoveries. Ellen Levine extended this argument in her cartoon caption: "Because of their raging hormonal imbalances, women make better mothers than men."[14]

Incompetent, governed by her emotions, and valued chiefly for a youthful appearance, woman in sum was treated as a laughable character, the stock target of jokes, caricatures, and stage comedy. Psychologist Naomi Weisstein summarized this conceptualization: "That is, part of the present social definition of woman is 'ridiculous person.' Women have always been in part defined as 'ridiculous persons,' but there was a time when 'wife' and 'mother' was, in principle, honored."[15]

These stereotypes were applied to historic women and continue to exert an effect, even if somewhat diminished. For example, why can't we perceive women humorists as just "people"? Yet women in humor and comedy still find themselves allied in the audience's mind with women humorists of the past. For example, writer Fran Leibowitz has been proclaimed "the new Dorothy Parker," and cartoonist Cathy Guisewite has been viewed in the tradition of Dale Messick, creator of "Brenda Starr."[16]

We conceptualize "women humorists" as a special category because humor is implicitly defined as a male realm, and the terms *comedian, cartoonist,* and *humorist* are implicitly gender-referenced. We thus feel compelled to distinguish comediennes, woman/lady humorists and woman/lady cartoonists from their male counterparts.

Viewed retrospectively, it is easy to see why women found obstacles in becoming successful humorists. It also becomes understandable that so much of women's humor has been directed toward changing that social system, through ridicule and the effort to substitute alternative gender models. As for psychological theories of women's humor, we can begin with the growing body of literature that suggests that women's psychology has not been adequately conceptualized or studied. It is then recognized that humor, a social category, is not merely a behavior affected by socialization but one whose recognition, evaluation, and significance depend in turn on socially determined attitudes and perceptions. A cognitive-social theory of women's humor is needed.

The doctrine of sexual spheres provided an argument against nineteenth-century woman's entry into the marketplace, higher education, and politics. Increasingly segregating men and women between marketplace and home, it offered categories of description and justification for psychological differences between the sexes.[17] Anthropologist Mahadev Apte documented social institutions governing women's access to humor codes, reporting consistent subordination across cultures: "By restricting the freedom of women to engage in and respond to humor in the public domain, men emphasize their need for superiority. Men justify such restrictions by creating ideal role models for women that emphasize modesty, virtue, and passivity."[18]

The language and cognition of gender are fundamental to most cultures. Psychologist Lawrence Kohlberg believed that a rudimentary understanding of gender codes emerged during the child's early development. He theorized that gender role behavior was acquired by a process of cognition: I am a boy/girl, so I must engage in boy-/girl-appropriate activities. Turning to more advanced life stages, Elizabeth Beardsley argued that linguistic conventions of "genderization" influence concepts of personhood and self-identity.[19]

Studies of social perception offer additional theoretical constructs for the study of humor and gender. To begin with, an attributional process has been posited to explain social perception and social causality: "Attribution refers to the process of inferring or perceiving the dispositional properties of entities in the environment. These are the stable features of distal objects such as color, size, shape, intention, desire, sentiment, and ability."[20]

The model emphasizes that both physical and psychological traits are in fact perceived by the human cognizer, who, in turn, ascribes their origin to a probable source. Kelley has refined the formulation as follows: "The attribution to the external thing rather than to the self requires that I respond *differentially* to the thing, that I respond *consistently,* over time and over modality, and that I respond *in agreement* with a consensus of other persons' responses to it."[21]

Following attribution theory, we can consider humor as a trait to be socially attributed, a quality with a psychological basis, not merely a structural one.[22] Take, for example, the notion of incongruity, which many theories have recognized as basic to humor forms.[23] We further acknowledge that perception of incongruity is subjective, depending on the viewer's expectations and past experience. To be accepted as funny, an intention or configuration of humor must be attributed to the person or event. Adding to the complexity of attributions, the audience predisposition to laugh depends on social factors as well as attitudinal and cognitive ones.[24]

We have been discussing humor as if the major psychological process were the inference or judgment of funniness. Yet there are a number of proposals for two-stage processing. A study by Linsk and Fine proposed two processes: perception and evaluation. They tested this model using cartoons varying in liberalism/conservatism and feminism/chauvinism. As predicted, subjects differed in both their classifications and humor ratings, supporting the dual-process model. Jerry Suls indicated that for disparagement humor, cognitive processes may actually preclude consideration of humor:[25] "It is conceivable that at this first stage the humor perception process may terminate for those who sympathize with the disparaged party. The reason is simply that the depiction of a sympathetic character being treated badly may cause the respondent to interpret the communication as not being a joke."[26]

Of course, there are other cognitive factors that could suppress humor, such as inability or unwillingness to take an appropriate social perspective. Consider the following anecdote described by journalist Elizabeth Janeway:

> A couple of years ago, *Esquire* decided to put out an issue on women, edited by women. One of the women in charge asked me to contribute a piece responding to the familiar query, "Why Does the Women's Movement Have No Sense of Humor?" I did so. The woman editor called me to say it was fine. Two weeks passed. One morning the mail brought the article back, with a letter explaining that while the women doing the job enjoyed it,

> masculine top brass didn't feel that it was the thing at all—distinctly not funny.[27]

Though in the above example men and women differed in their judgments, the net result was that a sample of women's humor was categorized as unfunny. A number of social factors reduce the probable attribution of humor to women's productions, and the most basic include the expectation that women are unlikely to use humor, the limited knowledge and value of women's experience, the low status of women in society, and characterizations of women's gender role. Given a social perception in which the definition of woman contradicts a belief in her deliberate efforts at humor, males (and females) espousing traditional stereotypes will not view the product as humorous.

Another factor stems from men's and women's contrasting interests and experiences. Women's activities are often defined as trivial and uninteresting, evidenced by the snicker accompanying mention of women's clubs, coffee klatches, or even women's colleges. Likewise, compare the amount of television viewing time devoted to women (engaged in activities typically of interest to women) to that for men. Hidden and relegated to private conversations between women, child rearing, domestic tasks, and even women's social concerns remain outside the realm of most men's familiarity. Yet if men are not expected to appreciate women's jokes, how does one explain the converse, that male humorists attract a universal following? Haven't women claimed to enjoy Will Rogers, Mark Twain, Charlie Chaplin, and George Burns?

It has been known for some time that humor in a social setting is initiated by someone of higher status. Women, of course, are recognized as being of lower status than males. When a person of low status initiates a joke, the judgment may be that it is inappropriate for that person to be joking. In that case, indignation supplants amusement, and any tendency to respond humorously is suppressed from the outset.[28]

Finally, consider women's role definitions. Can a woman be passive and control an audience? Can a person serve as attractive sex object and comedian? From cognitive theories, we posit these pairs as incompatible, and thus the social inference denies the humor. The cognitive or attributional model takes us some distance in understanding women's humor. It is not argued that this is the only explanation, or even itself a sufficient one, but rather it constitutes a set of factors that exert psychological control.

A different psychological approach focuses on the designation of women as a social subgroup and applies principles of group process to the construction and function of humor.[29] The unit of analysis becomes the group, both intergroup and intragroup, and issues include how women use humor, where it originates, and the social functions it serves with respect to this group.[30]

A social group endorses patterns of behavior, serving as a reference point and a source of identity. Any collective human category may designate a social group, which implies that groups may differ in the degree to which members adopt characteristic traits or are influenced in attitudes and values. For example, one may be a Catholic, a Republican, a Pennsylvanian, a Vassar graduate, a PTA member, and a woman. Each of these offers different levels of likely association, as well as unequal importance for personal identity.

Recent studies have emphasized the social group as pivotal in the genesis of humor. Principles formulated under such names as reference group, identification class, and disposition theory support similar conclusions. From research using Catholics, Jehovah's Witnesses, southern Baptists, and agnostics, Lawrence La Fave derived the following principle in 1961: "Jokes tend to be judged as funny by Ss whose reference (identification) group is esteemed, and whose outgroup is disparaged, and to be judged unfunny by Ss whose reference group is disparaged and whose outgroup is esteemed."[31] The notion of *reference group* (or *identification class,* which La Fave later preferred) entered the humor literature, and research continued with established social groups. One study from the La Fave group reported that promale males rated promale/antifemale jokes as funnier than profemale/antimale jokes. Selecting women members (and sympathizers) from campus women's liberation groups likewise revealed their appreciation of profemale/antimale jokes over promale/antifemale jokes.[32]

Examining women as a social group, we may identify five major obstacles to the development of women's humor: (1) little encouragement for humor, (2) little recognition of shared experience, (3) lack of a functional women's reference group, (4) failure to recognize sources of conflict, and (5) little consensus on traits to be caricatured.

In a chapter titled "The Role of Laughter and Humor in Growing Up Female," psychologist Paul McGhee argued that childhood socialization regards humor as incompatible with female gender role standards: "Because of the power associated with the successful use of humor, humor initiation has become associated with other traditionally masculine characteristics, such as aggression, dominance, and assertiveness. For a female to develop into a clown or joker, then, she must violate the behavioral pattern normally reserved for women."[33]

McGhee's analysis would suggest that most families would provide as much encouragement to a little girl clown as to a little boy sissy. Both have been judged inappropriate, and hence social role models and reinforcement contingencies will rechannel "deviant" behaviors. While social conventions may discourage potential women humorists, the model abandons adult women at the mercy of their early conditioning and gives insufficient attention to how women humorists, though exceptions, do emerge. It also presumes a perspective from which women as subordinates use humor in the same manner as men, only less effectively.

The recognition of common experiences and mutual perceptions strengthens intragroup social bonds. For males, puberty, manhood, graduation, employment, marriage, parenthood, and retirement tend to provide life structure and to convey social meaning. Current patterns in women's life cycles and societal affiliations, in contrast, have failed to foster awareness of commonality and shared feelings. Each marker event—puberty, graduation, marriage, employment, parenthood—has had a different connotation for males and for females, for females reinforcing or challenging the concept of femininity in a manner not comparable to that for males.[34] For example, common as retirement cartoons are in this society, one rarely finds one with a female protagonist (nor are women found alone on desert islands). In short, women's experience tends to be ambiguous, hidden, or lacking universality, which means that the foundation of most humor—one's own human experience—has failed to generate humor.

The need to recognize women's experience as the foundation of women's humor was recognized by journalist Kathleen Fury:

"[G]ood women's humor—or good humor by women . . . is humor that derives from the experience and feelings we have shared by virtue of having been born and raised female in our culture. It provides the laughter of recognition: 'Oh, yes. I've been there. I know about that.' "[35]

New openness about women's experience may help to create shared meanings. On the other hand, as greater diversity faces our pluralistic society, it may be too late to invent even that symbolic pattern. Lacking this, an important ingredient for distinctively women's humor will be missing.

Men's societies, fraternities, and informal gatherings evolved rituals of drinking, card playing, and recreation from which women were typically excluded. Whether male bonding claims any biological basis, business, politics, and education in contemporary society continue to convey a masculine orientation and stratification. Nineteenth-century women participated in sewing circles and observed formal conventions of social visitation. The psychological benefits of the women's society were eventually lost, until rediscovered by the women's movement of the late 1960s and 1970s. Activists set out to create support groups for women, such as consciousness-raising groups, women's centers, and classes in assertiveness training. Activities such as aerobics and belly dancing help women explore aspects of themselves and define female identities and women in society. The label "I am a woman" must not be merely a realization but preemptive as a relevant and positive self-identification in order for group identification to occur.

Naomi Weisstein understood that lack of a meaningful identification with gender could only impede the development of women's humor:

> It [women's rebellious humor] would seem to require that the group with whom one identifies provide some permanent although perhaps fragile shelter, some home base from which one goes out and deals with an oppressive world. While there are many occasions when women are together—in offices, in factories, in homes—our base has not generally been a social grouping of women, but some particular man with whom we live.[36]

The field of comedy is disproportionately populated by members of minorities—Jews and blacks, for example. The paucity of white male Protestants is attributed to the fact that other groups need humor. Following a comparison with Jews and blacks, Stoddard explained, "There is no comparable genre of women's humor because there is no widespread belief among women that they are, indeed, oppressed."[37]

Awareness of friction and social conflict is often a basis for humor. Anti-British humor flourished in the United States around the time of the American Revolution, and women cartoonists became a dominant force in the struggle for woman suffrage.[38] Nevertheless, for many aspects of women's inequality there is no direct agent to be found, even in those instances where discrimination is recognized. Women have been socialized to accept male privilege.

Most women remain reluctant to accuse or criticize men too openly, since, following Weisstein, much of their identity is as daughters, wives, and mothers of males, not to mention years of unquestioning obedience. It is similarly difficult to distinguish the class of men from particular men. Recognition of oppression may be essential for women's humor, and that agent (or a suitable target) specified.[39]

The language or symbolic codes of humor employ character types and traits. Humor may focus on the absentminded professor, the Caspar Milquetoast, the dirty old man, the jilted lover, and so on. Typical female types are the old maid, the club woman, the mother-in-law, and the dumb blonde. All have been conceived and perpetuated by society, although the old maid and the club woman have increasingly lost humor potency. The paucity of readily identifiable female types reduces the likelihood of humor.

Typical humor against women relies on stereotypes of "female gabbiness, wiliness, stupidity, stubbornness, lecherousness, extravagance, fecklessness, fickleness."[40] In the face of this, it is noteworthy that there is no dominant stereotype used by women for the purpose of sharing a sense of camaraderie and for making light of themselves.[41] There is no parallel in jokes to an overbearing "male ego," nor does a match exist for men's fears of impotence or homosexuality.

In published and performance forms by contemporary women humorists, some common characteristics are apparent. Women are active and central participants, in underground comix, for example, comprising 75 to 100 percent of the important characters.[42]

Yet their personas are not women but women-in-society, the end products of a century in which social science has demolished the myth of decontextualized gender. The most critical dimension of women's humor becomes the manner in which women's social roles are portrayed and/or challenged in women's humor. Five types of humor will now be considered: role-consistent humor, role-reversal humor, role-dilemma humor, role-transgressive humor, and role-transformative humor.[43]

Women humorists entering the male-dominated field of humor have often perpetuated stereotyped roles of women. Gracie Allen played a dim-witted, subservient partner to George Burns. Lucille Ball emerged as a bungling, misguided housewife. Helen Hokinson's club women were likable, well-meaning middle-aged matrons, though limited in insight and objectivity. In "Bobby Sox," Marty Links epitomized the 1950s teenager, who wouldn't think of phoning a boy herself and whose habits, attire, and beliefs are a puzzlement to her parents. Such cartoons were by women, about women, based on the conventional roles enacted by middle-class women.

The formula of role reversal as a comic device was increasingly applied to situations as the first serious challenges to male supremacy were felt in the nineteenth century. By the 1860s, Currier and Ives and *Harper's Weekly* published illustrations in which men did the washing and sewing and tended the children, while women ran the elections, drove the stagecoach, and went out on the town.[44]

In 1979, *New Woman* issued a collection of its cartoons titled *New Woman Presents Best Cartoons from the New Woman,* in which most examples offer nontraditional roles and role reversals. This humor functioned to highlight implicit assumptions about gender roles, dating, careers, and marriage. Like portraying a mouse in pursuit of a cat, ideas are funny simply because the anticipated order is reversed. Artists' signatures reveal that many of the contributors are men, in the initial years approximately 85 percent.[45]

In a typical cartoon, by Joseph Farris, a young woman declares to her date, "No, I wouldn't like to come to your apartment to see your etchings. Would you like to come to my studio and buy some of mine?" Sandy Dean likewise applies reversal when a woman executive remarks on the phone, "It's been nice chatting with you, Loretta, and remember me to the little man." An example by Martha Campbell depicts one man telling another, "It's not easy to get ahead these days. One doesn't know whether to propose to the boss's daughter or to the boss." All humor would be lost if the viewer were unfamiliar with male bosses, pretenses involving etchings, and the derogatory phrase "little woman."

Role-dilemma humor is centered in the contemporary roles and the challenges of feminine identity in a transitional society. This position is well illustrated by Cathy Guisewite's strip, "Cathy," launched in 1976 by its then twenty-five-year-old creator. The comic-strip character Cathy is torn by a conflict between an intellectual acceptance of feminist principles, upheld by her close friend Andrea, and the traditional values of her upbringing, continually reinforced by her mother. She dates Irving, a chauvinistic egotist, who places another set of demands on her. In a sample dialogue from 1978, Andrea and Cathy are seated at McDonald's, discussing women's issues:

> ANDREA: Just think, Cathy. With equality women will be able to pursue the same careers as men, without discrimination. We'll be protected by the same legal rights as men, without question!! We'll be able to earn as much as men, without fail!!
> CATHY: I think equality should go even farther, Andrea. I want to be able to eat as much as men without getting fat.[46]

The strip has quietly evolved into taking a more active social stance. In fact, commentaries on day care and the working mother which appeared prior to the 1988 elections were suppressed by some newspapers. A recent collection, *A Hand to Hold, An Opinion to Reject,* offers in its title some insight into the new Cathy. In one strip, Cathy's mother criticizes the practice of giving a baby a hyphenated last name. Cathy agrees it's terrible, adding, "Why can't they ever put the *woman's* name last? Why can't the *woman* be in the 'real last name' position, and the *man* in the patronized middle spot?"[47]

Parisian Claire Bretécher expressed role dilemmas in cartoon format from a series called *Les Frustrés.* In "True Confessions," one young woman questions another: "Tell me honestly . . . do you think I'm liberated or just an easy lay?" Ambivalence about motherhood is another topic, treated in an episode called "The Maternal Instinct." After struggling with the decision about whether or not she really wants a child, a career woman concludes, "The ideal would be to get knocked up without doing it on purpose."[48]

Role-transgressive humor is based on violations of conventional boundaries of social propriety. When a "lady" was defined as someone who never swore, avoided carnal language, and admitted no erotic sensibility, only men and wanton women were given free license with language.

The underground comix served as one arena for 1970s feminists, who produced works such as *It Ain't Me Babe Comics, Wet Satin,* and *Wimmen's Comix.* The themes were often erotic, presenting sex, violence, and rape from women's viewpoints. There were parodies of advertisements, as in *Manhunt! 1973:* "The inner cover ad promises instant enhancement of sex allure for $11.98, as a three breasted woman illustrates an 'add-a-Breast' kit. There is a clip-out coupon and testimonials: 'Tits are my business as a wet nurse.' "[49]

In the well-known collection of women's humor *Titters,* Stillman and Beatts attempted to parody male eroticism with the graphic use of both male and female bodies. The cover depicted a hip-to-neck close-up of a woman with the title "Titters" across the bustline. Representative articles and comics included "Fake Confessions," "The Myth of Male Orgasm," "My Secret Cabbage Patch," "Clampax Menstrual Poontons Instruction Booklet," and "Hedy the Hooker."[50]

While male comics from Lenny Bruce to George Carlin to Eddie Murphy have reveled in dirty words, use of sexual material by Joan Rivers, Marsha Warfield, Robin Tyler, or Sandra Bernhard still shocks some audiences. A feminist perspective is claimed in Robin Tyler's "reverse tits and ass jokes."[51]

It is understandable that the effect of such humor depends on the audience. Consider the routine by Anne Beatts: "I've finally figured out why men hate women. It's because we can always do it. Even if we're dead."[52] Beatts has reported that women laugh spontaneously, but only in a single-sex group. If the audience is mixed, they wait for men to laugh first. Cultural constraints remain strong, consistent with Freud's belief that erotic themes (for him, "smut") were a male prerogative, heightening humor's effectiveness by circumventing repression. Today, women's erotic language may evoke conflicting codes for males—whether to identify *with* her or be seduced *by* her.[53]

There have been erotic-toned routines by women since the days of Belle Barth, Irene Bordoni ("Let's Misbehave"), and Mae West.[54] And perhaps it is society's ambivalence concerning its appropriateness that enhances its success. Are women simply redefining male social territory as their own? Artist Trina Robbins, accused of portraying women as sex objects and of creating rape fantasies, responds that "what they're *really* about is POWER!"[55]

Role-transformative humor is the humor that most obviously and directly seeks to attack gender roles. Women have long recognized the use of humor to seek social change, whether for feminist causes or to fight basic injustices in society. Women are portrayed as victims of social oppression and conditioning in the 1973 collection by Ellen Levine, *All She Needs. . . .* Using a distinctive outline style of a female with sagging breasts, major themes portrayed include identity, sexuality, and male-female relations. One reflects, "When a guy gets screwed he's in trouble. . . . When a girl gets screwed she's a woman."[56]

Pulling Our Own Strings includes a number of examples meeting the definition of role-transformative humor. Bübül (Gen Guracar) presented a middle-aged housewife telling her husband, "No it's not menopausal depression, it's no pay, no sick leave, no pension, no identity." Betty Swords depicted a laboratory scientist telling another, "This is our experimental physics laboratory, this is our X-007 data processing center, and this is our woman." Another in the collection by Swords shows a husband retrieving the *Wall Street Journal* from his wife and announcing, "When I want your opinion I'll tell you what it is."

A prototypic liberated woman is found in Nicole Hollander's "Sylvia," a middle-aged housewife devoted to her TV, beer can, and munchies. Discussed in Patricia Williams Alley's essay in this volume, she challenges social expectations toward women in her attitudes, behavior, and attire.[57]

Harrison and Tyler, united in that rare phenomenon—a female comedy team—developed a number of comedy routines on stereotypic female roles, such as stewardess and housewife. In her subsequent solo act, Tyler proposed a social policy: "I would like to become the president of a major TV network, and then I would ban all the commercials that make women look like imbeciles—that would mean 24 hours of uninterrupted programming."[58]

Recognition of the social nature of humor was understood years ago by popular humorist Carolyn Wells, who claimed that much of Mark Twain's appeal stemmed from tradition or social convention. She commented: "People have been trained to believe that Mark Twain is a great humorist. So they laugh at his books and say they are funny when as a matter of fact the fun has no real appeal to them."[59]

When we acknowledge humor as enmeshed in social traditions of thought and behavior, much of the ambiguity surrounding women's humor vanishes. That is, if humor is socially defined, perceived, and conditioned, differences ascribed to the female psyche become manifestations of society's attitudes and values.[60] Moreover, the thorough analysis of women's social humor has been impeded by inadequate conceptual frameworks. Is the central locus of humor to be found in behavior, thought processes, or social interactions? Should its essence be posited as process, structure, or symbolic interaction?

From the social constructivist position, social realities determine what will be perceived and shape modes of social attribution. This paper has acknowledged cultural constraints as misconstruing women's experience, and therefore women's humor. Thus, social scientists are hampered by an incorrect assumption regarding humor and gender roles, namely, that humor productions of women, including both spontaneous and nonspontaneous forms, have been observed appropriately.[61] To the extent that women construct different social realities and codes, humor may differ in its functions and forms. To those outside the tradition, its message is incompletely decoded.

The next set of socially influenced behaviors are linguistic and behavior codes, for which gender role serves as generative and normative. Yet, despite increased recognition of humor as being intrinsically related to gender role, the link between role-derived standard and the individual remains unclear. Dominant theoretical approaches of this type include social dominance, role-appropriate behavior, and the end products of early socialization.[62] Each of these relationships posits a direct influence of gender role on behavior.

A third model of social influence on humor concerns the reference group. This posits collective identification among women and the image derived as central to individual identity. There is a certain paradox that women's social behavior for each historical period has been so clearly articulated, and yet women seem hindered in discerning a functional reference group.[63] Walker has noted this failure, despite her belief that "even American women have enough in common to be considered a group with shared interests and concerns."[64]

La Fave, however, recognized the conceptual limitations of the concept of reference group, especially its imprecise psychological significance, and advocated the concept of identification class. Like other theories, La Fave's approach is limited by its focus on behavioral manifestations of reference group rather than internal representations. There is a need to posit a representation or idealized image which promotes adherence to social standards, for which constructs of gender role and reference group prove inadequate.[65]

For social humor, we have noted the effect of several cognitive processes: perception, attribution, and judgments. These, in turn, have produced distinct outcomes for women's humor. First, the repeated lack of recognition of women humorists resulted in an assumption that they didn't exist. Second, women's humor is linked to women's social codes, which deviate from male standards. Third, traditional women were not encouraged to develop and exercise a sense of humor. Fourth, recognition of women humorists is a social judgment, evoking processes of social cognition. Giving women a typewriter, a drawing pen, or a comedy stage will not lead to far-reaching success unless women literary humorists, cartoonists, and stand-up comics can fit into the social categories of society.

It appears inescapable that certain women's humor is not fully appreciated by men—a fact that has hindered society's acceptance of women humorists. The dominant status group has failed to observe and sanction humor by women; women have failed to understand this loss of power and meaning resulting from the invalidation of perception/experience. Earlier in the century, humorist

Carolyn Wells grasped the psychological significance of role divisions, which she portrayed in her poem "Woman":

> Women are dear and women are queer
>   Men call them with a laugh,
> The female of the species,
>   Or a husband's better half.
> They sing their praise in many ways,
>   They flatter them—but, oh
> How little they know of Woman
>   Who only women know![66]

Notes

1. Not atypical is the humor collection that included nine studies using male subjects alone, two based on both males and females, one using females. Jacob Levine, *Motivation in Humor* (New York: Atherton, 1969). Women's humor has been omitted in major references, such as *The Psychology of Humor,* ed. Jeffrey H. Goldstein and Paul E. McGhee (New York: Academic Press, 1972); and the *Handbook of Humor Research,* ed. Paul E. McGhee and Jeffrey H. Goldstein, 2 vols. (New York: Springer-Verlag, 1983).
2. Naomi Weisstein, "Psychology Constructs the Female, or the Fantasy Life of the Male Psychologist," *Roles Women Play: Readings toward Women's Liberation,* ed. Michele H. Garskof (Belmont, Calif.: Brooks/Cole, 1971), 68–83; Jean Baker Miller, *Toward a New Psychology of Women* (Boston: Beacon Press, 1976).
3. Carol Mitchell, "The Differences between Male and Female Joke Telling as Exemplified in a College Community," diss. Indiana University, 1976 (Ann Arbor: UMI, 1977); Paul E. McGhee, "The Role of Laughter and Humor in Growing Up Female," in *Becoming Female: Perspectives on Development,* ed. Claire B. Kopp (New York: Plenum Press, 1979), 183–206; Leigh Marlowe, "A Sense of Humor," *Imagination, Cognition, and Personality* 4 (1984–85), 265–75; Alice Sheppard, "Funny Women: Social Change and Audience Response to Female Comedians,"

Empirical Studies of the Arts 3 (1985), 179–95; Alice Sheppard, "From Kate Sanborn to Feminist Psychology: The Social Context of Women's Humor, 1885–1985," *Psychology of Women Quarterly* 10 (1986), 155–70; Mary Crawford, "Humor in Conversational Context: Beyond Biases in the Study of Gender and Humor," in *Representations: Social Construction of Gender,* ed. Rhoda Unger (Amityville, N.Y.: Baywood, 1988).

4. Hazel Markus and R. B. Zajonc, "The Cognitive Perspective in Social Psychology," in *The Handbook of Social Psychology,* 3rd ed., ed. Gardner Lindzey and Elliot Aronson, Vol. 1 (New York: Random House, 1983), 137.
5. Mary Douglas, "The Social Control of Cognition: Some Factors in Joke Perception," *Man* 3 (1968), 361–76; Anton Zijderveld, "Jokes and Their Relation to Social Reality," *Social Research* 35 (1968), 286–311.
6. Peter L. Berger and Thomas Luckmann, *The Social Construction of Reality* (Garden City, N.Y.: Doubleday, 1966), 45.
7. The word *role* is derived from theater, French *le rôle,* a device that held a roll of paper on which the actor's script was written.
8. Carolyn Korsmeyer, "The Hidden Joke: Generic Uses of Masculine Terminology," in *Feminism and Philosophy,* ed. Mary Vetterling-Braggin, Frederick A. Elliston, and Jane English (Totowa, N.J.: Littlefield, Adams, 1977), 140.
9. A boy and his father are involved in an auto accident in which the father is killed. In the hospital operating room, the surgeon exclaims, "I can't operate, that's my son!" Janice Moulton, "The Myth of the Neutral 'Man,' " in *Feminism and Philosophy,* 124–25. A big Indian and a little Indian are sitting on a fence. The little Indian is the big Indian's son, but the big Indian is not the little Indian's father. How can this be? Judith Fryer, *The Faces of Eve: Women in the Nineteenth Century American Novel* (New York: Oxford University Press, 1976), 6.
10. Misogyny as endemic to American humor is discussed in Jesse Bier, *The Rise and Fall of American Humor* (New York: Holt, Rinehart and Winston, 1968); Merrie Bergmann, "How Many Feminists Does It Take to Make a Joke? Sexist Humor and What's Wrong with It," *Hypatia* 1 (1986), 63–82.
11. Marlowe, "A Sense of Humor," 268.

12. Mark Snyder, "On the Self-Perpetuating Nature of Stereotypes," in *Cognitive Processes in Stereotyping and Intergroup Behavior,* ed. David Hamilton (Hillsdale, N.J.: Erlbaum, 1981), 184.
13. For a discussion of nineteenth-century femininity, see Barbara Welter, "The Cult of True Womanhood: 1820–1860," *American Quarterly* 18 (1966), 151–74.
14. Ellen Levine, *All She Needs . . .* (New York: Quadrangle, 1973).
15. Naomi Weisstein, "Why Aren't We Laughing . . . Anymore," *Ms.,* November 1973, 89.
16. Lawrence J. Peter, "Why So Few Female Cartoonists?" *San Francisco Sunday Examiner and Chronicle,* January 14, 1979; "Laughter, How Much Do You Love Your Misery?" *Cultural Correspondence* 9 (Spring 1979), 5–6. Another example of gender domination is the fact that one of Dorothy Parker's biographers characterized her as a "tiny, big-eyed, feminine woman with the mind of a man"; John Keats, *You Might As Well Live: The Life and Times of Dorothy Parker* (New York: Simon and Schuster, 1970), 305.
17. Jessie Bernard, *The Female World* (New York: Free Press, 1981).
18. Mahadev L. Apte, *Humor and Laughter: An Anthropological Approach* (Ithaca, N.Y.: Cornell University Press, 1985), 81.
19. Lawrence Kohlberg, "A Cognitive-Developmental Analysis of Children's Sex-Role Concepts and Attitudes," in *The Development of Sex Differences,* ed. Eleanor E. Maccoby (Stanford, Calif.: Stanford University Press, 1966), 82–173; Elizabeth Lane Beardsley, "Referential Genderization," *Philosophical Forum* 5 (1973–74), 285–93, rpt. in *Women and Philosophy,* ed. Carol C. Gould and Marx W. Wartofsky (New York: Putnam's, 1976), 285–93; Elizabeth L. Beardsley, "Traits and Genderization," in *Feminism and Philosophy,* 117–23.
20. Harold H. Kelley, "Attribution Theory in Social Psychology," in *Nebraska Symposium on Motivation* 15, ed. D. Levine (1967), 193; Fritz Heider, *The Psychology of Interpersonal Relations* (New York: Wiley, 1958).
21. Kelley, "Attribution Theory," 194.

22. For purposes of this paper, we assume a class of events commonly referred to as humor. Scholars have not achieved a universal definition, nor from a constructionist psychological perspective would the definition apply solely to the object.
23. For a discussion of incongruity, see D. E. Berlyne, "Laughter, Humor, and Play," in *Handbook of Social Psychology,* 2nd ed., ed. Gardner Lindzey and Eliott Aronson (Reading, Mass.: Addison-Wesley, 1969), 3:705–852. It should, however, be acknowledged that incongruity is a necessary, not a sufficient condition; incongruous ideas or events may be experienced as annoying, appalling, or anxiety-provoking—not funny.
24. Joyce O. Hertzler, *Laughter: A Socio-Scientific Analysis* (Jericho, N.Y.: Exposition Press, 1970). The importance of overt laughter can be considered from self-perception theory, which holds that attributions result from our own behavior. That is, the movie must have been funny *because* I laughed. Daryl J. Bem, "Self-Perception Theory," in *Advances in Experimental Social Psychology,* ed. Leonard Berkowitz (New York: Academic Press, 1972), 6:1–62.
25. It should be pointed out that ability to define and measure both perception and evaluation does not indicate that one necessarily follows the other in the individual's mind. Jerry Suls, "A Two-Stage Model for the Appreciation of Jokes and Cartoons: An Information-Processing Analysis," in *The Psychology of Humor,* 81–100; Frederick L. Linsk and Gary Alan Fine, "Perceptual and Evaluative Response to Humor: The Effects of Social Identification," *Sociology and Social Research* 66 (1981), 69–79.
26. Jerry Suls, "Cognitive and Disparagement Theories of Humour: A Theoretical and Empirical Synthesis," in *It's A Funny Thing, Humour,* ed. Antony J. Chapman and Hugh C. Foot (New York: Pergamon, 1977), 43.
27. Elizabeth Janeway, *Between Myth and Morning: Women Awakening* (New York: William Morrow, 1974), 147.
28. Rose Coser, "Laughter among Colleagues: A Study of the Social Functions of Humor among the Staff of a Mental Hospital," *Psychiatry* 23 (1960), 81–95; Mary Jo Neitz, "Humor, Hierarchy, and the Changing Status of Women," *Psychiatry* 43 (1980), 211–23. See also Apte, *Humor and Laughter.*

29. This section is a revision of an earlier paper, "Humor and Gender," presented at Second International Humor Conference, Los Angeles, August 1979.
30. There is a distinction between gender role, the standards set by a society to which females are expected to conform, and women as a social group, maintaining an interactional base and functioning as a reference group for its members.
31. Lawrence La Fave, in William H. Martineau, "A Model of the Social Functions of Humor," in *The Psychology of Humor,* 110. Gary Alan Fine, "Sociological Approaches to the Study of Humor," in *Handbook of Humor Research,* 1:159–81.
32. Lawrence La Fave, "Humor Judgments as a Function of Reference Groups and Identification Classes," in *The Psychology of Humor,* 195–210.
33. McGhee, "The Role of Laughter and Humor," 183–84.
34. To graduate from college or engage in a career has long been regarded as less than feminine, whereas marriage and motherhood offer reassurance of role success. To be a mother and a worker sets up an incongruity, whereas *worker* and *father* are simply juxtaposed. In addition to uncertainty for women associated with education and career, there is ambivalence arising from menarche, pregnancy, and menopause.
35. Kathleen Fury, "Okay, Ladies, What's the Joke?" *Redbook,* June 1980, 164.
36. Weisstein, "Why Aren't We Laughing," 88.
37. Karen M. Stoddard, " 'Women Have No Sense of Humor' and Other Myths: A Consideration of Female Stand-up Comics, 1960–1976," *American Humor: An Interdisciplinary Newsletter* (Fall 1977), 11. Howard R. Pollio, John Edgerly, and Robert Jordan, "The Comedian's World: Some Tentative Mappings," *Psychological Reports* 30 (1972), 387–91.
38. Michael Wynn Jones, *The Cartoon History of the American Revolution* (New York: Putnam's, 1975); Alice Sheppard, "Political and Social Consciousness in the Woman Suffrage Cartoons of Lou Rogers and Nina Allender," *Studies in American Humor,* n.s. 4, 1–2 (1985), 39–50.
39. Weisstein, "Why Aren't We Laughing."
40. Erica Jong, "You Have to Be Liberated to Laugh," *Playboy,* April 1980, 208.

41. What I am suggesting is that to taunt young girls as "Carrie Nations" or "Vicki Woodhulls" would enhance a knowledge of and pride in women's history.
42. Delores Mitchel, "Women Libeled: Women's Cartoons of Women," *Journal of Popular Culture* 14 (1981), 598.
43. The question of "feminist humor" has been addressed by several theorists. Gloria Kaufman and Mary Kay Blakely, eds., *Pulling Our Own Strings: Feminist Humor and Satire* (Bloomington: Indiana University Press, 1980); Nancy Walker, "*A Very Serious Thing*": *Women's Humor and American Culture* (Minneapolis: University of Minnesota Press, 1988). Within the present typology, the latter three categories generally represent more radical positions, but an adequate designation must consider the attitude and intentions of the humorist. A working definition of *feminist* encompasses "ideas and actions directed towards ending female social subordination"; Susan Condor, "Sex Role Beliefs and 'Traditional' Women: Feminist and Intergroup Perspectives," in *Feminist Social Psychology: Developing Theory and Practice,* ed. Sue Wilkinson (Philadelphia: Open University Press, 1986), 97.
44. Monika Franzen and Nancy Ethiel, *Make Way!* (Chicago: Chicago Review Press, 1988).
45. *New Woman Presents Best Cartoons from New Woman* (Fort Worth: New Woman, 1979). Evelyn Sendecke, letter to the author, May 23, 1980.
46. Cathy Guisewite, *The Cathy Chronicles* (Kansas City, Mo.: Sheed Andrews and McMeel, 1978), 134.
47. "Newspaper Editors Bounce 'Cathy,' Say Comics No Place for Politics," *Daily Item* (Sunbury, Penn.), October 29, 1988, 2. Cathy Guisewite, *A Hand to Hold, an Opinion to Reject* (Kansas City, Mo.: Andrews and McMeel, 1987), 9.
48. Claire Bretécher, *The National Lampoon Presents Claire Bretécher* (New York: National Lampoon, 1978). Claire Bretécher, *Frustration* (New York: Grove Press, 1987).
49. Mitchel, "Women Libeled," 603.
50. Deanna Stillman and Ann Beatts, *Titters: The First Collection of Humor by Women* (New York: Collier, 1976).
51. Karen Stabiner, "The Belly Room Presented Comediennes," *Mother Jones,* July 1979, 47.

52. Fury, "Okay, Ladies," 165.
53. Sigmund Freud, *Jokes and Their Relation to the Unconscious,* trans. James Strachey (New York: Norton, 1960).
54. Joe Franklin, *Joe Franklin's Encyclopedia of Comedians* (Secaucas, N.J.: Citadel, 1979).
55. "Trina Robbins," *Cultural Correspondence* 9 (Spring 1979), 12.
56. Ellen Levine, cartoon, *All She Needs . . .*
57. Nicole Hollander, *Never Take Your Cat to a Salad Bar* (New York: Vintage, 1987).
58. Stabiner, "The Belly Room," 49.
59. In Thomas L. Masson, *Our American Humorists* (New York: Moffat Yard, 1922), 314.
60. Although the issue has been taken up previously (e.g., Stoddard, Walker), this provides another answer to the question, "Why do women have no sense of humor?" The question then becomes, "Why is there a failure to perceive women's humor?"
61. See Crawford, "Humor in Conversational Context," for a methodological critique.
62. These explanations include social dominance hierarchies (Coser, Neitz, Weisstein), role-appropriate behaviors (Crawford, Marlowe, Mitchell, Walker), and early socialization (McGhee).
63. Martha Banta, *Imaging American Women* (New York: Columbia University Press, 1987). See also Bernard, Walker, Welter, and Weisstein. Certain women's organizations gain high status (e.g., faculty wives, ladies' auxiliaries) but are often subordinate groups, defined by their relation to dominant male associations.
64. Walker, "*A Very Serious Thing,*" 103.
65. La Fave, "Humor Judgments."
66. Carolyn Wells, *An Outline of Humor* (New York: Putnam's, 1923), 751–52.

Toward Solidarity: Women's Humor and Group Identity

Nancy Walker

One important ambition of the women's movement in America, throughout its long if not continuous history, has been to promote in women a sense of community with one another—to alleviate women's feelings of isolation and powerlessness and to foster an understanding of shared problems and aspirations. While most of the overt goals have been political and economic—the right to vote, pay equity, access to leadership positions—a number have been personal: not just reproductive rights and freedom from sexual harassment but also the feeling of autonomy and personal power that is both a consequence of these freedoms and in some ways a precondition for them. Yet what feminists have encountered again and again is the fact that, unlike other oppressed groups, women do not constitute a group in the usual sense but instead are isolated from one another by their intimate relationships with men and, traditionally, by their habitation in the private sphere of homemaking and child rearing.[1]

Efforts to promote a sense of group solidarity have therefore been resisted by cultural realities that have dictated women's separation not only from the policy-making mainstream but also from one another. With rare exceptions, women have been a definable group only in what William Chafe has called an "aggregate" rather than a "collective" sense, sharing certain behaviors and problems by virtue of being women rather than because of a conscious decision to act in concert with other women.[2]

Thus, for example, the mid-century suburbia that Phyllis McGinley described as a "village of women" was also the breeding ground for the discontent that Betty Friedan documented in *The Feminine Mystique* in 1963. Rather than an organized discontent, what Friedan identified were feelings of individual, personal, isolated frustration arising not only from the blunted aspirations of intelligent, educated women but also from women's perception that each was alone in her problems. Indeed, McGinley's "village of women" emerges in her prose and light verse not as a community of people sharing the circumstances of their lives but rather as separate individuals who meet for bridge games or PTA teas and then retreat behind chintz curtains to await their commuting husbands. As much as McGinley attempts to make comic the repetitions of housework, the vagaries of husbands, and the raising of children, her verses reinforce the essential loneliness and triviality women so frequently felt in the suburban environment. In "Collector's Items," the speaker declares, "My life is filled with cereal." In "Beauty Parlor," the women do not speak to each other but concentrate on nail polish and movie magazines. And in "Occupation: Housewife," a middle-aged woman delays with bridge games "the encroaching desolation of her days."[3]

McGinley is one of a number of domestic humorists whom Friedan took to task in *The Feminine Mystique* for inviting women to "dissipate in laughter their dreams and their sense of desperation."[4] Yet humor is a common device for creating solidarity among members of minority groups: laughing at the oppressors minimizes their authority, and the ability to make fun of one's own oppression provides a psychic distance from it. As Lawrence Levine argues in *Black Culture and Black Consciousness,* the long tradition among blacks of "laughing at the man" has had a cohesive effect on members of the black community: by pointing out the foibles and pretensions of white culture, blacks have identified with one another in opposition to white hegemony. As a corollary, self-deprecating humor among blacks frequently turns upon and thus renders absurd and harmless stereotypes originating in the dominant culture, such as laziness, sexual prowess, a fondness for watermelon and black-eyed peas.[5] Other groups, notably Jews, have developed over centuries of persecution a humor that reinforces group identity and belonging. To make the other the target of humor is to claim superiority over even a culturally dominant group.

But among women, there appears to exist no corresponding tradition of "underdog" humor, a humor that, as Naomi Weisstein says, "recognizes a common oppression, notices its source and the roles it requires, identifies the agents of that oppression."[6] There are several reasons for the apparent lack of such a tradition. One is the fact that, as Chafe points out, women's legal and economic ties to—and dependence on—men have worked against female group identity and therefore the development of certain group codes, of which humor is one. Another reason is the pervasive ideology of the "lady," which became firmly rooted in the rise of genteel culture in the early nineteenth century and which mandates a passive behavior that is the very opposite of the irreverent stance of the humorist. The lady laughs at men's jokes; she does not invent her own. Finally, if there *were* a tradition of women's humor similar to that of blacks, Jews, and other minority groups, it would probably be a submerged, almost invisible tradition, unavailable as a source of strength to women as has been so much of women's history.

In fact, a more or less invisible tradition of women's humor does exist in this culture, but before examining the ways in which it has promoted or served as evidence of a sense of group identity for women, it is important to make some distinctions, first between oral and written humorous expression and also between political and nonpolitical humor. Acts of speaking and writing carry with them different sets of constraints, so that whereas in social settings women—in spite of notable exceptions such as Dorothy Parker—may not feel encouraged to tell jokes or be witty, writing humorous verse or satire, while a more isolated act, is also more nearly sanctioned by female socialization. Thus, at the same time that the very existence of a female sense of humor was being debated in the periodical press—primarily in the late nineteenth and early twentieth centuries—women's humorous writing flourished in such magazines as *Judge, Life, Vanity Fair,* and the *New Yorker.* Similarly, the social sanctions against women's political humor, especially when that humor concerns women's own political agenda, have been far stronger than those governing the expression of humor about the domestic setting that has been considered woman's "proper sphere." To write amusingly about cooking, cleaning, and children, and particularly to point to one's failures and frustrations in these areas, is to appear to occupy the subordinate role mandated by the dominant culture. But humor that openly advances a feminist cause challenges that dominance and posits a sense of solidarity which threatens its hegemony.

The humor of American women has in fact functioned as a means of establishing and representing a community of shared concerns about oppression. Despite the daunting effects of female socialization to be passive and dependent on male approbation, and without an understanding of their own humorous tradition, women have nonetheless used humor to connect with one another and to announce their superiority to cultural myths about their nature and behavior.

Humor and Female Socialization

Writing about growing up in the 1950s, Anne Beatts recalls, "real girls weren't funny. Real girls were pretty and fluffy and could do the splits in cheerleader try-outs." The only girls she remembers who were known for being funny in high school did not meet the test of a "real girl": "One of them was fat. One was handicapped. The others were 'tough.' "[7] Deanne Stillman remembers submitting parodies to *Mad* magazine and signing her name as "Dean" because "writing funny was something girls didn't do."[8] Stillman and Beatts, both comedy writers, coedited a 1976 collection of women's humor titled *Titters: The First Collection of Humor by Women,* the subtitle betraying their lack of awareness of two previous anthologies of women's humorous writing.[9] Both their assumption that women were not supposed to be funny—in person or in print—and their ignorance of a female humorous tradition point to the complex relationship between humor and female socialization.

Psychologists and sociologists who study gender differences in the creation and appreciation of humor necessarily base their findings on observations of social interaction rather than on the writing and reading of humorous literature. However, some of the patterns they observe are also characteristic of women's written humor, and certainly these patterns help to explain why women tend not to regard themselves as "natural" humorists. Some of the most comprehensive research on humor and gender differences has been done by psychologist Paul McGhee. While Freud believed that differences in the sense of humor between men and women were innate and that jokes, like dreams, originated in the unconscious mind as a means of circumventing inhibitions, McGhee and most other recent theorists maintain that joking is learned behavior and as such is influenced by social relationships. The well-documented fact that women are far less likely than men to attempt to be humorous in a social situation is dictated by women's need to adhere to culturally determined standards of ideal female behavior.

In "The Role of Laughter and Humor in Growing Up Female," McGhee cites studies demonstrating that among preschool children there is no significant difference between boys and girls in laughter and joke telling. But after the age of six, boys initiate humor far more frequently than do girls; furthermore, girls tend to laugh at humorous situations more often when there is an external signal, such as canned laughter accompanying a film, that sanctions such a response. One of the most significant aspects of McGhee's study is that girls age six or older who do tell jokes and engage in other humorous activity have two common characteristics: they have received less parental help in resolving problems and conflicts, and they are more physically active. In other words, they have taken on the so-called male attributes of independent thinking and physical prowess. Yet McGhee also points to humor as a relatively safe way for girls to express aggressive feelings: "While humor appears to be a form of interaction normally 'reserved' for males, highly aggressive and dominating behavior is clearly more in violation of the traditional female sex role than joking and clowning. Thus, channeling one's aggression into a humorous context may be a girl's best means of minimizing her violation of traditional sex-role expectations, while at the same time allowing herself some form of expression of aggression."[10] If aggression, for women, is most safely expressed in humor, this could explain why the only funny girls Anne Beatts remembers from high school were fat, handicapped, or "tough": the hostility they felt at being different from the "real girl" ideal was channeled into humor. Similarly, the many works of domestic humor by women, featuring housewives who struggle with diets, unruly children, malfunctioning appliances, and repetitious tasks, may be seen as efforts to protest the conditions of the homemaker's life through the covert means of humor rather than in a more direct, aggressive manner, allowing women to preserve their femininity.

The self-deprecation that characterizes women's domestic humor (the diets never work, the children remain unruly, despite the woman's efforts) has been common in much of women's humor, including Dorothy Parker's self-mocking poems and the comedy routines of Phyllis Diller. On the one hand, this suggests that women have internalized the cultural message that they are inferior. In fact, McGhee cites several studies in which women, particularly those with traditional views of women's role, preferred humor in which women were victimized by men to that in which men were the victims. McGhee suggests that "women may be more used to accepting subordinate roles and putdowns and so are freer to laugh at their own expense" (198). Yet there is a vast difference between laughing at a joke of which a woman is the butt and deliberately creating a humorous piece in which a woman is an inept housekeeper, a dumb blonde, or a gossip: the former may be a conditioned response to the humor of the dominant culture, while the latter is frequently a subversive attack on the status quo. Lorelei Lee, the narrator in Anita Loos's *Gentlemen Prefer Blondes* (1925), is one of American literature's most famous avatars of the dumb blonde figure, but the subtext of Loos's book is an indictment of a culture that requires women to depend on their appearance for male approbation and economic survival. As Zita Dresner points out, "the relationship between [Gus] Eisman [one of Lorelei's 'gentlemen'] and Lorelei is mutually exploitive and . . . the social moralism that traditionally condemned such relationships is also responsible for creating the conditions for such relationships by making woman's sex appeal her most marketable asset."[11]

Furthermore, self-deprecating humor may be evidence of strength rather than weakness. Freud posited that the self-critical jokes of Jewish culture served to promote unity and consensus, and McGhee suggests that the ability to laugh at oneself may be evidence of a better sense of humor than that of those who cannot: "One popular definition of a sense of humor has focused on the capacity to laugh at one's own shortcomings, to see the humor of one's own ways, to see the 'light side' of things, and to be able to laugh at one's own expense" (198). In the early years of the women's movement, feminists were frequently accused of lacking a sense of humor, partly as a consequence of the fact that they had stopped laughing at jokes that denigrated women. Naomi Weisstein points out that the ability to laugh at the humor of others has long been part of the definition of women's charm, and "when people tell us we've lost our sense of humor—it's as good as telling us we're ugly." Weisstein continues: "And it is, of course, as revealing. It means that we may actually be changing our social roles, that we have stopped trying to please. If we are no longer laughing at what is not funny to us, we may be, in a way, taking the first step in our being able to develop our own women's humor" (89). In the same year that Weisstein wrote her article, 1973, Erica Jong published her novel *Fear of Flying,* in which the heroine, Isadora Wing, frequently finds men and sex very funny and does not hesitate to say so. In a 1980 article, Jong recalls that the book was severely criticized by some radical feminists for reasons that a friend finally explained to her: " 'You're writing humorously about the battle between the sexes,' she said, '*and it's no laughing matter!*' "[12] One measure of the increased strength and confidence of feminism in the 1980s is women's ability to laugh at themselves—what Jong calls "a sign of health" (162)—as I will discuss later.

If responses to humor are the result of socialization, then changes in cultural expectations for women's behavior should affect those responses. McGhee suggests that this is true when he refers to the supposed humorlessness of feminists. Rejecting the notion that feminist women have somehow lost their sense of humor, he agrees with Weisstein that one's values determine what one finds amusing: "The victimizing of women in fantasy loses its humor precisely because the events depicted are perceived to reflect realistically the plight of women in our society" (200). The consciousness that women *are* victims, in other words, removes the incongruity that makes a situation humorous. Sociologist Mary Jo

Neitz similarly proposes that changes in the social order affect joking relationships. As an example, she observed a group of radical feminists on a college campus and found that the fact that they were "consciously attempting to subvert the sexual hierarchy" was reflected in the informal humor of the group's interaction. One type of humor, which is common among groups of contemporary feminists, plays on the self-denigration pattern of women's humor. One member of a group of women getting into a car together, for example, asks the others, "Do you think you can be safe with a woman driver?" The laughter here arises from the self-evident absurdity of the question.[13] The other common type of humor, which Neitz acknowledges might be extreme because of the radical nature of the group, is castration jokes, which "gloried in women's strength rather than colluding to hide it" (221). Castration jokes are obviously aggressive, and may even be hostile, but Neitz notes that they are a direct response to the epithet *castrating bitch* that has been hurled at feminists. Using humor to stand this accusation on its head is a sign of unity: "Politicized women have now apparently defined certain areas as essential to survival and cultural integrity, and to expression of group solidarity" (222).

Women in Groups: The Invisible Tradition

The effects of female socialization are most apparent when women are in social interaction with men. The behavior of women in groups composed only of women, as Neitz's example of the radical feminist group indicates, may be quite different: relieved of the necessity to act in a way that will please men—and relieved also of the competition for male attention—women are more likely to concentrate on what unites them *as women* and to feel free to express themselves. Such, of course, was the rationale for the women-only consciousness-raising groups of the 1960s and 1970s; interaction with other women allowed a sharing of concerns and fears that removed women from the isolation of their lives and allowed them to realize that the personal was indeed the political.

Nor were such groups new in the 1960s. Women's groups and clubs have been a major factor in women's social existence since the eighteenth century, and whether formed for social or political causes—child welfare, temperance, woman suffrage—or for more informal reasons such as quilting or playing cards, they have provided an opportunity for women to achieve a sense of collectivity and common purpose. Whether gathered for political action or entertainment, women have developed a humorous tradition that, hidden from the dominant culture and largely unrecorded, replicates the subversive and strengthening humor of a minority group.

The most comprehensive substantiation of this more or less invisible tradition is presented by anthropologist Mahadev Apte in *Humor and Laughter.* Apte cites numerous studies that indicate that in virtually every culture, cultural prohibitions curtail women's participation in humor; just as in American culture, male dominance extends to a control of the expression of humor. Exceptions to this pattern are primarily of two types: women of advanced age who, because of either respect for their seniority or their effective removal from the competition for male approval, are permitted to indulge in humorous activity; and women in groups composed only of women. Because men are excluded from these groups, it was not until increasing numbers of women entered the field of anthropology that such behavior could be studied, so that anthropological studies tended to perpetuate the assumption of female humorlessness, with men serving as the joker and trickster figures in most cultures. Yet within the all-women's groups, humor flourishes—as an expression of hostility to male hegemony; indeed, the more repressive the culture for women, the more directly women's humor is focused on the habits and foibles of men. Separate studies conducted in Iraq, rural France, and Sicily led Apte to conclude that "common topics for humor development in such gatherings include men's physical appearance, their social behavior, their idiosyncracies [*sic*], their sexuality, their status-seeking activities, and their religious rites"[14]—in short, all of the areas in which men claim dominance.

The humor that women create under these circumstances may be ribald or even obscene, such as the women in a tribe in Nepal who gather at the groom's house before a wedding to perform comic rituals that parody male sexual arousal. As Apte states, "when women act collectively, many of the behavioral constraints that they must observe as individuals can be disregarded" (78). A similar sort of freedom from "ladylike" behavior is described by folklorist Rayna Green in "Magnolias Grow in Dirt." Recalling visits to family in East Texas when she was a child, Green writes of the often bawdy humor that women shared with each other after dinner when the men had gone outside to talk about politics. The stories and jokes that the women in the family told on these occasions served several functions, one of which was to introduce the children to adult sexuality, and particularly to warn young women about men: "The tales and sayings tell young women what they can expect in private out of the men and the institutions they are taught to praise in public, and they inform them as they could never be informed in 'serious' conversation. Poking fun at a man's sexual ego, for example, might never be possible in real social situations with the men who have power over their lives, but it is possible in a joke."[15] The issue of power that Green raises here is similar to the findings of the anthropological studies that Apte reports in *Humor and Laughter:* whenever men control women's political, economic, and personal lives, humor that makes men the target must be shared in secret.

A second function of this bawdy humor that women share is also related to power, but in a different way. The sharing of such humor gives women a sense of collective power, the power of consensus among themselves. Further, Green points out, women who are good storytellers achieve status in their own group: "In the women's world, as in the men's, the premier storyteller and singer, the inventive user of language, commands respect and admiration" (33). Within the group of women, a skilled storyteller occupies the position of the joker or trickster figure who in many cultures is the only one allowed to mock the conventions and rules of the society. Closely related to this is the fact that the humor these women share is subversive. Instead of reinforcing the traditional image of women, the humor works against it: "Unlike the enormous repertoire of horror stories used to convince children (particularly young women) of the importance of maintaining the culture's public agenda ('why, I know one girl who sat on a park toilet seat and got a disease and she could never marry'), the bawdy tales debunk and defy those rules" (33).

Green also offers a logical and obvious reason why folklorists and humor researchers do not comment on this kind of women's humor or even report its existence: with the exception of a few, such as Vance Randolph, they have accepted the cultural stereotype that denies women's participation in humor, especially bawdy humor, and therefore have not thought to ask the right questions. Of course, trying to collect examples of this humor could be fraught with difficulties for men: "Had they gone collecting the stuff from women, they'd have either got it, been shot trying, or ruined their reputation with the men out by the pick-up" (30). Thus, the tradition of women's shared oral humor has remained invisible to the culture at large.

In women's written humor, however, there is also considerable evidence of women's identification with other women, a perception of shared problems, concerns, and goals. This consciousness of belonging to a group of people with whom one has common ties is conveyed primarily by two devices. One is a narrative strategy in which two or more women are conversing with each other without the presence of males. The strategy arises naturally from the same circumstances that give rise to the oral tradition that Apte and Green describe: women in kitchens, or talking over back fences, or meeting for coffee in the midst of a day of housework. As Trudier Harris observes in her introduction to Alice Childress's *Like One of the Family,* the stories women tell are in some senses synonymous with their everyday lives: "Instead of moving out of the usual realms of their environments to share experiences with others, women frequently tell their tales where they are—in the dining room or living room while they are shelling beans for dinner, ironing, or while chastising their children. . . . Tasks do not interfere with performance, and life and art are synonymous."[16]

Childress's "conversations" are a good example of the pattern of shared confidences in women's written humor. Her narrator, Mildred, is a black domestic worker who shares her experiences with white employers with her friend Marge, frequently in Marge's kitchen. The humor in Mildred's monologues to Marge derives from her refusal to bow to white preconceptions of her inferiority. When a woman for whom she works ostentatiously removes her purse from Mildred's vicinity, Mildred reveals the absurdity of this action by taking her own purse with her when she runs a brief errand, and when another employer, upon learning that she lives in Harlem, asks to see her health card, Mildred responds by asking the woman for proof of her own health. By sharing such stories with the sympathetic Marge, Mildred both gathers strength for her efforts to achieve equality and affirms her connection with a black female community. Earlier in the century, two popular characters—Anne Warner French's "Susan Clegg" and Mary Roberts Rinehart's "Letitia Carberry"—provided examples of single women deriving a sense of strength and belonging from close relationships with other women. The Susan Clegg stories, like Childress's sketches, consist of largely one-sided conversations between Susan and her neighbor Mrs. Lathrop about men, marriage, and social mores. Rinehart's "Tish" is one of a group of three women friends who share action as well as talk, participating in a series of comic adventures that testify to their independence but also to their reliance on each other.

The second technique for establishing an impression of women as a group is the author's direct address to the reader—an inclusion of the reader in the concerns of the writer, assuming shared values and problems. The most striking examples of this device occur in the long tradition of satires on advice literature that has been part of women's humor since the early twentieth century. Female humorists have responded to the flood of etiquette books and advice columns intended to instruct women in manners, morality, and appearance by mocking both the genre and its efforts to make women conform to a cultural ideal. Josephine Daskam's *Fables for the Fair* (1901), subtitled *Cautionary Tales for Damsels Not Yet in Distress,* is a series of sketches that show women risking spinsterhood by being too intellectual, too independent, or too successful; and Helen Rowland's 1913 *The Sayings of Mrs. Solomon* provides similar advice in a more direct manner—for example, "Go to the *lemon grove,* oh, thou Scholarette! For no woman with *brains* hath ever plucked a peach in the Garden of Matrimony."[17] More recently, Deanne Stillman's "Ann Van Brothers Talks to Teens about Your Hair, Your Figure, Your Diet, Your Sweat, and Your Face," Mary Bess Whidden's "Dear Nanny," and Judith Martin's very popular *Miss Manners' Guide to Excruciatingly Correct Behavior* continue this tradition.[18] In all of these works, the author assumes a community of like-minded readers who will be sympathetic to her position.

Toward Solidarity: The Early Twentieth Century

Humor has both mirrored and promoted solidarity among women most overtly and intensely during periods in which women have been politically active on their own behalf in large numbers. Unified political action both removes women from the isolation of their lives and provides the sense of confidence and superiority that facilitates humorous expression. Two such periods in the twentieth century—the decades just before and just after passage of the woman suffrage amendment in 1920, and the women's movement that began in the 1960s—gave rise to a distinctly feminist humor that reveals a consciousness of common oppression. The humor of the earlier period is more narrowly focused on the right to vote and gender relationships, while contemporary feminist humor deals with a broader range of issues and more clearly demonstrates women's ability to laugh at themselves. Both, however, are evidence of unified concerns and values in a community of women.

By the turn of the century, a number of factors had combined to give American women a feeling that improvements in their status and role were not only possible but imminent. The reforms of the Progressive Era, a relaxation of Victorian morality, and renewed hope regarding woman suffrage led to the establishment of a large number of women's groups for social betterment and self-improvement. One such group, which existed in Greenwich Village from 1912 to 1940, was Heterodoxy, which numbered among its members Zona Gale, Charlotte Perkins Gilman, Susan Glaspell, and Fannie Hurst. The club, whose name derives from the diverse political allegiances and personal life-styles of its members, met once every two weeks for lunch and discussion—usually heated and frequently witty—of issues and ideas. What united the Heterodoxy members, according to Judith Schwarz, was their support of women: "All of the Heterodoxy club were ardently pro-women supporters who felt strong friendships and contacts with other women were vital to their lives."[19]

In the Heterodoxy group were several of the leading humorists of the period. Lou Rogers was a cartoonist whose prosuffrage cartoons appeared in numerous periodicals in the years preceding the suffrage amendment; Alice Duer Miller and Florence Guy

Seabury wrote satiric poetry and essays about women's status; and Charlotte Perkins Gilman frequently used humor in her utopian novels and social criticism. In addition, members of the group, including its founder, Marie Jenney Howe, displayed a flair for parody and irony that arose directly from their association with a group of strong, supportive women. Howe's "Anti-Suffrage Monologue," for example, is a clever parody of the standard antisuffrage speech that emphasized women's supposed emotional rather than intellectual "nature." "Now," writes Howe toward the end of the piece, "I think I have proved anti-suffrage; and I have done it in a womanly way—that is, without stooping to the use of a single fact or argument or a single statistic" (99). Howe's monologue ends on the same note: "Oh, friends, on this subject I feel—I feel so strongly that I can—not think!" (100).

Feminist humor in this early period tends to be directly political before 1920 and after that date tends to focus on personal relationships, as dual-career marriages and male-female role reversal became somewhat more common. Miller's 1915 book of verse, *Are Women People? A Book of Rhymes for Suffrage Times,* like Howe's monologue, parodies antisuffrage arguments and speaks, as had Daskam's *Fables for the Fair,* to the lack of regard for women's intellectual capacity. In "Why We Oppose Votes for Men," Miller points to men's emotional behavior at baseball games as evidence that they lack the calm reason necessary for voting; and "Interviews with Celebrated Anti-Suffragists" includes the following statements:

> Woman's place is in my home.—Appius Claudius
> I have never felt the need of the ballot.—Cleopatra[20]

In "The Protected Sex," Miller responds to an editorial opposing coeducation on the grounds that boys may be scarred by losing intellectual competitions with girls:

> There, little girl, don't read,
> You're fond of your books, I know,
> But Brother might mope
> If he had no hope
> Of getting ahead of you.
> It's dull for a boy who cannot lead.
> There, little girl, don't read.
>
> (34–35)

Gilman's "If I Were a Man" is a fantasy in which a woman manages to inhabit her husband's body for a day, and the dual consciousness that results from this merger of selves juxtaposes the stereotypical views that each gender has of the other. Mollie overhears men talk of woman's "God-appointed sphere" and the Edenic myth that women brought evil into the world, but eventually her presence in Gerald's consciousness causes him to respond to such sexist comments by saying, "Women are pretty much *people,* seems to me," thus answering the question in Miller's title.[21]

Writing in the 1920s, Rowland and Seabury addressed women's roles and relationships in what seemed to be a new era of freedom and possibility. The expectations, if not the actual lives, of middle-class, educated women had been enlarged to include political power and careers as well as marriage and children. The effect of women's new goals on the lives of men is the subject of Seabury's "The Delicatessen Husband." Ethel Winship, a Vassar graduate and a "modern, self-supporting woman," works late at her job and hates housework, forcing her husband, Perry, to depend on a delicatessen for sustenance. Perry, with fond memories of a nurturing mother and home-cooked meals, views delicatessens not as a convenience but as an evil: "They were emblems of a declining civilization, the source of all our ills, the promoter of equal suffrage, the permitter of the business and professional woman, the destroyer of the home."[22] In addition to satirizing Perry for his inability to accept the "modern woman," Seabury traces the stereotype of the nagging wife to its source in women's entrapment in the home: "Ethel is an excellent chemist, and an exceedingly poor homemaker. If she had lived a hundred years ago, with no outlet for the forces of her nature, nothing to exist for except a domestic routine, she would probably have been one of those irritable, inefficient wives and tart mothers who make an entire family miserable, seeing their duty and doing it" (35). The satisfaction of a career was, in the 1920s as now, a mixed blessing for women who also had major responsibility for the household. The speaker in Rowland's *This Married Life* wants to advertise for a "substitute wife" for her husband—someone who will provide the services that a working woman is too tired or too busy to provide: "Somebody to greet him with a glad, bright smile and a bark of joy when I am kept late at the office. . . . Somebody to wait up for him when he stays out late, listen to his 'explanations' and pretend to believe them, while I get a full night's sleep. Somebody to remind him to write to his Mother."[23] As social scientist Lorine Pruette wrote in 1931, upon marriage "men appear to lose a large part of their capacity as adults: they can no longer feed themselves, house themselves, look after their health, or attend to their social responsibilities (most of them upon marriage lose the capacity even of writing to their own mother)."[24]

Yet, despite humor that seemed to speak to the common problems of professional women, feminism was on the decline by the mid-1920s. Women who had been united by the suffrage battle and other feminist causes in the early part of the century watched younger women succumb to complacency and a renewed feminine image promoted by the media. At no time during the 1920s were more than 30 percent of married women in the labor force, and in 1930 less than 4 percent of married women held white-collar positions.[25] Media attention to the problems of the working woman notwithstanding, she remained a rarity as most women followed traditional socialization to devote themselves to home and family. It was precisely this absence of women from the work force that precluded a sense of group identity that might have kept feminism alive as a social force. As Elaine Showalter puts it in *These Modern Women,* the "necessary preconditions" for radical feminism did not exist in the 1920s. Even though most of the issues raised by the contemporary women's movement were raised at the time, what was missing was a critical mass of women confronting various kinds of discrimination: "What was missing was a sufficiently sizable base of employed married women, experiencing firsthand the role conflict which the *Nation* women understood; and a feminist analysis which could interpret the role conflict and the discrimination as a collective political phenomenon rather than as a personal problem."[26] The feminist humor of the early decades of the century lost ground by the 1940s to the domestic humor that emphasized women's isolation rather than their identity as a group.[27]

Toward Solidarity: The 1970s and 1980s

During the early years of the women's movement that began in the late 1960s, women had to struggle to emerge from their isolation of preceding decades, and humor did not play a large part in feminism. Indeed, the anger and grim determination that characterized the early women's movement, like the civil rights movement that instigated it, led to renewed accusations that women—especially "women's libbers"—had no sense of humor. Typical are the comments of Harvey Mindess, who speaks of women's "reluctance to laugh at themselves and their mission" and accuses women of using caustic wit rather than "good-natured humor."[28] But women who were tired of centuries of humor at their own expense saw very little that was funny in their efforts to have their concerns taken seriously. Mary Kay Blakely explains in her introduction to *Pulling Our Own Strings* the problematic relationship between humor and liberation during this period:

> I heard the faint voice of self-consciousness in our humor, the nervous laugh of the messenger who doesn't want her head cut off for reporting the damaging news. . . . We are expected, somehow, not to offend anyone on our way to liberation. There's an absurd expectation that the women's movement must be the first revolution in history to accomplish its goals without hurting anyone's feelings. We are to be the Boston Tea Party that serves crumpets with its resolutions.[29]

Yet some writers, even in the early years of the movement, found humor in their own ambivalence and in some aspects of the movement itself. Judith Viorst captured the tension that many women felt between traditional roles and political activism in her poem "A Women's Liberation Movement Woman." Torn between dependence on male protection and anger at her subordinate position, Viorst's speaker begins:

> When it's snowing and I put on all the galoshes
> While he reads the paper,
> Then I want to become a
> Women's Liberation Movement woman.
> And when it's snowing and he looks for the taxi
> While I wait in the lobby,
> Then I don't.[30]

If Viorst expresses ambivalence about becoming part of a group of feminists, Nora Ephron points out that groups of women who gathered for consciousness-raising did not always accomplish their purpose. Ephron's 1973 essay "On Consciousness-Raising" is a witty description of the way her particular group descended from the goal of transforming the personal into the political to sharing recipes for stuffing a Thanksgiving turkey. Although supportive of the goals of consciousness-raising groups, Ephron points out that hers became a "running soap opera," with each woman stuck in her own unchanging story. "We were much too sophisticated," Ephron says, "to waste time discussing hard-core movement concepts like 'the various levels and forms that oppression takes in our daily lives.' What we wanted to talk about was men."[31]

As the movement matured in the late 1970s, feminists moved from talking about individual men to talking about men and institutions in general and finally to the point of being able to laugh at themselves—not the self-deprecating laughter of the underdog but the laughter that comes with security and confidence. It is this sort of laughter that Hélène Cixous describes in "The Laugh of the Medusa" when she calls for women to write *as* women, "in order to smash everything, to shatter the framework of institutions, to blow up the law, to break up the 'truth' with laughter."[32] The feminist humor of the early twentieth century did not, except in utopian works such as Gilman's *Herland,* imagine a new social order; rather, it parodied the existing order. Feminist humor of the 1970s and 1980s, however, uses irony and whimsy as well as satire in order to point up the absurdity of oppression. Flo Kennedy's famous line "a woman without a man is like a fish without a bicycle" goes beyond criticism to assume equality and independence.

The publication of *Pulling Our Own Strings: Feminist Humor and Satire* in 1980 was significant for several reasons. That a market for such a collection was believed to exist is in itself evidence of the growth of the women's movement. As a corollary, the volume proved how much humor the movement had given rise to: a few of the selections are by feminists of earlier eras, such as Alice Duer Miller and Elizabeth Cady Stanton, but most are by contemporary writers and comic artists—including, importantly, several men, such as Jules Feiffer and Garry Trudeau. Some of the humor is of the caustic kind that had bothered Harvey Mindess in 1971. Joanna Russ's "Dear Colleague: I Am Not an Honorary Male" strips bare men's comments to female colleagues by translating their real meanings. For example, "It was only a joke" translates as "I find jokes about you funny. Why don't *you* find jokes about you funny?" (180). Others, such as Gloria Steinem's well-known "If Men Could Menstruate," point to the absurd relationship between biology and power by asserting that if menstruation were a factor in male physiology, it would be honored rather than feared and degraded.

But more important than the tone or subject of individual selections is the fact that most of the writers convey an assumption of being understood by readers who share not only the experience being described but also the writer's attitude toward women and equality. Efforts by psychologists to measure the factors involved in response to feminist humor have been inconclusive,[33] but numerous studies have shown that agreement with the ideological stance promoted in humor is necessary for a positive response from reader or listener. Again and again, these writers speak of "we housewives" and "we women" and speak to the reader as "you." This sense of unity is explained by Mary Kay Blakely as a survival technique: "With our humor we learn how to live in a society, despite its sexism, without compromising too many of our principles or sacrificing too much of our happiness. We use our humor as a cure for burnout" (12).

Several recent phenomena testify that humor has become, in the 1980s, an effective instrument for unity among women. One is the emergence of lesbian feminist humor. Susan J. Wolfe has emphasized the bonding effect of lesbian humor, particularly when women tell humorous stories about coming out and early sexual experiences. Further bonding is created by the fact that some lesbian humor is initially inaccessible to heterosexuals because of its grounding in and reference to lesbian culture. To say, for example, that calling a lesbian a clone is a compliment does not make sense unless one understands the rejection of heterosexuality and thus of reproduction by heterosexual means. Wolfe notes that "many of us are becomings secure enough in our own politics to start spoofing them" and that "jokes about political correctness have become commonplace among Lesbian feminists." In a group that is opposed to every conceivable "ism," she says, "it is *fairly* easy to fall into political error in word and deed."[34] Gail Sausser's book *Lesbian Etiquette* is another example of the ability to laugh healthily at oneself while promoting feminism and tolerance. Sausser's essays address such topics as handling a visit from a lover's parents, dealing with dating, and confronting the straight world. Sausser pokes fun at the extremes of lesbian culture, such as food fetishes—"I swallowed gallons of carrot juice"—while at the same time using humor to oppose homophobia. In "Gays Need Better P.R.," for example, she says, "we are the answer to overpopulation, unwanted pregnancy, and sexual repression—let's get some credit for it."[35]

Two of the most significant signs that women have achieved a new relationship with humor are the dramatic increase in the number of female stand-up comics and the popularity of comic strips such as Nicole Hollander's "Sylvia" and Cathy Guisewite's "Cathy." The fields of stand-up comedy and syndicated cartooning have been particularly resistant to women artists for years, and major advancements by women in these areas in the 1980s proves that there is a large audience for feminist—or at least nonsexist—humor in a variety of media. The new female comics, who make up about one-third of current performers, refuse to practice the self-deprecatory humor that seemed the only avenue for those in Phyllis Diller's era, when the put-down of women was a staple of male stand-up comedy. So pervasive has been the comedy routine with women as its major target that a 1984 article about new female comedians was subtitled "Can You Be a Funny Woman without Making Fun of Women?" Julia Klein, author of this *Ms.* article, noted that many female comedians do not overtly define themselves as feminists, but their subject matter has a definite female focus: "They return repeatedly to the incongruities of relationships between men and women; they comically detail the life of the urban single woman; they do set pieces on the perils of premenstrual syndrome and birth-control methods. Their politics, for the most part, are intensely personal. Ronald Reagan is of less interest than sexual rejection, the Pill, and the disgusting nature of cottage cheese."[36] In short, these comics use as material what it is like to be a woman today, and they seem to be reaching large audiences with similar concerns.

In like manner, female cartoonists, such as Hollander, Guisewite, and J. J. Danielson, confront issues central to women's lives without disparaging either women or the issues. Guisewite's Cathy handles a demanding job, fends off fashion trends that she knows are intended to manipulate her, and worries about dieting and dating. Hollander's Sylvia is more iconoclastic, taking on the role of an informal therapist who says precisely what she feels and frequently expresses what women *wish* they could say. In one strip, for example, Sylvia relaxes in the bathtub while her daughter knocks on the door and says, "Ma, I gotta get in there! Ma, how long are you going to stay in the tub?" Sylvia replies, "I'm staying in here until Phyllis Schlafly admits she's a female impersonator. You better take a bath next door." Hollander describes Sylvia as "the part of women that's strong and self-confident and has a humorous vision of the world."[37]

To be strong and self-confident and have a humorous vision of the world, while not precisely a stated goal of the women's movement, is certainly one of the results of liberation. As Erica Jong puts it, "the ability to joke about something implies an underlying security of belief" (162). Although it is impossible to document the precise effects that women's humor has had on the progress of the women's movement at this or any other time, it is clear that laughter *with* others is evidence of shared values and perceptions, and the proliferation of humor by women in recent years is a symptom of vitality and self-confidence. Humor can trivialize and even wound, but it can also bring us together in a feeling of common humanity that is necessary to work for full liberation.

Notes

1. It should be noted that this situation has changed rather dramatically in recent years. In 1984, 59 percent of married women with children were in the labor force, and a variety of social changes have promoted a shift from what Alice Walker has called "suspended women" to "emergent women." Yet it should also be noted that the increase in women's freedom and autonomy has affected primarily white, middle-class women, not minority women, who tend either to remain in traditional roles or to be single heads of households. See Rochelle Gatlin, *American Women since 1945* (Jackson: University Press of Mississippi, 1987), esp. chaps. 7–9.
2. William H. Chafe, *Women and Equality: Changing Patterns in*

American Culture (New York: Oxford University Press, 1977), 3–11.

3. Phyllis McGinley, *Times Three: Selected Verse from Three Decades* (New York: Viking, 1961), 182, 135. Subsequent page references will be given in parentheses in the text.
4. Betty Friedan, *The Feminine Mystique* (New York: Norton, 1963), 57. One of Friedan's points is that the professional writer, such as McGinley, Jean Kerr, or Shirley Jackson, led a far more fulfilled professional life than did the women who read her humorous works, so that her pretense of being "just a housewife" was false and deflected women from developing a proper rebellion against their subordination. But it seems far more likely that women's humor of this period provided one of the few available senses of community among women. See Nancy Walker, "Humor and Gender Roles: The 'Funny' Feminism of the Post–World War II Suburbs," in *American Humor,* ed. Arthur P. Dudden (New York: Oxford University Press, 1987), 118–37.
5. Lawrence W. Levine, *Black Culture and Black Consciousness: Afro-American Folk Thought from Slavery to Freedom* (New York: Oxford University Press, 1977), chap. 5, "Black Laughter."
6. Naomi Weisstein, "Why Aren't We Laughing . . . Anymore," *Ms.,* November 1973, 88. Subsequent page references will be given in parentheses in the text.
7. Anne Beatts, "Can a Woman Get a Laugh and a Man Too?" *Mademoiselle,* November 1975, 140.
8. Deanne Stillman, *Getting Back at Dad* (New York: Wideview Books, 1981), 5.
9. Kate Sanborn, *The Wit of Women* (New York: Funk and Wagnalls, 1885); Martha Bensley Bruère and Mary Ritter Beard, *Laughing Their Way: Women's Humor in America* (New York: Macmillan, 1934).
10. Paul E. McGhee, "The Role of Laughter and Humor in Growing Up Female," in *Becoming Female: Perspectives on Development,* ed. Claire B. Kopp (New York: Plenum Press, 1979), 192. Subsequent page references will be given in parentheses in the text.
11. Zita Zatkin Dresner, "Twentieth Century American Women Humorists," diss., University of Maryland, 1982, 64–65.
12. Erica Jong, "You Have to Be Liberated to Laugh," *Playboy,*

April 1980, 162. Subsequent page references will be given in parentheses in the text.

13. Mary Jo Neitz, "Humor, Hierarchy, and the Changing Status of Women," *Psychiatry* 43 (August 1980), 220. Subsequent page references will be given in parentheses in the text.

14. Mahadev L. Apte, *Humor and Laughter: An Anthropological Approach* (Ithaca, N.Y.: Cornell University Press, 1985), 76. Subsequent page references will be given in parentheses in the text.

15. Rayna Green, "Magnolias Grow in Dirt: The Bawdy Lore of Southern Women," *Southern Exposure* 4 (1977), 33. Subsequent page references will be given in parentheses in the text.

16. Trudier Harris, Introduction, *Like One of the Family: Conversations from a Domestic's Life,* by Alice Childress (1956) (Boston: Beacon Press, 1986), xvi.

17. Helen Rowland, *The Sayings of Mrs. Solomon: Being the Confessions of the Seven Hundreth* [*sic*] *Wife* (New York: Dodge, 1913), 22.

18. Deanne Stillman, "Ann Van Brothers . . . ," in *Getting Back at Dad;* Mary Bess Whidden, "Dear Nanny," in *Provincial Matters* (Albuquerque: University of New Mexico Press, 1985); Judith Martin, *Miss Manners* (New York: Atheneum, 1982).

19. Judith Schwarz, *Radical Feminists of Heterodoxy: Greenwich Village 1912–1940* (Lebanon, N.H.: New Victoria Publishers, 1982), 1. Subsequent page references will be given in parentheses in the text.

20. Alice Duer Miller, *Are Women People? A Book of Rhymes for Suffrage Times* (New York: George H. Doran, 1915), 53. Subsequent page references will be given in parentheses in the text.

21. Charlotte Perkins Gilman, "If I Were a Man," in *The Charlotte Perkins Gilman Reader,* ed. Ann J. Lane (New York: Pantheon, 1980), 38.

22. Florence Guy Seabury, "The Delicatessen Husband," in *The Delicatessen Husband and Other Essays* (New York: Harcourt, Brace, 1925), 28–29. Subsequent page references will be given in parentheses in the text.

23. Helen Rowland, "If She Could Advertise," in *This Married Life* (New York: Dodge, 1927), 69–70.

24. Lorine Pruette, "Why Women Fail," in *Woman's Coming of*

Age, ed. V. F. Calverton and Samuel Schmalhausen (New York: Horace Liveright, 1931), 256–57.

25. Nancy F. Cott, *The Grounding of Modern Feminism* (New Haven: Yale University Press, 1987), 182–83.

26. Elaine Showalter, ed., *These Modern Women: Autobiographical Essays from the Twenties* (Old Westbury, N.Y.: Feminist Press, 1978), 26.

27. However, as I have argued elsewhere, a close look at women's domestic humor from 1940 to about 1965 reveals what might be considered a prefeminist attack on the cultural subordination of women. See "Humor and Gender Roles."

28. Harvey Mindess, *Laughter and Liberation* (Los Angeles: Nash, 1971), 198–99.

29. Gloria Kaufman and Mary Kay Blakely, eds., *Pulling Our Own Strings: Feminist Humor and Satire* (Bloomington: Indiana University Press, 1980), 10. Subsequent page references will be given in parentheses in the text.

30. Judith Viorst, *It's Hard to Be Hip over Thirty* (New York: Norton, 1968), 16.

31. Nora Ephron, "On Consciousness-Raising," in *Crazy Salad: Some Things about Women* (New York: Knopf, 1973), 71–78.

32. Hélène Cixous, "The Laugh of the Medusa," trans. Keith and Paula Cohen, *Signs* 1, no. 4 (Summer 1976), 888.

33. The problems involved in such studies include choosing a definition of feminism and the selection of materials to which subjects are to respond, both of which can be affected by the bias of the researcher. Two psychologists at Western Carolina University conducted three studies of different age groups, each including both males and females. The groups were asked to rate themselves on a scale of sympathy with feminist principles and then to respond to cartoons and slogans from a feminist product catalogue. The researchers were interested in the correlation between feminist identification and positive response to feminist humor, and indeed the correlation was high, except for the women in the college-age group. But those who *agreed* with the slogans presented did not always find them *funny,* leading the researchers to conclude that "perhaps appreciation of feminist humor requires a shared conviction that gender-based stereotypes must be changed." Judith M. Stillion and Hedy White,

"Feminist Humor: Who Appreciates It and Why?" *Psychology of Women Quarterly* 11 (1987), 219–32.

34. Susan J. Wolfe, "Ingroup Lesbian Feminist Political Humor," paper presented at the Midwest Modern Language Association, Minneapolis, November 1980.
35. Gail Sausser, "Gays Need Better P.R.," in *Lesbian Etiquette* (Trumansburg, N.Y.: Crossing Press, 1986), 49.
36. Julia Klein, "The New Stand-up Comics," *Ms.*, October 1984, 122.
37. Quoted in Kathy Witkowsky, "Cartoon Verite: She Strips to Conquer—Nicole Hollander's 'Sylvia,' " *Vogue*, February 1986, 222.

PART TWO

American Women Humor Writers

Nineteenth-Century Women's Humor

Nancy Walker

Women, like men, have based their humor on the incongruity between the ideals and the realities of American culture. However, instead of concentrating on the gap between ideal and real in the public arenas of politics and business, women have pointed to incongruities in the more private areas of home and human relationships. America's best-known female humorist, Dorothy Parker, exemplifies this tendency in her light verse, such as the famous couplet "Men seldom make passes / At girls who wear glasses." This is not to say that male humorists have ignored what was called in the early twentieth century "the war between the sexes"; the point is rather that personal life instead of public life has been the primary focus of women's humor, whereas the reverse has been true of men's humor.

Kate Sanborn's 1885 collection, *The Wit of Women,* intended to counter the idea that women lack a sense of humor, is a chatty, anecdotal book that provides brief selections from the work of dozens of writers, most of them unknown to twentieth-century readers. Sanborn's definition of *wit* is anything but narrow; the book includes puns, poems for children, dialect stories, satire, and bits of witty conversation. Most of the selections, however, reflect Sanborn's genteel New England heritage, and her biases are clear. Although she includes many puns, for example, she disdains them: "It is also affirmed," she writes, " 'that women cannot make a pun,' which, if true, would be greatly to their honor."[1] Nonetheless, *The Wit of Women* provides ample evidence that long before Erma Bombeck, American women in great numbers wrote humorous literature.

Sanborn provides a clue to the popularity of some female humorists of the nineteenth century when she mentions their names but does not include their work (or much of it) on the grounds that it is already familiar to her readers—"why not," she asks, "save space for what is not in everyone's mouth and memory?"[2] Among the more well-known humorists she counts Frances Whicher, "Gail Hamilton" (Mary Abigail Dodge), Phoebe Cary, and Caroline Kirkland. Writing between the 1830s and the 1870s, these women demonstrated the range of themes and forms that characterize much of nineteenth-century women's humor. Women's experience of life both in settled communities and on the frontier was quite different from that of men, and the subjects of their humorous prose and poetry reflect their much greater concern with the household, interpersonal relationships, and the role of women in American society.[3]

The work of Frances Whicher (1814–1852) shares with that of much "traditional" nineteenth-century humor the use of dialect. In the sketches collected as *The Widow Bedott Papers* in 1856, Whicher tells of life in rural New York State from the perspectives of two women: the Widow Bedott, a pretentious, gossipy husband hunter; and her sister, Aunt Maguire, a slightly more sensible women who points out the foibles of others more often than she demonstrates them herself. The sketches deal with the world of the small-town woman of the period: housework, children, and social occasions such as the church-sponsored sewing society. The characters are unconcerned with politics, except the social politics of the community; women inhabit an environment that does not extend beyond home, family, and neighbors. Within this environment, the Widow Bedott and Aunt Maguire both embody and point to the ridiculous behavior of people whose lives consist of routine, petty detail.

For example, in the piece "Aunt Maguire Continues Her Account of the Sewing Society," the women argue about how often to meet, the purpose of the money they will raise with their sewing, and who makes the best cake and preserves. As Aunt Maguire reports, "ther tongues went a good deal faster 'n ther fingers did."[4]

The humor in the Widow Bedott sketches comes from the ironic distance between the author, Frances Whicher, and the women and men who populate them. Although Whicher expects her readers to laugh at the silliness and pretensions of her characters, she makes it clear that the competition among the women for both men and social prestige is a result of social pressure rather than innate weakness or defect. In the small world Whicher portrays, woman's worth is validated only by the "feminine" qualities of attractiveness to men and good housekeeping skills. When the widow, having failed to snare Mr. Crane in matrimony, does succeed in capturing the Reverend Sniffles, she reveals in a letter to her daughter that she has made a good move socially: "It's melanchony to be alone in the world, but then ministers don't grow on every bush."[5] The dialect in which her characters speak may make *The Widow Bedott Papers* difficult for the modern reader (e.g., "perdickerment" for *predicament* and "curus" for *curious*) but no more difficult than the work of other dialect writers, and it is a rich source of the humor in the sketches, reflecting the early-nineteenth-century writer's concern for the "common man" (or woman).

Both Caroline Kirkland (1801–1864) and Mary Abigail Dodge (1833–1896) deal with a different kind of women's experience in the nineteenth century: life on the frontier. If small-town women turned to social climbing as a result of their restricted lives, women who followed their husbands to remote, unsettled areas west of the Appalachians had to cope with the absence of not only a social structure but often the basic necessities of life. For male humorists of the period, such as Bret Harte, Artemus Ward, and Thomas Bangs Thorpe, the hardships of pioneer existence were translated into tall tales of heroic men subduing the wilderness—uncertainty became transformed into bravado. But the women, who frequently went went out of a sense of duty to their husbands instead of any pioneering urge, were far more likely to make humor out of the chaos of trying to maintain households in primitive surroundings. Kirkland, who wrote as "Mrs. Mary Clavers,"[6] accompanied her husband to Michigan in the 1830s, and in *A New Home—Who'll Follow?* (1841), she makes it clear that there was nothing heroic for a woman in this frontier environment. Kirkland writes, for example, of the settlers' habit of borrowing what they need from their neighbors—everything from flour sifters to saddles—with the result that a housewife cannot depend on having what she needs for her own family: "Not only are all kitchen utensils as much your neighbor's as your own, but bedsteads, beds, blankets, sheets, travel from house to house. . . . sieves, smoothing irons, and churns run about as if they had legs. . . . I have lent my broom, my thread, my tape, my spoons, my cat. . . ."[7] The habit of borrowing reaches its zenith in the request from a nursing mother that she be allowed to borrow another woman's baby when her own is unable to nurse. Kirkland's narrator comments, "I could not help thinking that one must come 'west' in order to learn a little of everything."[8]

Later in the century, "Gail Hamilton" (pseudonym of Mary Abigail Dodge) reacts to a similar isolation in *Twelve Miles from a Lemon* (1874). Using the lemon as a hallmark of civilized life and a synonym for the nearest town, Dodge details the difficulty a woman has in getting a meal prepared when she must depend on random deliveries of meat, milk, and eggs. When someone suggests that she keep her own hens for eggs, she replies in a manner that foreshadows Betty MacDonald's 1945 humorous novel, *The Egg and I:*

> Because eggs are no sooner hatched than all the forces of nature rise up together to destroy them. Hatched, do I say? Before they are hatched the fox comes. While they are yet eggs the cats smell them out and suck them. When they have broken shell and become chickens, the first thing they do is get lost. If there is a bit of late snow it shall go hard but they will roam around till they find it, and then they will stand on it and shiver and die.[9]

The itinerant peddler is regarded as a "missionary" who brings "us outside barbarians" the "appliances of civilization."[10] *Twelve Miles from a Lemon* includes satiric essays on a number of topics in addition to frontier living, but all of them deal with women's experience and either implicitly or explicitly urge changes in attitudes toward or conditions of women's lives.

In *The Wit of Women,* Kate Sanborn notes that some have called Phoebe Cary (1824–1871) "the wittiest woman in America." Cary seems to have had a reputation like Dorothy Parker had in the 1920s and 1930s for being a clever conversationalist, adept at what would today be called one-liners.[11] Her humor, as represented in her collection *Poems and Parodies* (1854), has a sophistication in direct contrast to Frances Whicher's dialect sketches; her style has more in common with that of Ambrose Bierce and Oliver Wendell Holmes than with that of the frontier humorists. The speaker in her polished verse is highly literate and somewhat aloof, and she often writes parodies of well-known works of literature. Cary's concerns, however, are the relationship between women and men and the ways women conform to societal expectations. In the poem "Girls Were Made to Mourn," Cary echoes Whicher's Widow Bedott as she addresses the belief that an unmarried woman is somehow incomplete. Whicher approaches the subject by showing the lengths to which a woman will go to have a husband; Cary's speaker openly questions the requirement:

> If I'm designed to live alone,—
> By nature's law designed,—
> Why was this constant wish to wed
> E'er planted in my mind?

Another stanza reminds us of the dependency of the Widow Bedott and others:

> See yonder young, accomplished girl,
> Whose words are smooth as oil,
> Who'd marry almost anyone
> To keep her hands from toil[12]

The most obviously feminist humorist of this period—and also the most widely read, according to book sales—was Marietta Holley (1836–1926). Whereas Gail Hamilton and others used irony and sarcasm to reveal women's deeply felt desire for equality, Holley posed direct rational challenges to the values of a culture that subjugates half its population. In twenty-one books published between 1873 and 1914, Holley's character Samantha Allen combines the dialect of a rural farm wife with a commonsense feminism that brings to the fore the issues that most immediately concerned women's rights advocates of the day: the right to vote, temperance, entry into the professions, equal pay for equal work, and many more. As Jane Curry, editor of a recent anthology of excerpts from Holley's books, put it, "When one reads the Samantha books, she begins to view the 19th century not as 'then' so much as it was the beginning of 'now.' "[13] Holley's work is thus a striking combination of traditional technique and contemporary issues: the use of dialect and misspelling was going out of style even as Holley wrote, but her insistence on women's equality is relevant a hundred years after her first books were published.

As the uneducated person of common sense, Samantha Allen qualifies as an *eiron*—a wise innocent—and much of the humor in the Samantha books depends on stereotypical clashes between the simple and the pretentious. When Samantha travels from her rural home, as she does in *Samantha at Saratoga* (1887) and *Samantha at the World's Fair* (1893), among others, she marvels at the grandeur so unlike her farm house, but she displays the *eiron*'s insight. Seeing the statues in the great hall of the World's Fair, for example, she comments knowledgeably about the role women have played in American culture: "Then there wuz Tradition. Them wuz two old men, as wuz nateral—wimmen wuzn't in that—woman is in the future and the present. Them two men, a-lookin' considerable war-like, wuz a-talking' over the past—the deeds of Might. They didn't need wimmen so much there, and I didn't feel as if I cared a cent to have her there."[14] Samantha as "wise innocent" sees that men, not women, have started wars, and is content that women are not part of a warlike statue to "Tradition," but she is confident that women will play a large role in the "future." At home, Samantha argues incessantly with her husband, Josiah, and her neighbor Betsey Bobbet about the proper role for women. Betsey, the stereotypical husband-hunting spinster, is a foil to Samantha's commonsense feminism; Betsey's claims that "women's speah" is to cling to man "like a vine to a stately tree" are met by Samantha's outrage: "Women's speah is where she can do the most good; if God had meant that wimmen should be nothin' but men's shadders, He would have gosts and fantoms of 'em at once. But havin' made 'em flesh and blood, with braens and souls, I believe He meant 'em to be used to the best advantage."[15] Most such conversations take place in Samantha's kitchen, where she is simultaneously doing laundry, making preserves, and baking pies. Occupied with household duties, like other women, Holley's character nonetheless has a sophisticated understanding of social issues, and she brings into the open the concern for sexual equality that earlier female humorists had addressed in a more subtle manner.

Notes

"Nineteenth-Century Women's Humor" originally appeared in Nancy Walker, *The Tradition of Women's Humor in America* (Huntington Beach: American Studies Publishing, 1984), 8–14. Reprinted with permission.

1. Kate Sanborn, *The Wit of Women* (New York, 1885), 16. For a discussion of the ways in which nineteenth-century female humorists dealt with this subject, see Nancy Walker, "Wit, Sentimentality, and the Image of Women in the Nineteenth Century," *American Studies* 23, no. 2 (Fall 1981), 5–22.
2. Sanborn, *Wit of Women,* p. 69.
3. See Linda Ann Finton Morris, "Women Vernacular Humorists in Nineteenth-Century America: Ann Stephens, Frances Whicher, and Marietta Holley," diss., University of California, Berkeley, 1978.
4. Frances Whicher, *The Widow Bedott Papers* (New York: J. C. Derby, 1856), 293.
5. Ibid., 188–89.
6. The use of pseudonyms by women who wrote humor in the nineteenth century was not motivated by the desire to hide a female identity that caused, for example, Mary Ann Evans to write as "George Eliot." Most female humorists used women's names and pseudonyms and shared with male humorists of the period the habit of creating a humorous persona not to be confused with the more serious or more sophisticated author.
7. Mrs. Mary Clavers [Caroline Kirkland], *A New Home—Who'll Follow?* (New York: Charles S. Francis, 1841), 106.
8. Ibid., 112.
9. Gail Hamilton [Mary Abigail Dodge], *Twelve Miles from a Lemon* (New York: Harper and Brothers, 1874), 14–15.
10. Ibid., 21.
11. Sanborn, *Wit of Women,* 100–101.

12. Phoebe Cary, *Poems and Parodies* (Boston: Ticknor, Reed, and Fields, 1854), 166–67.
13. Jane Curry, ed., *Samantha Rastles the Woman Question* (Urbana: University of Illinois Press, 1983), 1.
14. Josiah Allen's Wife [Marietta Holley], *Samantha at the World's Fair* (New York: Funk and Wagnalls, 1893), 229.
15. Josiah Allen's Wife [Marietta Holley], *My Opinions and Betsey Bobbet's* (Hartford: American Publishing, 1882), 238.

Domestic Comic Writers

Zita Z. Dresner

The adoption of the persona of housewife is not peculiar to twentieth-century women's writing. From Anne Bradstreet in the seventeenth century to Erma Bombeck today, American women writers have used domestic images, settings, voices, and characters to express in both serious and humorous poetry, verse, novels, stories, and articles their perspectives on their own lives and on the social, political, and cultural environments in which they have lived. However, the emergence of domestic or housewife humor—a body of humorous writing in which the autobiographical persona of a harried housewife describes her frantic and often unsuccessful efforts to cope with life in the slow (family- and home-centered) lane—can be viewed as a post–World War II phenomenon for a number of reasons.

The 1940s are often considered a decade of liberation for women because the job opportunities created by World War II brought more than six million women into the labor force by 1945, thus increasing the number of working women by 50 percent and doubling the number of working wives. When the war ended, however, and it became clear that the vast majority of female workers wanted to keep their jobs, those business executives and government bureaucrats who had originally used their resources to woo women into the labor force launched a virulent antifeminist campaign against women's continued employment. Historians have clearly documented how in the postwar period these groups, with the overwhelming concurrence and aid of the mass media, promoted the idea that the employment of women in traditionally "masculine" occupations was "unfeminine" and that the employment of wives and mothers, in general, was "un-American." Moreover, at the same time that women were admonished to return to their "true place" in the home, they were also blamed for destroying society by undermining the American family through leaving home to work in the first place.

Beginning in the late 1940s, women were accused in print of responsibility for a plethora of social ills, from male impotence to alcoholism to juvenile delinquency, at the same time as they were glorified for their nurturing and caretaking abilities.[1] "One of the by-products of the war, therefore," William Chafe writes, "was a deepening sense of bewilderment among many American women over how to define their identity"; and this confusion was kept alive by magazines that, beginning with *Life*'s feature in the summer of 1947 on the "American Woman's Problem," presented almost weekly at least one article on this "problem."[2] A frequently espoused solution to the "problem" and, according to Philip Slater in *The Pursuit of Loneliness,* the most significant factor in the "ultra-domestication" of the American woman of the 1950s, was the "magnification of the child-rearing role."[3] Following the 1947 publication of *Modern Woman: The Lost Sex* by Ferdinand Lundberg and Marynia Farnham, middlebrow publications like *The Atlantic* and *Saturday Review,* as well as women's magazines, reiterated Lundberg and Farnham's view that women would be perfectly happy if they would only accept the fact that they "had been created to be biologically and psychologically dependent on man" and would embrace again the home and child rearing as the core of their existence.

Along with the baby boom that lasted from the 1940s to 1960, the tremendous growth of suburban communities between 1950 and 1968, the reduction in the age at which women married, and the number of women who dropped out of college to marry (60 percent by the mid-1950s) all attest to the extent to which women accepted the popular emphasis on family togetherness and the joys of femininity as the road to happiness. Betty Friedan's 1963 blockbuster, *The Feminine Mystique,* clearly documents the ambiguity and anxiety that many American women felt about their identity and place. In analyzing the decline and fall of the mainly white, middle-class American woman from the end of World War II to

1960, Friedan showed how the clash between the realities of these women's lives and the illusions they were socialized to accept and perpetuate resulted in what she called "The Problem That Has No Name."[4]

It is no coincidence that female domestic or housewife humor developed during this same period, for it is in many ways another by-product of the "bewilderment" that was generated by the post-war antifeminist sentiment, another response to the confusion that existed about woman's identity, purpose, and place. However, rather than encouraging radical solutions to the "woman problem," as Friedan's women's liberation movement intended to do by calling for equality between men and women and by challenging the political, social, and economic systems that reinforced women's subjugation, domestic humor tended to provide women with a temporary tool for coping with those negative feelings about themselves and their lives; it spoke directly to those who have been pressured, overtly or covertly, into acknowledging housewifery as their sole occupation and raison d'être.

Housewife humor, consequently, has been castigated as antifeminist for encouraging women to accept the home as their place and for supporting the notion that domesticity offers women adequate outlets for satisfying their needs and utilizing their talents. Friedan, for example, writes in *The Feminine Mystique:*

> there is something about Housewife Writers that isn't funny—like Uncle Tom, or Amos and Andy. "Laugh," the Housewife Writers tell the real housewife, "if you're feeling desperate, empty, bored, trapped in the bedmaking, chauffeuring and dishwashing details. Isn't it funny? We're all in the same trap." Do real housewives then dissipate in laughter their dreams and their sense of desperation? Do they think their frustrated abilities and their limited lives are a joke?[5]

Patricia Meyer Spacks expresses similar concern about the effects of housewife humor: "The Erma Bombeck–Jean Kerr–Betty MacDonald comic tradition is profoundly conservative in its social implications, preserving the image of feminine incompetence, siphoning off anger, suggesting that if it's funny to be a bad housewife, there may be some dignity to being a good one."[6]

It is the contention of this essay however, that while domestic humor may be merely another current in the mainstream of what Eric Bentley defines as modern American "commercial comedy,"[7] because it upholds rather than attacks the status quo, the enormous popularity of books by "housewife writers" who describe the domestic scene in a humorous way, as well as the recent work of humor scholars, suggests that the appeal of this humor cannot be so simply dismissed as reactionary. Moreover, such an oversimplification fails to consider the ways in which humor functions covertly to inspire rebelliousness.

In assessing the nature of domestic humor, it is important to reemphasize a point made by Elizabeth Janeway (and others) that guilt and insecurity have characterized the homemaker, as well as the working woman, since the postwar period. First, the isolation of middle-class women in a personal universe of home and family tended to cut housewives off from and make them fearful of assuming responsibility for issues and events activating the male-dominated public arena of business and politics. The more removed women become from objectively significant experience, feminists have argued, the more importance they attach to trivial concerns such as dull floors, graying hair, body odor, and ring-around-the-collar; these concerns become the only issues about which they feel they can do anything. Moreover, having little opportunity, in the home-centered lives they have chosen, to utilize their own intellectual abilities or nondomestic talents, housewives have been reduced to receiving a great deal of their experience vicariously—to defining the success and value of their lives in terms of the actions and achievements of their husbands and children.[8]

The domestic humor that emerged during the period, therefore, seems to have both grown out of and appealed to the anxiety and frustration many housewives experienced in attempting to meet the conflicting demands of their prescribed role and to assimilate the endless barrage of often contradictory "expert" advice offered by the popular media on how to keep their homes spotless and beautiful, their budgets balanced, their meals nutritious and exciting, their children physically and emotionally healthy, their husbands happy, and themselves energetic and attractive. The humor recognized and responded to the new pressures and needs women confronted as they struggled to adapt the requirements of their traditional role to the rapid social, cultural, and technological changes that undermined the usefulness and significance of that role.[9]

Perhaps the most basic need met by domestic humor was the need for communication, felt by both the writer and her audience. This need undoubtedly became more acute with increased mobility after World War II and with the shift in emphasis away from responsibility to an extended family to total immersion in a nuclear family. Following their husbands to places where they had no friends or relatives and where they were often isolated in apartments, suburban bungalows, or (as in the case of Betty MacDonald and Shirley Jackson) in rural environments where they were viewed as outsiders, women often lacked others with whom to share their domestic experiences and feelings; also, they often kept silent out of fear that their experiences and feelings might mark them as pariahs. With the exodus to the suburbs between 1955 and 1965, housewives frequently found themselves trapped in bedroom communities, surrounded by look-alike houses, children, and other young women whose existences, like theirs, revolved around housekeeping, childbearing, and child raising, and who, like them, did not think to question or rebel against what society, culture, and biology prescribed as their appropriate and natural functions. However, those women who had the talent and felt the motivation to write about their domestic lives found a wide and receptive audience.

Over the past decades, humor studies have emphasized the fostering of group solidarity as a major social function of humor. The millions of housewives who read about experiences so close to their own, described by someone who spoke in the voice of a next-door neighbor, undoubtedly felt themselves less alone in their bewilderment about their roles and responsibilities. For, as much of the literature of the 1950s and 1960s suggests, despite the car pools, card games, PTA meetings, "koffee klatches," and welcome wagons that became symbols of the surburban scene, young housewives often suffered from emotional as well as physical isolation. Moreover, competition often characterized women's lives in these middle-class communities as much as it did their husbands' survival in the growing corporate world. Consequently, domestic humorists from Betty MacDonald through Judith Viorst and Erma Bombeck also provided relief from the anxiety that many housewives may have experienced but would probably not have admitted to their family or friends.

Being on the defensive, housewives have been particularly prey to those feelings of inadequacy that purveyors of consumption are so adept at manipulating. Consequently, another function of domestic humor has been to lessen the reader's sense of insecurity by illustrating that she is not the only one who finds the popular images of happy and successful homemakers impossible or unsatisfying to mirror. For example, when MacDonald describes her inability to keep her farmhouse spotless, when Kerr talks about being overwhelmed by the demands of child rearing, when Bombeck laments her inability to achieve the results touted for products in advertisements, or when Viorst obsesses about becoming middle-aged and middle-class, the reader discovers that she is not peculiar or abnormal when she feels unable to cope or vulnerable to failure. As she recognizes and identifies with the counterimage of the frustrated, imperfect housewife depicted in domestic humor, the reader can perhaps see herself as part of an in-group of women who have a shared reality of experiences and concerns. To the extent that she may laugh with and at the humorists who describe their lives as an unending struggle to bring order out of chaos, she can also laugh off her own negative emotions as she confronts the same problems.

In addition to relieving the reader's anxieties about her own incompetence by describing housewives who may be even more overburdened or less efficient than she, domestic humorists also suggest that the activities that form the housewife's daily existence are not as crucial to determining her worth as the popular culture would have her believe. For the domestic humorists, in offering themselves as the butt of their humor, emphasize the futility of their attempts to achieve perfection; they do not merely define themselves as helpless victims of hopeless situations whose plight is laughable because deserved. To define domestic humor this way is to take it too literally and, literally, too seriously. Rather, when the domestic humorist describes her frustrations and deficiencies, she also points out what Louis Rubin has called a central motif of American humor: "the contrast, the incongruity between the ideal and the real, in which a common, vernacular metaphor is used to put a somewhat abstract statement involving values . . . into a homely context."[10] Thus, when MacDonald caricatures the compulsive but joyless housekeeping activity of Mrs. Hicks, or Bombeck pokes fun at the young housewife so caught up in the housewife mythos that she decorates her garbage cans and waxes her driveway, they are using the behaviors, products, and propaganda that identify the average woman's existence to raise questions about the value of that existence and, therefore, about the validity of evaluating women solely on the basis of their performance as housewives.

These humorists, then, help the reader to recognize what Gerald Mast defines as one of comedy's elemental lessons: "mortal perfection is a contradiction in terms."[11] By depicting themselves as women who cannot accomplish all that is expected of them, and by poking fun at those expectations, domestic humorists suggest that the demands on women to epitomize what Friedan labeled the feminine mystique are unreasonable; therefore, judging oneself and one's worth against that yardstick is absurd. This does not mean that the housewife who reads these writers will suddenly stop trying to be efficient housekeeper, interior decorator, gourmet chef, nurse, teacher, child psychologist, chauffeur, handyman, hostess, mistress, beauty queen, nurturing mother, and supportive wife. However, what domestic humor can do, to varying degrees, is demonstrate the irrationality of the "normal" obligations attached to woman's role. The ability to recognize and laugh at the incongruities between the ideal "norm" and the realities of the average woman's life, as described in domestic humor, may be the first step a reader will take toward permitting herself, and others like her, some flexibility in deviating from the impossible cultural standard without guilt and shame.

These ideas about the nature and functions of domestic humor can be seen in the work of those who have written and performed domestic humor, from Cornelia Otis Skinner in the late 1930s to Roseanne Barr today. However, in response to the comments of Friedan and Spacks noted earlier, the work of Betty MacDonald, Jean Kerr, and Erma Bombeck will be used to illustrate how domestic humor developed during the thirty years following World War II and what purposes it may have served.

Although Betty MacDonald has been castigated for initiating in *The Egg and I* a new genre of female self-deprecating humor that supported postwar antifeminist back-to-the-kitchen sentiment, her stated purpose in writing the book was not to ridicule female incompetence but rather to provide "a sort of rebuttal to all the recent I-love-life books by female good sports whose husbands had forced them to live in the country without light and running water . . . [to] give the other side of it . . . a bad sport's account of life in the wilderness."[12] And, in fact, almost the entire content of the book shows the young Betty's gradual awareness that the domestic chores and routines to which she is restricted by her husband's decision to take up chicken farming in a remote area of Washington's Olympic Mountains are meaningless. Far from illustrating that "if it's funny to be a bad housewife, there may be some dignity to being a good one," as Spacks declares, the book implies that there is, at best, little connection between a woman's efficiency as a housekeeper and her value and fulfillment as a human being.

While much of the humor is at the expense of the "I" in *The Egg and I,* the "I" is the young housewife that MacDonald had been and through whom the author is able both to make fun of the "I'll-go-where-you-go-do-what-you-do-be-what-you-are—and-I'll-be-happy philosophy" inculcated in young women of her generation (12) and to give the lie to the notion "that it is a wife's bounden duty to see that her husband is happy in his work"—no matter the cost to her (11). Conditioned by her mother's example and precepts, which reinforced society's view of woman's role, and intimidated by her husband, Bob, to whom she feels inferior and for whom she is compelled to prove herself a perfect woman and wife, the young Betty offers little or no protest against the demands made on her by her husband and by the isolated, rigorous, primitive existence he chose for them both. She plunges into the work he assigns her with an enthusiasm matched only by her total lack of preparation for it, having lived most of her previous life in a solid, middle-class Seattle environment.

Inevitably, MacDonald shows Betty failing in her drive for perfection—not because she is incompetent but because her expectations of herself are as unreasonable as Bob's expectations of her. Unable to recognize the irrationality of her situation, however, Betty dwells on her obvious inadequacies as a farmhand and allows herself to become more and more vulnerable to and anxious to disprove Bob's intimations of her failings as a homemaker. Thus, she assents, for example, to his decision to put a white pine floor in the farmhouse and then to his demand that she keep it spotless (71–72) or to his decision to do without electricity and indoor plumbing, and then to his demand that she nevertheless keep his work clothes perfectly clean, starched, and ironed (67–68). Thus, MacDonald ridicules not Betty's ineptitude as a homemaker but her foolishness as a female for being conned by the myth that a woman's happiness and worth depend on her husband's satisfaction and for pretending to be content despite all evidence to the contrary. The targets of MacDonald's humor are both the fierceness with which the young Betty struggles to be Bob's and society's illusion of the ideal helpmate and her blindness to the foolishness of those efforts—a blindness that gradually lifts as the book progresses and the value of those efforts begins to be questioned.

The education of the young Betty, and of the reader, is essentially a lesson in disillusionment, taught with the devices of humor: understatement, overstatement, caricature, and irony. These devices enable the young Betty gradually to see things as they really are and to recognize that many of her previous notions about marriage and country life are deceptive. The detailed descriptions of the daily drudgery of rural existence undermine the popular idyllic image of living in the country in tune with nature. Similarly, Betty's observations of the decadence and depravity of the Indians destroy her prior conception of the Indian as a "noble savage," just as her awareness of the cruelty, hypocrisy, and negativism of her neighbors clashes with her previous idea of country people as simple, kindly, virtuous, and cheerful folk. As the young Betty sheds her illusions about the things and people around her, including her husband, she is brought face to face with what seems an irresolvable predicament: how to extricate herself from her oppressive environment. In dealing with this predicament, Betty does engage in self-deprecating humor in an attempt to deny or dismiss her negative feelings, as Spacks points out, but MacDonald suggests that, given Betty's upbringing and social conditioning about woman's place and marital commitment, the humor serves as a survival technique and, as in much minority humor, a defense against more destructive alternatives, such as madness or suicide.

This defensive function of humor is also evident in the caricatures drawn by MacDonald of the women around Betty, who provide her with mirror reflections of herself. Although Spacks states that Betty finds herself wanting in comparison with the other women in the book, in actuality, as Betty looks at the women who inhabit the area surrounding the chicken farm, she fears becoming like them. Her immediate neighbors, Mrs. Hicks and Ma Kettle, are the two extremes between which she has to mediate to keep her balance. A formidable and compulsive housekeeper and pillar of the community, Mrs. Hicks is a pinched, miserable person whose mean-spirited snooping, endless ailments, and hypocritical gestures of friendship attest to the lack of fulfillment her cleaning and cooking offer her. Ma Kettle, in contrast, is warm, earthy, and honest; but Betty comes to understand that Ma's ability to take things as they are is a defense against disappointment and that Ma has had to pay a price for her surrender to her husband in her fight to keep her home and family from going to hell: a loss of self-respect.

The other women characters MacDonald describes also serve as warnings to the young Betty. Mrs. Maddock, who has not been off the ranch for twenty-seven years, is "as dark and dreary as her house" (219). Mary MacGregor has become the local drunkard and laughingstock after losing her husband to lockjaw because she "run a pitchfork into her old man's behind" when she caught him "layin' up with the hired girl" (130). Mrs. Wiggins, a more advanced case of Mrs. Hicks, is so starved for a topic of malicious gossip that she accompanies her husband on a business call to Bob just so she can spy on Betty, who, she has heard, smokes cigarettes and reads books (132–33). Mrs. Weatherby, who rambles on about "the theatah" and "the dahnse," oblivious to the filth and squalor in which she lives, prompts Betty to remark, "I had an awful foreboding that given time *I* could be like Mrs. Weatherby" (250–52). Finally, in the last chapter, a crazy woman appears in Betty's yard while Bob is away, scaring Betty half to death. When Ma Kettle explains that the woman lives in a mental institution and is just visiting relatives in the vicinity, Betty exclaims, "That valley woman must be even more isolated than I if she's that desperate for companionship to come to a stranger's house" (273–75).

The last chapter of the book presents other evidence of Betty's recognition that her life has reached a point of desperation no longer containable through humor. The second paragraph, for example, begins: "our future prospects were very good but my enthusiasm was at a low ebb. . . . My life on the ranch had reached some sort of climax and it was the aftermath which worried me. We were just about to go into another long, dreary winter and I felt harried and uncertain as though I was boarding a steamer with no passport and no luggage" (272). Further, the humor that Betty, earlier in the book, used to mitigate the growing alienation she felt in describing the relationship between Bob and herself as "a halloo from the brooder house porch to the manure pile; . . . a few grunts at mealtime as we choked down our food and turned the leaves of seed catalogues and Government bulletins," vanishes in the last chapter. In telling him about the incident with the crazy woman, Betty explains, "I didn't even try to convey my terror because I knew by then that Bob and I were poles apart as far as emotions were concerned," adding two pages later that being alone together makes her and Bob so uneasy that they "act like neighbors who suddenly find themselves in a hotel room together." These comments lead into a description of the unending, depressing isolation anticipated by Betty as she contemplates the coming of winter, in which day after day brings "the regular, gradual closing in of the mountains with rain, rain, rain, moaning winds and loneliness" (276).

If *The Egg and I* had ended at this point, the reader would be confronted with a portrait of the author as a young woman whose self-denial and self-surrender have dehumanized and trapped her in a situation from which she sees no exit—a depressing ending that MacDonald herself probably could not have countenanced. On the other hand, if the ending had conformed to the actuality of MacDonald's life—her leaving her husband, at about the time the book concludes, to return to Seattle and then divorcing him—this first book by an unknown writer probably would not have been published, since such an ending, especially for what was ostensibly a humorous *bildungsroman,* would have flown in the face of the popular postwar notions about woman's place, the family, and the good old American pioneer spirit. Thus, whether by her own choice or the coercion of her publisher, MacDonald has Betty suddenly change, in the book's final pages, from despair to euphoria at Bob's surprise announcement that he has, without consulting her, purchased a new chicken farm, one with running water and electricity—improvements that will, at best, help to ease only Betty's physical burdens.

Because of the comedic "happy" ending, the book does have the effect of making light of the serious issues it raises and may also, as Spacks contends, confirm the trap—not, as Spacks claims, for MacDonald, who got out, but for the reader, who is left with the false impression that Betty's problems of emotional and intellectual frustration and stagnation can be resolved, as modern advertising would have women believe, by new appliances and other material goods. Nevertheless, for those readers who may have found the conclusion unimportant, or recognized it as simply a literary artifice, and for whom identification with Betty, as she moved from ignorance to awareness, was the essential element of their reading experience, MacDonald may have accomplished her purpose of helping free them from collusion in their own subjugation.

If MacDonald describes her younger self as having allowed herself to be caught in the circularity of an oppressive domestic existence, Jean Kerr, whom Spacks sees as MacDonald's direct descendant, broadened the circle enough to alter the shape and substance of that existence. Publishing *Please Don't Eat the Daisies* in 1957, twelve years after *The Egg and I,* Kerr reflected and appealed to the millions of women who drifted back into the work force, often part-time, during the 1950s, once their children were grown, or who, following the postwar directive to devote themselves to home and family, found themselves, after ten or more years of housekeeping, wanting or financially needing something else to do. Although Kerr, like MacDonald, does exploit the image of the inadequate, overburdened housewife, her writing encourages flexibility in the definition of woman's role because it reveals her as both a housewife and a playwright. In fact, the overall portrait of Kerr that emerges from her best-known and earliest humorous autobiographical works, *Please Don't Eat the Daisies* and *The Snake Has All the Lines* (1960), is not that of a woman confined to a narrow domestic existence and overwhelmed by the demands of her family. Rather, she presents herself as a woman who has been able to integrate a career with motherhood, domestic obligations with social pleasures, and the mundane occupations of running a household with the intellectual activities involved in her husband's and her own career in the theater. Her books, therefore, serve the dual purpose of communicating with the reader about the everyday world of the surburban household and, at the same time, describing a more glamorous world of the theater, travel, and parties—a world the reader can enjoy vicariously.

For Kerr, the family provides a haven from her professional obligations, and her career provides her with relief from the homemaking demands that she is unable or unwilling to meet. Consequently, when she makes fun of her inadequacies as a homemaker, she not only enables the reader to identify with her but also justifies her career in terms that are both nonthreatening to and supportive of the full-time housewife. This dual function of her humor can be seen in her introduction to *Please Don't Eat the Daisies* when she explains that she began writing solely to make enough money to hire someone to help with the domestic and child-care chores that prevented her from being able to sleep late in the morning—the one luxury in life for which she would sell her soul. Moreover, there is no indication that her family in any way suffers from her pursuit of a writing career. On the contrary, her family life appears ideally all-American: close, warm, healthy, fun-filled, bustling with physical and intellectual activity. Kerr's readers are therefore treated to a demonstration of woman's ability to successfully combine marriage, motherhood, and career.

For example, an area that is a trouble zone for MacDonald—the marital relationship—is basically untroubled for Kerr, who, unlike MacDonald, presents herself and her husband as being unusually compatible: they both enjoy their family, love the theater, have fun socializing, write for a living, and, when they go house hunting, fall for the same crazy old place. For Kerr, the worst flaws possessed by her husband, Walter, and by husbands in general are that they are overanxious about their children, unwilling to deal with anything they consider to be part of the domestic sphere relegated to their wives, forgetful of things their wives ask them to do or buy, overattached to old clothes, honest at times when they should be tactful, childish in their need for attention and the ways they go about eliciting it, given to pomposity, unable to sleep without snoring, most concerned about being reasonable when their wives are most upset, and unaware of the importance of maintaining a romantic relationship with their wives after the first year of marriage and/or after the first child.[13] In other words, they fit the image of the stereotypical American male of the period.

Kerr's attitude toward her children is like that toward her husband: like all boys, her sons are active and often mischievous, but the problems they cause are minor and their parents would not have them any other way, as the following passage from *Daisies* illustrates:

> One day recently, after Christopher had left for school, I discovered that he had used my brand new lipstick to draw a pirate's treasure map on the floor of the garage. I was just waiting to get my hands on him when he arrived at four o'clock, all smiles. . . . And I was just starting to call to him when I heard him ask his father, "Hi, Dad, where is La Belle Senorita?" Now what do you do in a case like that? Damned if I know.[14]

Moreover, while the care, pleasure, and individuality with which Kerr describes her sons indicates their importance to her, she also emphasizes that she has time and space to herself, respected by her husband and children, to pursue her writing career.

If Kerr has any negative feelings about the choices she has made in her life, they are well hidden by an unadulteratedly good-natured tone that seems as genuine as MacDonald's sardonic one. For Kerr's gripes are minor—"tiny irritations," as she describes them in "Letters of Protest I Never Sent,"[15] that do not have to be taken seriously because they do not really interfere with normal functioning. What creates problems for her are such basic vicissitudes of life and career as house hunting, looking for an automobile that will accommodate her family, getting her sons off to school in the morning, waiting for reviews of her work, and getting through the out-of-town tryout period of a show. In addition, she is annoyed by and turns her humor against pretentiousness and phoniness of all kinds: professional interior decorators who intimidate their clients into believing themselves and their homes to be tasteless; writers who move to the country and suddenly claim to be (and express themselves as) simple, natural folk; popular advice experts who guilt-trip women into believing that they are inadequate mates or mothers or females; and hospital personnel who treat adult patients like irresponsible children for feeling unwell. She also pokes fun, as a parodist, at popular fads that she finds ridiculous or misguided: overrated books, avant-garde movies, Mickey Spillane, permissive theories of child rearing, marriage counseling, dieting, and the female obsession with youth and beauty promoted by the media.

The appeal of these pieces to the female reader has already been implied: the image Kerr presents of a woman capable of successfully spanning the worlds of the suburbs and Broadway speaks both to the frustrated full-time homemaker and to the part-time housewife who seeks reinforcement for (or, perhaps, relief from guilt she has about) working outside the home. What enables the former to identify with Kerr is that, for all of her professional accomplishments, Kerr still appears concerned about many of the things that worry the average woman. Her persona is not that of a sophisticated career woman, exuding self-assurance and charm, but of an insecure individual who, like her readers, remains vulnerable to the opinions of others and never takes her success for granted. When she makes fun of her inability to keep everything under control, her weight problems, or her susceptibility to the claims made for beauty products, she establishes a peer relationship with the women who read her, despite the differences that exist between her life and theirs. Moreover, by suggesting that her writing resulted not from personal ambition but rather from her need to pay someone to make up for her deficiencies in the homemaking area, she implies that those readers who can successfully manage their households by themselves are at least equal, if not superior, to her.

At the same time, when she directs the humor outward, targeting husbands and children or popular attitudes and fads, she reassures her readers that they do not have to buy everything the culture promotes. For example, when she declares that permissiveness is not the key to child rearing and that children can be well adjusted and still be taught discipline and good manners,[16] she supports other women in rebelling against the "experts" who predict dire consequences for mothers who fail to follow their dictums. In "Aunt Jean's Marchmallow Fudge Diet," she challenges the prevailing equation of beauty with hollow cheeks, a flat chest, and no hips by asserting that women can be "well-endowed" and still loved by their husbands: "What I have discovered—attention, Beauty Editors everywhere!—is that the women who are being ditched are one and all willowy, wand-like, and slim as a blade."[17] And in "Mirror, Mirror, on the Wall, I Don't Want to Hear One Word out of You," she again uses ironic contrast to reiterate the same point that it is absurd for women to be so concerned about keeping young and beautiful:

> Of course you're not the enchanting girl he married. Nor could you be—with those kids, and that dog racing through the house, and practically no help, and a washer that's always on the blink? . . .
>
> Besides, why should *you* be all that enchanting? How does *he* look these days? Is *he* still the lean and handsome athlete who first caught your girlish fancy? . . . Do you catch him poring over articles instructing him how to look younger and sprucer so *he* can make *your* little heart palpitate? Boy, that will be the day![18]

In these pieces and others, Kerr suggests that people in general, and women in particular, should fight against those feelings of insecurity or inadequacy that make them distrust their own judgments and, thereby, get duped into accepting popular culture's ideas about how they should look, how they should behave, how they should raise their children, and how they should relate to their spouses. Because she refuses to knuckle under to self-proclaimed authorities, her autobiographical humorous writing is not as conservative as Spacks and Friedan imply. True, Kerr champions no great political causes dedicated to restructuring society and woman's position in it, but she also does not support the idea that homemaking constitutes the be-all and end-all of woman's existence or that women are intellectual dodos. On the contrary, within the scope of what she chooses to talk about—the concerns and activities of middle-class housewives of the 1950s and 1960s—she supports individuality over conformity. To that extent, her humor is liberating because it encourages women to be themselves by satirizing what is often promoted as the norm.

Although Erma Bombeck continued writing in the tradition of housewife humor popularized in the 1950s, her work also incorporates some elements that reflect the changes that developed during the late 1960s and 1970s in ideas about woman's place and status within both the family and American society. For example, Bombeck, even in her earliest work, is free both of MacDonald's illusions about woman's place and of Kerr's need to balance her roles as playwright and housewife, justifying the former in terms of her deficiencies in the latter. In fact, Bombeck's work, from *At Wit's End* (1965) to *Aunt Erma's Cope Book* (1979), is based on her assumption that at some point in their lives, housewives experience frustration, depression, and alienation because they discover that housework is essentially drudgery, that mothering takes less time and is less appreciated as children grow up, and that marital intimacy declines as men devote increasing amounts of time and energy to professional growth and outside interests while their wives remain in the same place doing the same things day after week after year.

Using an autobiographical persona that is generalized to reflect the typical Middle American housewife, family, and suburban community, Bombeck neither stigmatizes nor glorifies women who have chosen the life she describes. Instead, she makes fun of many of the trappings of suburban living and reveals the absurdity of much that constitutes the image of the ideal woman-mother-homemaker. Her method is to debunk the "happy homemaker" myth glorified in the popular culture by focusing on the realities of the American housewife's existence. Like Joan Rivers and Phyllis Diller did in their stand-up routines, Bombeck emphasizes the tedious, monotonous, and frustrating aspects of the housewife's life, often poking fun at the exciting, interesting, and stimulating "adventures" suggested for women by television advertising, women's magazine articles, newspaper columns, and self-help books. By pretending to take the media seriously, she shows the pathetic emptiness of women's lives when their greatest experience is being accosted in the supermarket by a sales representative who asks them to compare brands or in the laundry room by some lunatic who has broken into their house to tear their towels in half; when their most assertive act is firing their deodorant; and when the success of their marriage is based on how their husband's shirts smell. Bombeck also exposes how the media prey on women's lack of self-confidence when she burlesques women's obsessions with improving themselves physically and psychologically by offering in her own books parodies of those diets, courses, and self-help manuals that are designed to make women feel guilty for everything from not being physcially fit to not being the "Total Woman."

At the same time, Bombeck recognizes the seriousness of the problem presented by the triviality of the housewife's routine. For example, in "What to Do Until the Therapist Arrives with the Volleyball," Bombeck, in lampooning popular advice articles for women, also notes that "One of the occupational hazards of motherhood and housewifery is that you never get the time to sit down and read an entire book from cover to cover,"[19] thereby underscoring the context in which suggestions that women undertake home reading courses of the classics are absurd. On the other hand, in discussing why housewives feel so dumb, so out of touch with the world, so lacking in self-esteem, she expresses the frustration that many women must feel when she writes, "Just once I want to stand up at a PTA meeting and say, 'I entertain a motion that we adjourn until we have business more pressing than the cafeteria's surplus of canned tomatoes, and more entertaining than a film on *How Your Gas Company Works for You*' " (38). The feeling of irrelevance is emphasized again in another part of the book when, in acknowledging her husband's observation that she has nothing to talk about in the evening because she does nothing interesting during the day, she exclaims, "What did I do all day? The only big thing that had happened was I used the wrong aerosol can for my deodorant and I didn't have to worry about clogged-up nasal passages in my armpits for twenty-four hours" (47).

The triviality of women's lives and the meaninglessness of housework come together often in the writing of Bombeck, who unabashedly depicts her household as a shambles of dirty laundry, unwashed dishes, broken appliances, dusty furniture, and moldering decorations. Again like Rivers and Diller, who routinely made jokes about their atrocious cooking and allergy to cleaning, Bombeck sympathizes with those whose homes look like disaster areas and whose children "send Mother's Day cards to Colonel Sanders." Moreover, she suggests that if it's funny to be a bad housewife, it's even more absurd to try to be a good one, because to do so is to give importance to the tedious, thankless, repetitive chores that constitute "women's work."

In *The Grass Is Always Greener over the Septic Tank* (1976), Bombeck not only sympathizes with but defends antihousework housewives by conferring on them group status and identity—that of "Interim Mothers," who are "just biding their time until the children are grown"—and by contrasting them favorably with the prohousework contingent—the "Super Moms," who are "faster than a speeding bullet, more powerful than a harsh laxative, and able to leap six shopping carts on double stamp day."[20] An "Interim Mom" herself, Bombeck depicts the "Super Mom" as more to be pitied than admired: "Super Mom was the product of isolation, a husband who was rarely home, Helen Gurley Brown, and a clean-oven wish" (136). When a Super Mom moves in across the street from Bombeck, the Interim Mothers view her as a blockbuster and gradually break her down by their resentment and their example. Finally, she comes to recognize the error of her ways, meeting her final test when she is at Bombeck's house one afternoon and her child runs into the room yelling, "Mommy! Mommy! I was on the side using a toothpaste with fluoride and I have only one cavity." When the woman, after looking at her child silently for a full minute, finally remarked, "Who cares?" Bombeck says that, finally, "She was one of us" (140).

In her parodies of ads for consumer products aimed at women, in her detailed descriptions of the average housewife's day, and in her often farcical depictions of family life, Bombeck continually emphasizes that the lives housewives lead are actually dehumanizing, as the following passage from *I Lost Everything in the Post-Natal Depression* implies: "I always wondered if someone ran an ad in the New York *Times:* WANTED: Household drudge, 140 hour week, no retirement, no sick leave, no room of own, no Sundays off. Must be good with animals, kids and hamburger. Must share bath, would 42 million women still apply?"[21] In this context, the incompetence of the housewife or her failing to measure up to cultural expectations becomes a virtue, because it represents a refusal to accept housekeeping as a satisfying career; this mom no longer buys the propaganda that being a Super Mom or Total Woman will provide a sense of fulfillment or success. In illustrating over and over again the basic recognition that motivated her to begin writing—that housewives are at the bottom of American society and will remain there until they begin to do for themselves—Bombeck provides an antidote to women's magazines and commercials for household products, which manipulate women to seek a sense of productivity and worth in their devotion to the homemaking role. Bombeck proclaims instead that the Super Mom is a Super Sucker, the person who would answer the newspaper ad Bombeck imagines, only to end up bitter and angry at the waste of her life.

While not a political revolutionary, Bombeck illustrates that women can and should enlarge their lives, and she accepts as a basic premise that women need and ought to have something more in their lives than keeping house. Having gotten herself into something else without feeling guilty about it and, at the same time, without rejecting the role of wife and mother, Bombeck is able to write about where most women live without condescension or hostility and with a genuine, if gentle, satirical voice. While she does not call on women to leave their homes and families, as some feminists were doing, Bombeck does not, on the other hand, intend her humorous writing to confirm women in their acquiescence to socially prescribed gender roles, as Spacks and Friedan infer. At the least, this demonstrates the notion that housewifery as an end in itself is as false and barren as the American commercialism that extols it.

Although housewife humorists do not call upon women to reject their traditional role, they can liberate the reader from the guilt and shame she may feel about being dissatisfied with her life or frustrated by the demands of home and family. At the same time, the purpose of domestic humor is less to promote freedom from marriage, motherhood, and homemaking than freedom from the idea that having and raising a family (with its accompanying precept that woman's happiness derives solely from making her husband and children happy) must and should constitute woman's lifelong and full-time occupation.

The domestic humorist cannot and probably does not want to poke fun at divorce, child abuse, marital brutality, sexual deviance, or the pathological depression that makes some women incapable of performing the most elemental tasks. To do so would threaten and alienate rather than entertain and reassure an audience of women who, despite complaints about the burdens their role imposes, find pleasure or security in it that they don't want to give up or fear to lose. However, by teaching flexibility through laughter and by undermining the value of striving to be the ideal woman, domestic humor can grant its readers more freedom to be themselves and to consider their own needs. This freedom can, in turn, as domestic humor has reflected, permit women to change the definitions and obligations attached to their traditional role and to enlarge the boundaries of their lives.

Notes

This essay is a revised version of an earlier paper, "The Housewife as Humorist," which appeared in *Regionalism and the Female Imagination* (Fall–Winter 1977), and of chapters in "Twentieth-Century American Women Humorists," Ph.D. diss., University of Maryland, 1982.

1. See, for example, Lois W. Banner, *Women in Modern America: A Brief History* (New York: Harper and Row, 1974); William Chafe, *The American Woman* (New York: Oxford University Press, 1972); June Sochen, ed., *The New Feminism in Twentieth Century America* (Boston: D. C. Heath, 1971); Eugenia Kaledin, *Mothers and More: American Women in the 1950s* (Boston: Twayne Publishers, 1984); and Leila J. Rupp and Verta Taylor, *Survival in the Doldrums: The American Women's Rights Movement, 1945 to the 1960s* (New York: Oxford University Press, 1987).
2. Chafe, *The American Woman,* 199.
3. Philip Slater, *The Pursuit of Loneliness* (Boston: Beacon Press, 1971), 66.
4. Betty Friedan, *The Feminine Mystique* (New York: Norton, 1973).
5. Ibid., 50.
6. Patricia Meyer Spacks, *The Female Imagination* (New York: Alfred Knopf, 1972), 282.
7. Eric Bentley, "The Comic Spirit in America," in *The American Theatre Today,* ed. Alan S. Downer (New York: Basic Books, 1967), 54–55.
8. These points have been developed by, among others, Betty Friedan in chap. 2 of *The Feminine Mystique;* Helen Z. Lopata, *Occupation Housewife* (New York: Oxford University Press, 1971); Elizabeth Janeway, *Man's World, Woman's Place* (New York: Morrow and Co., 1971), 163–77; Alice S. Rossi, "Equality

between the Sexes: An Immodest Proposal," in *The New Feminism in Twentieth Century America,* 87–112; Cynthia Ozick, "Women and Creativity," in *Woman in Sexist Society,* ed. Vivian Gornick and Barbara K. Moran (New York: Basic Books, 1971), 442–49; Susan Strasser, *Never Done: A History of American Housework* (New York: Pantheon Books, 1982), chaps. 12–16; and Kaledin, *Mothers and More.*

9. These ideas are developed in detail in Kaledin and Strasser.
10. Louis D. Rubin, Jr., ed., "The Great American Joke," in *The Comic Imagination in America* (New Brunswick: Rutgers University Press, 1973), 5.
11. Gerald Mast, *The Comic Mind* (New York: Oxford University Press, 1973), 323.
12. Betty MacDonald, *The Egg and I* (New York: J. B. Lippincott, 1945), 83. Subsequent page references will be given in parentheses in the text.
13. Jean Kerr, *The Snake Has All the Lines* (Garden City, N.Y.: Doubleday, 1960), 120–28.
14. Jean Kerr, *Please Don't Eat the Daisies* (Garden City, N.Y.: Doubleday, 1957), 153.
15. In Kerr, *The Snake.*
16. Ibid., 60–70.
17. Kerr, *Please Don't Eat,* 175.
18. Kerr, *The Snake,* 167.
19. Erma Bombeck, *At Wit's End* (Garden City, N.Y.: Doubleday, 1965), 23. Subsequent page references will be given in parentheses in the text.
20. Erma Bombeck, *The Grass Is Always Greener over the Septic Tank* (Garden City, N.Y.: Doubleday, 1976), 136. Subsequent page references will be given in parentheses in the text.
21. Erma Bombeck, *I Lost Everything in the Post-Natal Depression* (Garden City, N.Y.: Doubleday, 1979), 145.

Hokinson and Hollander: Female Cartoonists and American Culture

Patricia Williams Alley

Cartooning is a rich source of female humor, but, like other mediums of female humor, it is often difficult to find many examples. Alice Sheppard, writing about early-twentieth-century women cartoonists, says, "There appears to be a profound gap between currently held perceptions of women's role in the history of American cartooning and the facts concerning their contribution". She goes on to say that "women had successfully penetrated the field of graphic humor" but "have rarely been emphasized or even included in theoretical and historical discussions of American cartoonists".[1] Today most major newspapers run only four or five women cartoonists on a page of about sixty or so. Both the explanation and the indictment for the lack of visibility of female cartoonists may be partially explained by the unique nature of the cartoon. As Nancy Walker, in the recently published study of female literary humor, suggests, each medium of female humor presents a different set of issues and problems, including those of production, setting, and audience.[2]

The problems with production, setting, and audience in cartooning rest partially on the dual nature of cartoons which combine written and visual materials. British caricaturist Max Beerbohm recognizes that cartooning calls for a special talent when he sets up the essentials for good cartoons. The good cartoonist, he says, must first "get at the soul or pith of the subject swiftly"; second, incorporate "simplicity, a quick and firm line"; third, produce a "statement with the minimum of explanatory text"; fourth, establish "a quality of kindliness or irony, sardonic or satiric and always humorous." In addition, the cartoonist must have a knowledge of the fundamentals of anatomy, must know how to get freedom and looseness into drawings of figures and animals, must be able to express action, show differences in textures, and add the expressive details.[3] Finally, a good cartoonist must have a sense of humor and the powers of observation of what's going on in the world as well as the talent for transfering the humor into drawings and captions.

After a cartoonist masters these skills of the medium, she must still gain acceptance into the medium settings, newspapers and paperbacks, and that is often as hard to attain as publication in a book or recognition as a director in the film medium. Finally, the cartoonist must capture an informal audience who can "read" and connect both drawings and captions. The audience comes from the popular culture milieu already saturated with cartoon options.

In spite of drawbacks in melding two art forms, Samuel Clemens recognized the benefits of combining writing and drawing, and he chose to have his characters illustrated rather than write long descriptions of them. Twain felt the pictures conveyed the physical attributes of a character better than the written word.[4] Many of the modes of humor are the same in other mediums—satire, parody, even sarcasm—and they are the same for men and women. However, as in other mediums, most female cartoonists are not pushing to represent men's worlds but to reach success in their own and often in a different way. Most female cartoonists offer insights into problems not usually approached by men, and they often present the solutions with more care and concern. That is not to say that they maintain a diatribe against men; they do not. They ask the questions that arise from a female perspective. Most female cartoonists try to balance the cartoons by raising controversial issues and entertaining an audience at the same time. They act as a psychological mirror for the culture.[5]

Sociological studies show that cartoons offer a rich source for studying American culture and more specifically social trends and attitudes. Several of these studies, but particularly "Women in July Fourth Cartoons: A 100-Year Look," focus on women in cartoons for insight into role changes. They find the cartoons a "rich source of information" because they communicate with complexity and completeness by using a primary visual sign plus secondary signs such as language which allow for complex messages about women. In addition, cartoons appear continuously over a long period of time, and "they provide a consistent source of long duration" and "reflect woman's place in American culture."[6]

Although the Meyer study just described focuses on political cartoons, a successful format is provided that can be used in another context. The three criteria—appearance, dominance, and role—are useful touchstones for comparing two cartoonists, Helen Hokinson from early in the century and Nicole Hollander, a contemporary cartoonist, to determine changes over time in dominant cultural patterns. However, these two women cartoonists also introduce ideas not necessarily in harmony with the ideology of the dominant culture as the Meyer study reports it. Their women characters differ in some ways. They succeed in portraying the culture of their times accurately but viewing it differently from most of their contemporaries; therefore, they bring a different perspective to the cartoon medium and female humor.

In the following sections of this essay, the biographical sketches of Hokinson and Hollander and their early work place them in time; the next section demonstrates the cartoonists' work as reflective of their respective cultures. Finally, I use the Meyer criteria for a more thorough comparison of the two cartoonists and their work with the cartoons of their contemporaries to show their unique perspectives.

Comparative Biography and Early Works

When Helen Hokinson (1893–1949) arrived in New York in 1920, she had come a long way from Mendota, Illinois, and her early drawing attempts. Encouraged by her father, she practiced her "funny pictures" on the stiff board that came in the Shredded Wheat packages—the ones that were put between the biscuits.[7] Later, she sold fashion sketches to some of the best department stores in Chicago. She moved to New York, enrolled in an art school, and collaborated with Alice Harvey in producing a short-lived comic strip (ironically called "Sylvia in the Big City") for the *New York Daily Mirror.*[8] Her classmates and her teacher urged her to take some of her sketches to the fledgling magazine the *New Yorker.* She submitted a sketch and was asked to bring in more. In two weeks, she returned to be greeted by "Where were you last week?"[9] They wanted fresh material every Tuesday for consideration at their art meeting. Her first sketch was published on July 4, 1925, and thus began a twenty-four-year career with the *New Yorker,* lasting until Hokinson was killed in a plane crash in 1949.[10]

Beginning in 1929, Hokinson divided her time between her New York City apartment and the secluded Connecticut cottage she shared with an elderly Canadian friend, Miss Henderson, and a successful businesswoman, Lulu Fellows. Her cottage showed the efforts of one feature of the life of her cartoon ladies: gardening. In addition, she liked bridge, cooking, reading, backgammon, the French impressionists, and Ray Bolger's dancing. She never read the *New Yorker* but instead read mysteries, Trollope, and Gaboriau. She liked James Thurber in book form rather than in the magazine; so said her collaborator, James Reid Parker. He became her caption writer after a mutual friend introduced them. They entered into a business agreement in which they set aside Friday afternoons and evenings as definite work periods to examine each other's files, outline future work, and rework rejections.[11]

Nicole Garrison Hollander's life parallels Hokinson's in some interesting ways although representing a culture a half-century later. Born in Chicago in 1939, Nicole Garrison grew up on the west side. She attended public schools. Her family encouraged her to develop her skills in drawing and painting as well as in wit and humor. She says, "My grandmother, who was a corset fitter, was a very feisty, quick lady. And my mother, who is director of patient relations at Highland Park Hospital, is very witty." Women in her family, it seems, practiced being amusing, telling stories cuttingly. According to her, she learned to read in order to follow the Sunday funnies; "The Phantom," "The Little King," and "Prince Valiant" were her favorites. However, she was not allowed to collect comic books, and certainly not *True Romance* nor *Tales from the Crypt.*[12] Her father was a strong union member from whom she received her political viewpoints.[13]

She attended the University of Illinois in Urbana-Champaign but later moved back to Chicago. There she married a sociology teaching assistant and changed her name to Hollander. She lived in Princeton and Boston and traveled in Europe. After a divorce, Hollander moved to California for a short time. Like Hokinson, she too was an illustrator in Chicago. In the 1970s, she was working as a graphic designer with an MFA in painting from Boston University. Later she began her career with the *Spokeswoman,* a national feminist newsletter out of Chicago. She was welcomed in the same manner as was Hokinson at the *New Yorker. Spokeswoman* publisher Karen Wellisch says she remembers Hollander walking into her office "waving a piece of paper, and saying, 'Look at what I did.' " Hollander herself has said: "I had always wanted to do something that expressed the way I felt politically, but no one had ever let me do it. All my illustrations for children's books, textbooks, whatever, always came back with comments like 'That's too ironic,' 'Too biting,' too this, too that. With *The Spokeswoman,* it was the first time that anybody had said, 'That's great. That's just fine.' "[14]

Both women shared other characteristics: a flair for dressing in bright colors and in styles that defied tradition. Hokinson is said to have worn Romany combinations of orange, pink, scarlet, magenta, and cobalt, "occasionally enhancing the effect with a chrome-yellow hat and a cherry-colored sweater."[15] At a celebration party for the publication of one of her books, Hollander wore "a bright green scarf blazing up against a very nondesigner wool turtleneck sweater" and gray Reeboks.[16] Hollander, speaking at the University of Washington in 1987, wore a short skirt, long dangling black earrings, and short gray hair.

Both women used their mothers as the main source for their characters. Hokinson attended club meetings with her business-college-educated mother who staunchly defended women's right to participate in "practical" business.[17] Hollander dresses Sylvia like the pictures of her mother and her mother's friends in the 1930s and 1940s.[18] Both were successful—Hokinson, cartoonist for the prestigious *New Yorker* magazine, and Hollander, cartoonist with eleven books published, greeting cards and calendars selling everywhere, and syndication in (at last count) forty-five newspapers—up from twenty-five in 1984. (Actually, 300 to 1,000 is considered by the syndicates as success.)[19]

The first sketches of both cartoonists were not totally formed, as we might expect. Seeing her friend off on a boat, Helen Hokinson pulled out her sketch pad and Eberhard pencil and drew a woman waving. The finished view, although a simple one from the rear, "vividly depicted the woman's character and the circumstances of her life. Her soft and plump middle-aged figure and the way she wore her summer dress and floppy hat showed her to be well to do."[20] Most of Hokinson's cartoons aimed for a particular group of people who could recognize themselves and laugh, namely the upper-middle-class, urbane reader of the *New Yorker,* well-to-do but not rich and not particularly stylish. Actually, "Helen Hokinson had taken so firm a grip on fat women [and their dialogue] that for any other artist to try them was almost presumptuous".[21]

In Hollander's first cartoon strip, appearing in the *Spokeswoman,* frame one depicts a woman with a little slice of pie on her plate who eyes a man with a big slice of pie on his. In the second frame, she points up to distract his attention. In frame three, she has the big slice and he has the little one. The drawing is simple, and the woman is different from the Sylvia drawings. Her first Sylvia-in-embryo was the September entry in a calendar, according to Hollander, "not yet named, her politics a little shaky, her profile undeveloped, but with backless mules and cigarette firmly in place."[22] As Hollander's cartoons, called "The Feminist Funnies," became a monthly staple of the *Spokeswoman,* Sylvia evolved. Several of her features are recognizable in the cartoon with Sylvia in front of her TV set talking back to it. She is wearing her fluffy bathrobe and backless mules and is holding her can of beer; a cigarette dangles from her mouth. Although an early version, this character is obviously Sylvia, and, like Hokinson's early "ladies," reflects the attitudes prevalent in her culture much the same way that the lives of Hokinson and Hollander reflected their cultures.[23]

Later Cartoons as a Reflection of the Cultures

The later single-frame and strip cartoons of Hokinson and Hollander reflect even more accurately the life of the times. Reviewing Hokinson's 1948 book *When Were You Built?* Lewis Nichols claims that "cartoon books . . . tell pretty much what is going on" and "What went on in Westchester County, Plainfield, and Englewood, New Jersey and the lower reaches of Connecticut was, of course, Helen Hokinson's business,"[24] as was what went on in the suburbs of Darien, Larchmont, and a handful of other places mentioned in the cartoons. "Westchester County, an area of hills and lakes north of the Bronx, tripled its population between 1900 and 1930. Here commuters lived in affluent communities such as Scarsdale, Larchmont and Chappaqua."[25]

The man in the Hokinson cartoon in fig. 1 might well have been one of those commuters to the financial centers. The characters in this cartoon had probably lived in the suburbs a bit earlier and set the pace for the middle class who moved there later but couldn't quite afford the maids and chauffeured limousines the Hokinson lady is sometimes seen with. Suburbanites collected early American furniture at this time. The tea or lamp table and the chair occupied by the man offer almost enough detail to classify them as perhaps being made between 1740 and 1780. The round table looks something like a Chippendale tea table, and the chair legs look like the European copies being made in Philadelphia much earlier.[26] Obviously, the lady has not been influenced by the modern, sleek chrome furniture that some in the suburbs were proudly showing at that time.

The cartoon lady would have been familiar with the modern or international style in the new Waldorf-Astoria in New York City, however. The kind of affluence both monetary and cultural that this woman represents is possible in the suburbs or the "exurbs"[27] of a city where finance and the arts command national attention. The Hokinson woman often attended functions in Manhattan, probably because in the late nineteenth and early twentieth centuries "Manhattan became the capital of the creative arts with music at the Metropolitan Opera, ballet at Lincoln Center, and paintings at scores of galleries and museums."[28] She may have traveled into

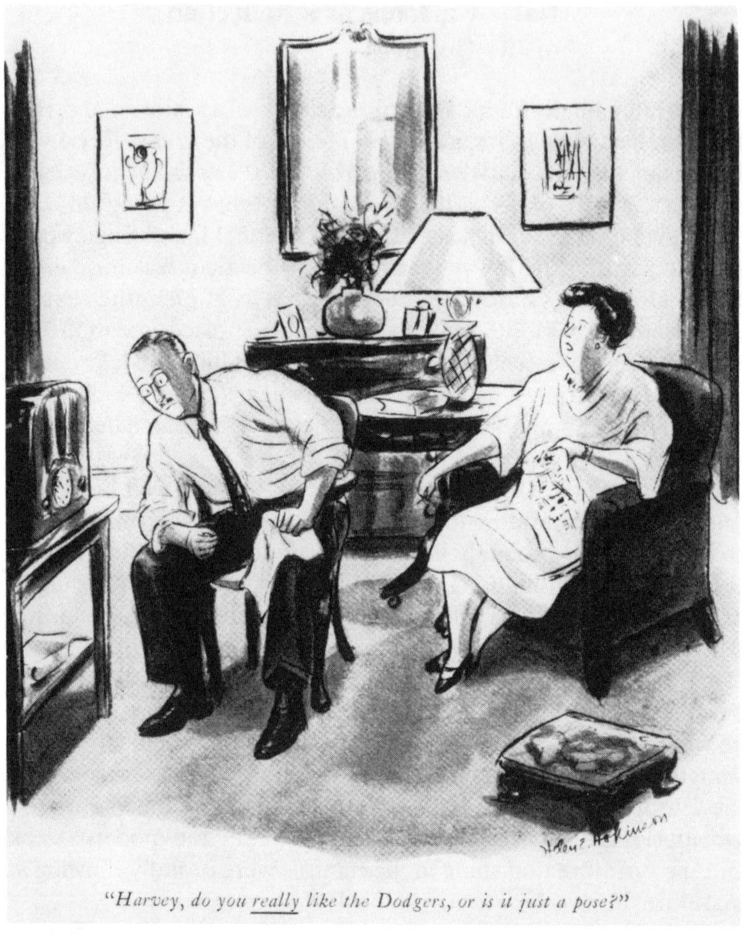

Fig. 1. Hokinson cartoon from the *New Yorker,* September 19, 1942. Drawing by Helen E. Hokinson; © 1942, 1970 The New Yorker Magazine, Inc. Reprinted by Special Permission. All Rights Reserved.

New York City for the events over and through the new bridges, tunnels, expressways, and parkways being built which Hokinson drew in her cartoons.

Because New York City was the art and music center of the nation, the woman may have seen—and certainly Helen Hokinson herself did—Rodin, Cezanne, Picasso, and Marin, who were much admired by some and much abhorred by others in New York after the Armory Show of 1913. The moneyed suburban lady may have heard Enrico Caruso at the Met or watched Arturo Toscanini conduct the New York Philharmonic, or she may have been lectured to by radio. The cultural explosion that brought art to the masses was not to happen until after World War II. While Hokinson's cartoons reflected current events, World War II is not in evidence. Occasionally a uniformed person, perhaps a visiting officer, attends a dinner party, and occasionally the Hokinson woman volunteers to aid the Red Cross, but she is generally unaffected by larger national events such as wars and depressions.

Reflecting cultural attitudes, Hokinson's ladies wouldn't appear in the bathtub or at a bar and, of course, not in front of a television as Hollander's Sylvia often does. Her surroundings are plusher than Sylvia's soft chair and bare TV. Whereas the ladies often wear fur coats, Sylvia more often wears a bathrobe and her hair is in curlers. Sylvia wisecracks a lot. Besides the latest feminist causes, Sylvia-as-counselor advises on everything from dinner menus to funerals; Sylvia-as-writer devises ideas for television game shows; Sylvia-as-friend discovers fantasy fears such as attending class reunions and not being the most accomplised person there. Politics abound. Animals, particularly cats, take on human characteristics. Mr. Herman, 109 years old, is interviewed by Patty, the reporter.

Hollander is reflecting her times, but the strongest influence is the feminist movement in the 1970s work. In her first book of cartoons, *I'm in Training to Be Tall and Blonde* (1979), she satirizes female stereotypes on television, from ethnic groups, and as housewives. Sylvia infrequently appears in this volume. The focus is on feminist issues such as male-female relationships and women in and out of history. Hollander keeps apprised of current issues in her frames. In the 1980s, the feminist issues are not quite so prominent as in the late 1970s, but the 1980s preoccupation with economics appears often. Hollander's new character, and one of her best, changes from Super Cop to Super Mom to several other Super's. She aims at the conscience of each of us.

The likenesses between Hokinson and Hollander and their characters indicate that the culture for women has not changed entirely. They titled their books in a similar fashion. For example, Hokinson's *When Were You Built?* compares closely with Hollander's *My*

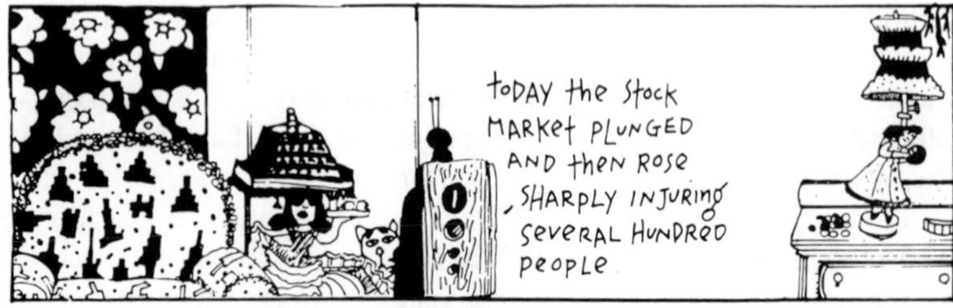

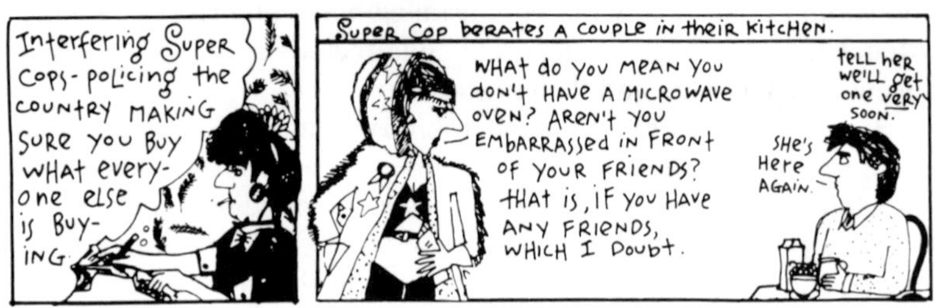

Fig. 2. Copyright © 1987 by Nicole Hollander. Reprinted from *Never Take Your Cat to a Salad Bar,* by Nicole Hollander, by permission of Random House, Inc.

Weight Is Always Perfect for My Height, Which Varies and *Okay! Thinner Thighs for Everyone.* Although the cartoonists are small women, the women characters in both strips worry about their weight. They are over forty. They diet and hate it, or they fight the notion that they should diet. Their clothes are not stylish, and they are never pretentious. They struggle with children and with men who are the straight characters, the supporting characters.

Both Hollander's Sylvia and Hokinson's ladies work at home, one in the era of wives at home in a nuclear family and one in the era of the growing group of writers working at home, single or retired women, often with children or young adult children at home. Sylvia is a writer because Hollander wanted to be one, and she is older because, as Hollander says, "I think I created someone who is a little bit older than I am now so I could see how I might act when I get to be that age. . . . Specifically, I'm thinking of how women become invisible after a certain age. No one listens to them; no one sees them."[29] Sylvia's flamboyance fights that tendency. The characters of both women are sophisticated about society but irreverent of it. They see the absurdity of situations. The comments of the *New Yorker* editors in a tribute after Hokinson's death best express her quality of humor in seeing absurdities: "Her work was the product of loving observation and a boundless delight in all absurdity, none more than that she found in herself, and the pleasure she gave other people was really a reflection of her own."[30] The same could be said of Hollander. Both use the subject matter of the times as their source material.

Some cultural changes are reflected in the differences between the cartoons. Hokinson's ladies are often naive and sometimes even out of touch, while Sylvia is savvy and always in the know. However, Hollander would probably agree with Hokinson's evaluation of humor evoked by her women characters: "I like my girls. They don't say anything I don't say. . . . A stupid remark isn't humorous, but an intelligent woman making a confused remark sometimes is. I rather admire my girls' point of view."[31]

Hollander uses Sylvia for the opportunity "to express a sense of outrage at all the things that bombard me from television, from newspapers and magazines, from other people's opinions about how everything should be."[32] Sylvia makes fun of those comments. Whereas the minor characters in Hokinson's frames are women alike, children alike, husbands alike, Hollander's minor characters reflect the complexity and diversity of late-twentieth-century culture. These minor characters include a realistic daughter who reverses the mother-daughter cultural roles by trying to get her mother to eat health food. She can hardly believe her mother's audacity in such habits as hogging the bathroom and communicating with fantasy creatures such as Gernif, the outer-space Venusian. Hollander's characters return again and again in her strips; Hokinson uses similar but different ladies and minor characters. The settings change from Hokinson's homes and art museums and concerts to Hollander's bathrooms, bars, and fortune-tellers' rooms. Hollander's strips call for much more communication through language, particularly since they attack more complex issues such as politics, whereas Hokinson's frames call for more quick one-liners. Hollander appeals to the popular culture addicts who read daily newspapers, and Hokinson appeals to the more sophisticated *New Yorker* weekly reader. However, the comparison indicates a common vision even though the culture changes. Much of the audience of one could easily be the audience of the other if they were produced in the same time period.

Historical Comparison: Hokinson and Hollander and Their Contemporaries

Because of some similarities in view, such as the empathy for women and their individual problems, not to mention their artistic and linguistic skills, Hokinson's and Hollander's cartoons are alike in several ways. However, because of the changes in time and culture, their cartoons, as we have seen, reflect substantial differences. A comparison of their work with other cartoons historically reflects how they deviated from the patterns of cartooning in their respective time periods. The comparison is aided by the Meyer study showing the dominant cultural patterns in cartoons.

In the earliest cartoons, the only female figures stood for ideas, not people. They were symbols. One from 1776 (fig. 3) one from 1912 (fig. 4) illustrate the prevalence of symbolic female figures for a long period of time. A female character alone is significant. The Meyer study shows that female images were scarce in most cartoons from 1890 to 1949 and that women were evident in about half of the cartoons from 1950 to 1976. Hokinson and Hollander use women in all their cartoons and thus can be considered subversively working against the trends. They are subversive in another way. Although the working stiffs in men's cartoons such as "Beetle Bailey" and Dagwood in the "Blondie" strip often have to be fall guys to be funny, Sylvia and the ladies always have the last word; they are never fall gals.

Appearance

The Meyer study uses three categories to look at female appearance in general cartoons: glamorous, matronly, or lifelike. None of the women in Hokinson's and Hollander's cartoons even pretends to be glamorous, but they are matronly and lifelike. Meyer says the usual matronly attributes are a hat, overweight or square figure, and attire that includes a housedress, apron, or high-necked long-sleeved dress intended to conceal the body.[33] Although these characteristics may have been used by both Hokinson's and Hol-

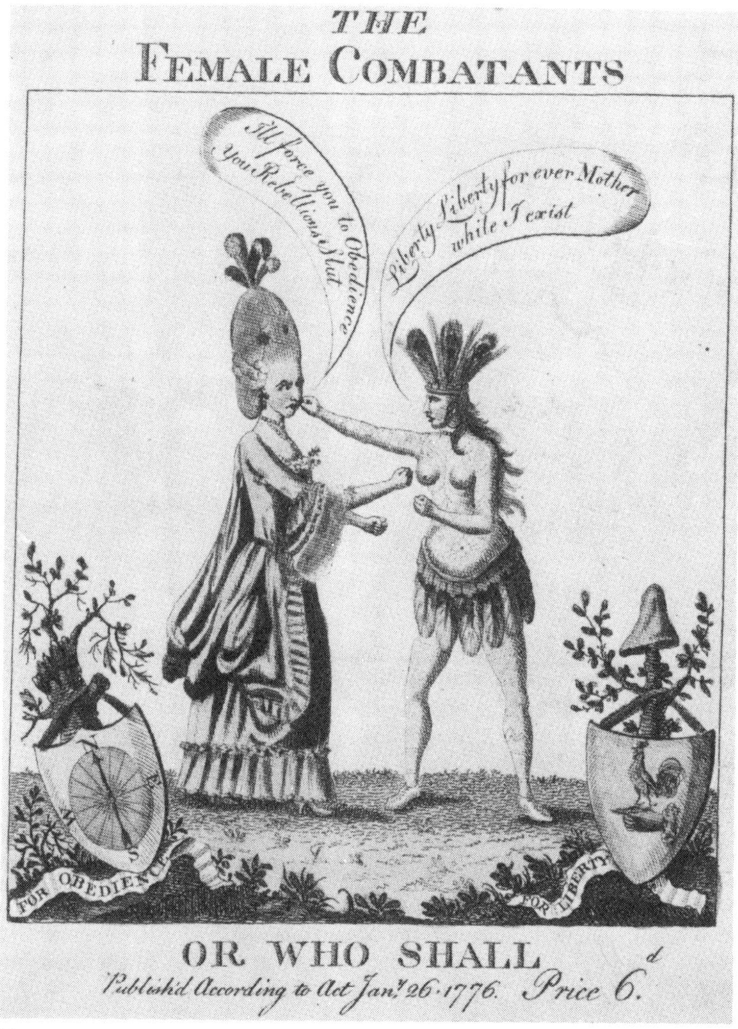

Fig. 3. Anonymous cartoon from the Revolutionary War, 1776.

lander's contemporaries to make a statement about dowdiness in women (see local newspapers for contrasting current examples in "The Wizard of Id," "The Lockhorns," and "Andy Capp," and early *New Yorker*s for examples from Hokinson's contemporaries),

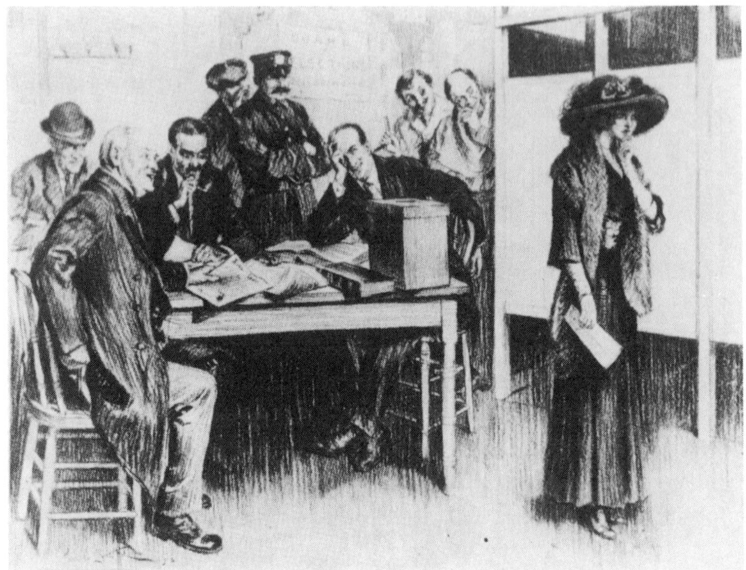

Fig. 4. Cartoon from *Harper's Weekly,* 1912.

both Hokinson and Hollander flaunt the costuming of their characters, much as they flaunted their own personal clothing. Hokinson's ladies don't seem to care too much about fashion, and Hollander's Sylvia spends most of her time in a huge, cuddly bathrobe when she is not in the bathtub.

Hokinson and Hollander seem to defy those who would dictate fashion over comfort. E. H. Gombrich recognizes the importance of an identifying characteristic for cartoon characters: "Dress and headgear, for instance, always acquire their own aura and significance in any culture," and he claims they are stocks in the cartoonist's armory.[34] The cartoon medium allows the advantage of seeing the costume. Hokinson's contemporaries did worry about fashion, and so do Hollander's contemporaries (again, see local daily comic strips such as "Cathy," drawn by Cathy Guisewite, for instance).

Women saw the Hokinson characters as lifelike in appearance. They identified closely with them, perhaps because Hokinson saw the small frustrations and humiliations of life as comic. She recognized that for the person involved, these frustrations are deadly serious, if only temporary.[35] These women drawn between 1925 and 1945 represent the fat ladies (see all Hokinson figures) with the feelings of Everywoman. They have been commonly called "sheep-shaped ladies,"[36] "ample dowagers," "benevolent creatures," "well-fed, well-bred stouts," "gregarious matrons,"[37] and "well-upholstered young-at-heart[s]."[38] A group of Akron, Ohio, women named their reducing club the Helen Hokinson Girls' Club. Another woman wrote to Hokinson from Needham, Massachusetts, "More power to you and the girls. The more I grow to look like them, the more I love them."[39] The Hokinson woman as a type must live outside the New York area, too. She may in fact still live—her lady in the voting booth is familiar, as is her lady in the liquor store; the latter might even have been a 1980s feminist.

But the prototype for the 1980s feminist is Nicole Hollander's Sylvia, about the same age as Hokinson's women, perhaps, but of a lower-middle-class or blue-collar working class: This lifelike, fiftyish, chenille-robed lady with her hair up in curlers, a cigarette dangling from the side of her mouth, and a can of beer in her hand observes and comments on our odd world as she divides her time between her television set, her kitchen table, her bathtub, and Harry's Bar.[40]

She has appeared in books with provocative titles such as *I'm in Training to Be Tall and Blonde; Mercy, It's the Revolution and I'm in My Bathrobe; Ma Can I Be a Feminist and Still Like Men?;* and *My Weight Is Always Perfect for My Height—which Varies.* Sylvia has perfect logic, the guts to say anything, and, as a result, evokes one laugh after another. Glamorous, she is not. Hollander is clear on her feelings about glamorous women—without words, she portrays decidedly unglamorous women, and sometimes she enforces the message with words.

Dominance

The second standard for studying cultural trends in cartoons, according to the Meyer study, is dominance. Dominance is portrayed by the relationship between the main character and the other characters in the cartoon. Dominance is judged by "considering whether women were shown alone or as equal to or subordinate to

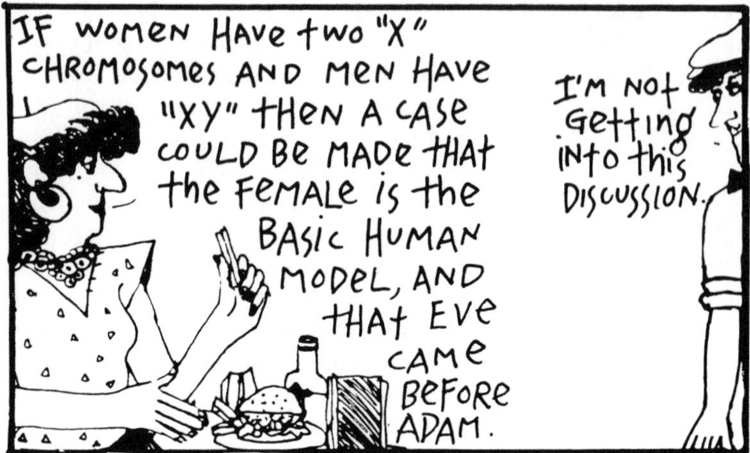

Fig. 5. Copyright © by Nicole Hollander. Reprinted from *Never Take Your Cat to a Salad Bar,* by Nicole Hollander, by permission of Random House, Inc.

men in action, spatial location, and verbalization".[41] A consistent but small minority of cartoons sketched women alone—that is, without companion.[42]

What about Hokinson's women and dominance? We might suppose them to be a stereotype, but we get some surprises if we do. In the 1920s cartoons, according to Meyer, significant activities were done only by men. In contrast, women were passive and unobtrusive for the most part.[43] Hokinson's ladies, however, do not fit the mold. Hokinson's character played opposite children, young people, and men, and in the drawings and captions she illustrates the interactions between them. However, the main foil for the women is the milquetoast male, probably her husband. The husband in the drawings has a receding hairline, delicate features, small round wire-rimmed glasses, and a small mustache. He is the supporting character, the "straight man" for the woman, much as are the maids, chauffeurs, clerks, and animals. Because this supporting character is always silent, listening to the comments by the more prominent women, the humor conveyed through him is also totally in the drawings.

The contemporary Sylvia, on the other hand, indicates the newer cultural acceptance of women being more frequently depicted and even at times dominant. Recently, according to Meyer, the male

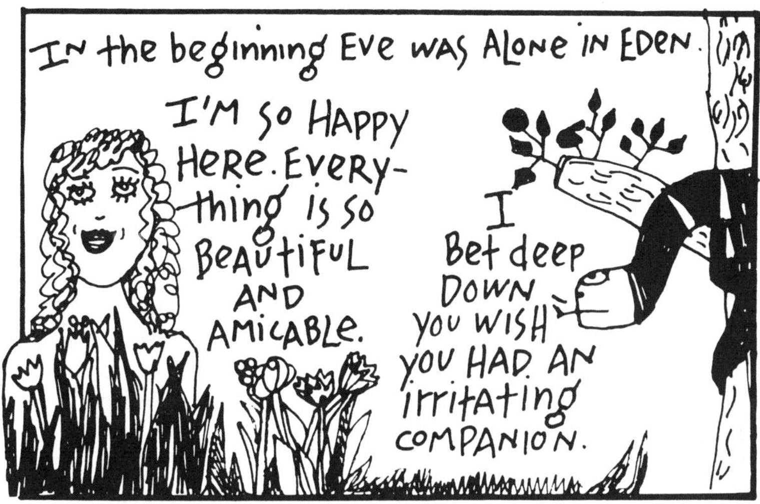

Fig. 6. Copyright © 1987 by Nicole Hollander. Reprinted from *Never Take Your Cat to a Salad Bar,* by Nicole Hollander, by permission of Random House, Inc.

"still appeared as more important. . . . [He] stood slightly in front of the woman, upstaging her."[44] Sylvia deviates decidedly from the cartoons showing male dominance. Sylvia is always dominant, as are the other women in Hollander's cartoons. Sylvia's crowd includes her daughter Rita (the ever-perplexed), her best friend Beth Ann (the ever-straight), Harry the bartender, Gernif the Venusian, Grunella the fortune-teller, and Patty Murphy, intrepid TV reporter. None of them ever upstages her. Women are often the same height or even taller than men, for instance.

Role

As with the first categories, Hokinson and Hollander deviate from the dominant culture representations in cartoons. They often indicate role by their individual techniques. These women are never pictured as victims because in each case the writer-artist is writing with a positive vision of women. In addition, treatment of subject matter is particularly important. One study shows "a rise in 'tendentious' humor as opposed to nonsense humor . . . [and]

when women were presented, they were the 'victors' rather than victims, 72% of the time."[45] Tendentious humor with victors fits both Hokinson and Hollander. Hokinson's humor derives from breaking down global problems into the lady's hometown suburban terms, minimalizing—or, assuming that her actions affect large events, maximizing—thus reflecting her ability to treat a large subject in small, concrete terms or expanding a small domestic issue into a global crisis. "Although more realistic portrayals of women emerged during the fifties, sixties, and seventies, there were only three cases in the whole time period in which women were drawn as challenging the Establishment, one each in the 1920s, 1960s, and 1970s."[46] Then came Hollander's strips in the 1980s—acerbic, bittersweet, witty, antiestablishment comedy, particularly when men and women see life differently. Hollander can be "at once funny, wrathful, and excruciatingly perceptive"[47] in such subject matter as unsung women, knotty problems, and sex, marriage, and other irreconcilable differences. Hollander offers a "slice of the true-life realism that finally does justice to the wacky off-centeredness of reality today,"[48] by using as subject matter panty liners and hemorrhoids. The contemporaries of Hokinson and Hollander were more likely to draw cartoons indicating mainstream roles and subject matter. (See figs. 4 and 5.)

Several other women drew cartoons for the *New Yorker* at the same time as Hokinson. They chose as subjects mostly young women, children, and men. Few chose the older woman as the subject for their drawings, and if they did, the women characters as well as the whole drawing were easily distinguished from Helen Hokinson's. For instance, Hokinson's friend Alice Harvey exhibited quite a different style. When women were drawn in cartoons, they usually had the more fashionable shorter skirts and slimmer figures, as did the Jazz Age ladies of Barbara Shermund. Mary Petty, who also contributed to the *New Yorker,* drew devastating commentaries on upper-crust New York life. Nearly all her characters were members of the "decadent old families whose blood but not their bank accounts had run thin."[49]

Hokinson did not follow the trend of women cartoonists in the *New Yorker* of picturing the frivolous younger set or the calcified older elite. The men who drew for the *New Yorker* used a wide variety of subject matter: Peter Arno, very wealthy New Yorkers (the top 400) in leisure time; Charles Addams, grotesques; William Steig, representatives of "People are no damn good"; Saul Steinberg, pure fantasy. In 1938, William Murrell saw their humor as "malicious jeering at upper-middle-class and upper-middle-aged women." He chided these "idle singers of an empty day" for being cruel and cynical and inhuman.[50] Shy Helen Hokinson and her cartoons do not match this zany bunch; however, when she found Peter Arno was paid more for his lecherous-looking men than she was for her "four-square ladies,"[51] she stopped sending in drawings until a suitable adjustment was made. She didn't need the advice of a much later *Ms.* magazine headline screaming, "How to Ask for Money and Get It." Helen Hokinson's cartoons were clearly distinguishable from her contemporaries on the *New Yorker.* Her cartoons were also clearly distinguishable from women contemporaries such as Lou Rogers and Cornelia Barns, who were drawing more radical feminist cartoons for social causes.

Several female cartoonists are as popular now as Hollander, such as Lynda Barry, Roz Chaste (the only woman cartoonist published in the *New Yorker* at this time), Cathy Guisewite, and Lynn Johnston. Each cartooning style is completely different, as are the purposes of each cartoonist. Barry sends us back to our childhoods and the strange but accurate rendition of our "kid" years. Chaste's strange, offbeat characters remind us of the zany cartoonists in past *New Yorker*s. Guisewite's young career women continually diets, argues with her mother, and struggles with her men friends; she occasionally raises feminist issues. Canadian Johnston, syndicated in U.S. papers, depicts the everyday struggles of a nuclear family. In several ways, Hollander and Hokinson are more similar to each other than they are to their contemporaries.

All of the evidence indicates that Hokinson and Hollander took unconventional stands even for women in a vocation largely occupied by men. They had to be good in two mediums: words and drawings. But they had to appeal to an audience in order to be published. Their purposes partially determined their audiences. William Murrell, a historian of American graphic humor, suggests two divisions for modern cartoons that may dictate how purpose and subject matter determine audience: "there are, broadly speaking, two main types of humorous drawing: that which makes humor an end in itself, the light humor of episode or situation; and the other, the humorous statement of a political, social, or personal viewpoint by means of ridicule. The sole purpose of the first is to provoke laughter; the purpose of the second is to awaken perception through laughter."[52]

Unlike these graphic historians and critics, we may take cartoons for granted, not dividing them into categories. However, these studies are useful because, as E. M. Gombrich says, "In studying the cartoons, we study the use of symbols in a circumscribed context," and we "look at these strange configurations . . . for what they may reveal about our own minds."[53] True, surprise is necessary for humor, but surprise founded on recognition. We recognize ourselves in Hokinson and Hollander, and yet we still are often surprised—we still learn.

Perhaps because of their educations in art, neither Hokinson's nor Hollander's drawings have been much criticized. Hokinson has received practically no criticism about any of her work either during the time she produced or since then, perhaps because she was different but not radically so. Hollander's ideas have sometimes been criticized by men who claim they don't understand her.[54] She is perhaps the most radical female cartoonist in the United States, but she may not be the most radical internationally. For instance, French cartoonist Claire Bretechér, now publishing in *Ms.* and *Esquire,* draws a mother dumping her baby in the garbage after she hears the exciting happenings at the office from a former colleague. The work is humorous, but U.S. audience opinion is unclear. Hollander, however, speaks to many who recognize their own familiar American culture.

The male contemporaries of Hokinson and Hollander usually praised them also. John Mason Brown eulogized Helen Hokinson: "Hers was the rarest of satiric gifts. She could ridicule without wounding. She could give fun by making fun, and in the process make no enemies."[55] And James Reid Parker, who wrote some of her captions, claimed he "admired Helen Hokinson above all the other members of her profession."[56] For women a half-century and a strong feminist movement later, the humor in the cartoons remains fresh.

The few reported comments by men about Nicole Hollander include a range of understanding and emotions. Mordecai Richler in the *New York Times Book Review* says, "Please send me more feminists like the saucy Nicole Hollander . . . her wit is unflagging and very much to the point."[57] Michael Denneny, a St. Martin's Press editor, is quoted in *Mother Jones:* "I thought the humor was just terrific, very sharp; it had a real political edge to it."[58] St. Martin's published the Sylvia books after Doubleday turned them down as being too feminist. On the other hand, inflamed by a strip that took Michael Jackson and Prince in vain, another writer scrawls: "I've never liked your strip but this time you went too far badmouthing Prince. He's more man than you can Handel [*sic*]."[59]

For a woman, making a living drawing cartoons is still difficult. Hollander has been turned down by several newspapers because they already carry Cathy and Sally Forth, very different women characters. The newspaper editors say women already have those two strips with which they can identify, and they consider that enough on a page of fifty or so strips.

In the tradition of female humorists, Hokinson and Hollander had similar problems but some enriching differences. Surpassing the culturally based problems of women getting published, Hokinson and Hollander stuck with their principles, producing realistic female characters in dominant roles while still appealing to wide audiences, succeeding in making a living humorously cartooning real women.

Notes

1. Alice Sheppard, "There Were Ladies Present: American Women Cartoonists and Comic Artists in the Early Twentieth Century," *Journal of American Culture* 7 (Fall 1984), 38.
2. Nancy Walker, *A Very Serious Thing: Women's Humor and American Culture* (Minneapolis: University of Minnesota Press, 1988), xi.
3. Quoted in Dorothea Daly, "The Flower of American Caricature," *Art News* 38 (March 1940), 18.
4. Thomas Craven, ed., *Cartoon Cavalcade* (New York: Simon and Schuster, 1943), 3–4.

5. Monika Franzen and Nancy Ethiel, *Make Way! 200 Years of American Women in Cartoons* (Chicago: Chicago Review Press, 1988).
6. Katherine Meyer, John Seidler, Timonthy Curry, and Adrian Aveni, "Women in July Fourth Cartoons: A 100-Year Look," *Journal of Communication* 30 (Winter 1980), 21. Hereafter referred to as the Meyer study.
7. Isabella Taves, *Successful Women and How They Attained Success* (New York: E. P. Dutton, 1943), 263.
8. *The National Cyclopaedia of American Biography* (New York: James T. White, 1956), 41:145.
9. Taves, *Successful Women,* 263.
10. Hokinson's books of cartoons include *The Ladies, God Bless 'Em!* (New York, E. P. Dutton, 1950); *My Best Girls* (1941); *There Are Ladies Present* (1952); and *When Were You Built?* (1952).
11. James Reid Parker, "Helen," memoir in *The Ladies, God Bless 'Em!* (New York: E. P. Dutton, 1950), 8, 12.
12. Marcia Froelke Coburn, "On the Draw," *Chicago* 33 (August 1984), 147.
13. Ellen Cantarow, "Don't Throw That Old Diaphragm Away!" *Mother Jones* (June–July 1987), 25.
14. Coburn, "On the Draw," 147.
15. Parker, "Helen," 11.
16. Cantarow, "Don't Throw," 23.
17. Albert F. McLean, Jr., "Hokinson, Helen Elna," in *Notable American Women, 1607–1950: A Biographical Dictionary,* ed. Edward T. James (Cambridge: Harvard University Press, 1971), 201.
18. Nicole Hollander, lecture, University of Washington, July 11, 1987.
19. Coburn, "On the Draw," 146.
20. Dale Kramer, "Those Hokinson Women," *Saturday Evening Post* 7 (April 1951), 98.
21. Dale Kramer, *Ross and the New Yorker* (Garden City, N.Y.: Doubleday, 1951), 202.
22. Nicole Hollander, *The Whole Enchilada: A Spicy Collection of Sylvia's Best* (New York: St. Martin's Press, 1976), 9.
23. Nicole Hollander's books of cartoons include *I'm in Training*

to Be Tall and Blonde (1979); *Mercy, It's the Revolution and I'm in My Bathrobe* (1982); *Hi, This Is Sylvia* (1983); *Okay! Thinner Thighs for Everyone* (1983); *Sylvia on Sundays* (1983); and *Never Take Your Cat to a Salad Bar* (1987).

24. Lewis Nichols, "Three Tested Recipes for Laughter," *New York Times Book Review* 5 (December 1948), 5.
25. David Maldwyn Ellis, *New York: State and City* (Ithaca: Cornell University Press, 1979), 44.
26. Milton W. Brown et al., *American Art: Painting, Sculpture, Architecture, Decorative Arts, Photography* (New York: Harry N. Abrams, 1979), 52–56.
27. A. C. Spectorsky, *The Exurbanites* (New York: J. B. Lippincott, 1955), 1.
28. Ellis, *New York,* 6.
29. Coburn, "On the Draw," 146.
30. "Helen E. Hokinson," *New Yorker* 12 (November 1949), 160.
31. Jeanine Dobbs, "There's a Little Helen Hokinson in All of Us," *Ms.* (February 1977), 17.
32. Coburn, "On the Draw," 147.
33. Meyer study, 22.
34. E. H. Gombrich, "The Cartoonist's Armoury," *Meditations on a Hobby Horse: And Other Essays on the Theory of Art* (London: Phaidon Press, 1963), 142.
35. Craven, *Cartoon Cavalcade,* 3–4.
36. Ellen Hart Smith, "Kind Hearted, Immortal Hokinson Ladies," *New York Herald Tribune Book Review* 26 (October 1952), 7.
37. "Our Times, A Cartoonists' Eye-View," *Saturday Review* 310 (November 1956), 80–82.
38. "The Hokinson Girls," *Time* 14 (November 1949), 80–81.
39. John Mason Brown, "Helen Hokinson," *Saturday Review of Literature* 10 (December 1949), 81.
40. Nicole Hollander, *That Woman Must Be on Drugs* (New York: St. Martin's Press, 1981).
41. Meyer study, 22.
42. Ibid., 26.
43. Ibid.
44. Ibid., 26–27.
45. Jennings Bryant, Joanne Gula, and Dolk Zillmann, "Humor in

Communication Textbooks," *Communication Education* 29 (May 1980), 132.

46. Meyer study, 25.
47. Nance Eberle, "A Review of *I'm in Training to Be Tall and Blonde*," *Chicago* (June 1979), 206.
48. Nicole Hollander, *My Weight Is Always Perfect for My Height—Which Varies* (New York: St. Martin's Press, 1982).
49. Kramer, *Ross and the New Yorker,* 136.
50. William Murrell, *A History of American Graphic Humor, 1865–1938* (New York: Macmillan, 1938), 2:203.
51. Kramer, "Those Hokinson Women," 26.
52. Murrell, *A History,* 263.
53. Gombrich, "The Cartoonist's Armoury," 127.
54. Cantarow, "Don't Throw," 23.
55. Brown, "Helen Hokinson," 8.
56. Parker, "Helen," 8.
57. Mordecai Richler, "Batman at Midlife: Or, the Funnies Grow Up", *New York Times Book Review* 3 (May 1987), 35.
58. Cantarow, "Don't Throw," 43.
59. Ibid.

PART THREE

Performers

Slapsticks, Screwballs, and Bawds: The Long Road to the Performing Talents of Lucy and Bette

June Sochen

Women stand-up comics are fashionable these days. It was not always thus. Indeed, according to erudite and popular opinion, women comics were an incongruous, indeed rare, lot. As already suggested, philosophers like Bergson and Schopenhauer had declared that women had no sense of humor; ergo, they could not perform humor. This weighty opinion held sway largely among male commentators on the subject until very recently. But the practice, the reality, for women wanting to be funny in public has always been more various, vital, and interesting.

Women comics in all of their variety—as slapsticks, screwballs, and bawds—have had a continuous history in this century. They have not always had warm receptions, nor have they had equal opportunity to perform alongside male comics, but they have existed and have provided scores of people with good laughs. They have been part of the rich tradition that Lucille Ball perfected on television in the 1950s and Bette Midler popularized on concert stages in the 1970s. The road to Lucy and Bette has been an exciting and uneven one.

Comic performances are difficult, if not impossible, to capture in print. They are intensely personal experiences for the viewer and the performer. They are felt, shared, and then no more. During the course of the show, the viewer is involved with the comic, laughs at all of the right times and places (if the comic is effective), and usually forgets most of the one-liners as well as the longer jokes by the end of the evening. The general idea of key routines may be remembered and reviewed at a later point, but there is little or no analysis of the humor. How did she make us laugh? What was funny about that skit? These questions usually remain unanswered.

Perhaps they are better left unanswered. Humor is to be experienced and enjoyed, with only a pleasant glow remaining afterwards. Why destroy the happy mood with intellectual dissection? (In the hope of enhancing the memory and recalling the humor.) Won't the organic whole of the performance be destroyed by a bit-by-bit critique? (Probably.) Can a writer capture and describe accurately the performance style of a comic? (Only indirectly by detailing the dress, the gags, the facial expressions, and the content of the material.) The writer approaches the humor of the performer and hopes that the reader, by filling in the particulars and recalling memories of similar experiences, can capture the vitality and skill of long-gone performances. In this way only can a writer preserve in print the always mobile comedy of Lucille Ball and Bette Midler.

Lucille Ball, particularly, participated in the rich era of Hollywood slapstick and screwball comedy and performed in situation comedy on the radio. Bette Midler grew up watching the movies of the 1940s and 1950s and integrated the fashions and songs of those eras in her comic routines. Both women had important predecessors. Both have been dedicated professionals who were very self-conscious about their work and tried to create high-standard performances. Both have possessed comic genius, a natural gift, that also requires cultivation, training, and experience. Both have been eclectic performers, very much in the American tradition of borrowing styles, mixing and matching, and emerging with their unique personalities; their styles synthesized earlier comic traits but in so doing transcended them. Both women are, contrary to popular opinion, living proofs of the vitality of women's skill at making us laugh.

In this century, women comic performers existed in most of the entertainment media, with a few notable exceptions. Women comics were not seen on the burlesque and vaudeville stages. That province belonged to men. The comedy was gross and physical—sight gags with baggy-pants clowns throwing pies in peoples' faces and having them thrown right back. In the burlesque houses, especially, the only role women played in the comic routines was as the straight person, the naive ingenue who asked the question "How can I find a good man?" and therefore presented herself for the butt of the joke. "I have never been kissed; will you teach me how?" offered endless possibilities for the male comic. The joke was always on the sweet young thing. She did not create or initiate the humor; rather, she was the hapless object of it.

The ethnic humor common on the vaudeville stage did not lend itself to women comics, either. The German, Irish, and Yiddish entertainers who made fun of their own groups were usually men. There were a few examples of man-and-woman comedy teams in vaudeville, but rarely, if ever, would an audience see a stand-up woman comic. It was beyond the imagination of the entrepreneurs and, by extension, of the culture. After all, women were stereotypically viewed as empty-headed, lacking in knowledge, wit, and a sense of humor. Further, it was an extremely unladylike thing to present yourself as funny, as physically unattractive, and/or as awkward and, worse yet, grotesque. Male comics were never beneath exposing themselves to all of these charges.

Slapstick comedy, the main style performed in vaudeville and burlesque, of course, was a physically rough-and-tumble style. Even the verbal humor was accompanied by a lot of pushing and shoving. Punching your partner, flaying your arms and legs regularly, and presenting yourself as a physical klutz were integral parts of the comic routine. All of these features were decidedly unladylike. They all defied the culture's expectations of proper behavior for women. Women could be in the chorus line, or the featured singer, or finally as the romantic interest in the show, but as the comic attraction, assuredly no. Showing personal weakness, an essential trait of humor, was considered funny when big, burly men did it, but women? After all, members of the "fairer sex" were known to be physically weak; that was their nature. What was funny about that? Indeed, it would be viewed as unfair, as bullying the vulnerable and defenseless, to make fun of women's physical or alleged intellectual weakness. Thus, it made eminently good cultural sense, something no one had to discuss or defend, to feature male comics and relegate women to second bananas or no role at all.

But in the new media of this century, the radio and silent film (and, later, sound film and television), women comics did play a larger role, though male comics still dominated. We can never forget the close interaction between cultural expectations and values on the one hand and the visibility of women comics on the other; this dynamic has always played an essential role in determining the imaginative possibilities available to women in comedy. As social mores relaxed and young women of this century went to school for longer periods, worked outside the home before and during marriage, and socialized freely, cultural attitudes about them changed. New possibilities, new roles opened up for them, including comedic ones. Lucille Ball, although she had toiled in the show-business vineyard for many years, succeeded in the new, still untested medium of television. The small screen turned out to be very congenial to the talents of a funny woman. It is no accident that Bette Midler's career flourished during a period of sexual liberation and in settings new to women performers—the gay Continental Baths and the pop concert stage. Women have always been funny and have always appreciated humor, but they have only been able to perform comedy when audiences showed the imagination, the accepting values, and the capacity to appreciate their humor.

Silent film, though it, too, featured male comics in perhaps their most creative environment, gave some women comics opportunities that they took great advantage of. Though film historians emphasize the comic genius of Charlie Chaplin and Buster Keaton, Mabel Normand, Marie Dressler, and Constance Talmadge were also extremely successful in that medium. Silent film was, above all, a visual art and entertainment forum. Just as the audience watched a vaudeville performance and enjoyed the movement and the liveliness of the performers, so, too, in silent film. Indeed, the moving camera, its chief novelty, required the performers to move around a lot. Big, burly Marie Dressler could rival male comics in physical, slapstick comedy while Constance Talmadge could play the dumb blonde, the nitwit, another stereotypical image of women that had ample exposure in vaudeville. While Dressler banged a frying pan on the head of her erstwhile lover, Talmadge batted her eyelashes, looked innocent, and uttered a faux pas. The empty-headed woman who, paradoxically, seemed to know precisely what she had in mind tickled audiences' funny bones. Again, the image suited cultural expectations about woman's alleged nature.

The radio, a verbal medium, and silent film, a visual one, epitomized the two essential dimensions of comedy. Fast talk and fast action. A good talker was essential for the radio, someone with a sense of timing, an expressive voice, and witty material with which to deliver the punch. Silent film relied on physical humor, on sight gags, spectacle, and the audacious. The eye beheld excitement, suspense, and pathos. And the effective comic provided audiences with the laughs, the tears, and the drama for which they paid their hard-earned coins. In silent film the eye was constantly assaulted with the actions on the screen, while in radio the ear absorbed and translated into humor the double entendres, the mispronounced words, and the mistaken identities.

Surely Chaplin's ability to evoke pathos in film was admirably suited to the new phenomenon, the moving picture, but so was Mabel Normand's. She was, physically, the female equivalent of Chaplin. Indeed, she made numerous movies with him and appeared as his female counterpart. Normand exploited the visual dimension as well, by moving around a lot and displaying an athletic demeanor. She was a small, petite woman with large brown eyes that were extremely expressive. In a series of comedies for Mack Sennett, the acknowledged king of silent film comedy, she flew an airplane, threw a pie in Ben Turpin's face, ran with the Keystone Kops, and generally gave as good as she got from Turpin, Chaplin, and Fatty Arbuckle. She appeared in constant motion, enrapturing her many fans with her audacity and willingness to be both comic and vulnerable. She combined the images of clown and pathetic character, the sweet, well-meaning ingenue and the naughty child; she initiated comic situations and also played the inadvertent victim.

During the 1910s, Normand was a big box-office success. But in the 1920s, her personal life was filled with sensational troubles resulting in the abrupt end of a brilliant comic career. Unknowingly, a young girl who had observed her work as well as that of others on the Mack Sennett comedy unit's productions became an effective performer in the Normand tradition. She was the impressionable and witty Carole Lombard. While Lombard made her mark in sound film, indeed in screwball comedy, she learned comic techniques from Sennett's slapstick comedy routines. It would be Lombard's witty delivery of nonsensical lines that assured her of comedic success rather than the peripatetic Normand's slapstick, physical style. Women comics became verbal comedians in the new screwball comedies of sound film, while male comics continued to hit each other on the head with the screams and the noises now heard, rather than imagined, by the audience. But in silent comedy, women ran toward, or away, from the Keystone Kops, fooled men, slapped an opponent, and fell on banana peels.

Verbal comedy, though it gives women more opportunities for expression than physical comedy, also has its pitfalls and limitations. Surely women talk too much, declares our culture, speaking trivialities and nonsensical statements about small matters such as household chores and child-raising problems; but this verbal excess disqualifies them from true verbal comedy. After all, who wants to hear about mumps or scouring pads that don't scour? So the content of women's verbosity has never been seen as appropriate or desirable material for verbal comedy. That is, on the stage or screen. Women have written domestic humor for 150 years, but their audiences have been overwhelmingly female, thus keeping the male half of the population immune to their humor. But clever adapters of women's alleged nature to the entertainment world explored and exploited the stereotype to make women acceptable verbal comics on the radio.

They discovered the screwball and situation comedic forms. Both exaggerate allegedly female traits: women as silly, childlike creatures who are overwhelmed by most of life's challenges, including how to use a defective scouring pad. Gracie Allen on the radio and Carole Lombard in the movies both perfected the screwball comedy genre. They used language creatively (Lombard asks William Powell, the butler in *My Man Godfrey,* "Can you buttle?"), and they always possessed their own sweet logic. Gracie once told her husband, George Burns, who played her straight man, "Why, if you don't believe me when I'm telling the truth, when I'm not telling the truth, you might think I was lying." The unique vision of women screwball comics—and the format belonged to women—made for easy, indulgent laughter from the audiences. Aren't women cute and simple, much like children? asked, or at least thought, male audiences. The men in their lives always had to explain the situation to them. Reasoning and logic went beyond their mental capacity.

Situation comedy builds on this same view of women, but it places them within their rightful place, the home, and makes jokes about their domestic situation. Isn't it funny if the housewife is baffled by the loss of a sock? The culture's low opinion of domesticity is the basis for the easy time comedy writers have in making fun of situations experienced regularly in the home. Vaudeville skits preceded radio and television situation comedies, but it was in the last two media that they achieved their greatest successes. The quick verbal exchanges on the radio, occurring in familiar settings, were only enhanced when the visual element could be added on television. The unanimous audience view that domesticity is a natural source of humor for women confirms the low opinion both sexes had for that topic.

Lucille Ball, trained as a dancer, became the timely exploiter of this dual tradition. She had observed slapstick comedy at the end of the silent film era, participated in some screwball comedy in Hollywood during the 1930s (she was also a good friend of Carole Lombard), and began her situation comedy on the radio in the 1940s. Television became the perfect medium for her talents: her athletic skills combined with her verbal genius were effectively captured on the small screen. Physical comedy, typified by slapstick, and verbal comedy, best achieved in situation comedy for women, offered audiences the full range of humorous possibilities. An interesting cultural sidelight, of course, is the fact that verbal humor, as seen in stand-up comedy routines, was until very recently almost exclusively the domain of men. Women may be witty givers and receivers of comic material in a domestic relationship, but the individual star, the solo verbal virtuoso, is male. Women may be fast talkers within the family environment, but, without explanation, they do not possess this same quality when alone on a stage.

Of course, it is not without explanation. The solo comic describes, in humorous detail, political bunglings, current event debacles, and philosophical musings, all subject matter beyond the reach and imagination of women—or so it is thought by the cultural arbiters. Until recently, the domestic world of women made them ill equipped to engage in political satire. Housewives may have had choice observations on the behavior of their local politicians, but because they did not have the vote until 1920 and were never elected to political positions, men did not listen to their political commentary. Without an audience, political humorists, like all humorists, cannot perform. Perhaps women exchanged wry remarks in their kitchens, but their words are lost forever. Women can comment humorously on their domestic disasters, indeed can often be the victims of their own actions, and will receive understanding laughter from both sexes. Women will laugh because they have often shared the experience, and men will laugh because they are relieved that they have not.

By this route, we approach the career of Lucille Ball. As a young woman yearning to become a performer, she watched silent film eagerly and, by a circuitous path, became the premier, and pioneer, television comic in history. Her first movie was *Roman Scandals* (1933) starring Eddie Cantor, a major force in radio comedy. She danced in Goldwyn productions, played the second banana in a series of movies, and spent three seasons on CBS radio as the female lead in a situation comedy called "My Favorite Husband." This show became the foundation for the "I Love Lucy Show," brought to television in 1951. And, as they say on television, the rest is history. But the incredible success of that series, which played for nearly six years, 179 half-hour episodes, requires explanation or at least an attempt at analysis.[1]

Situation comedy, though featuring a central character, cannot succeed without a talented ensemble of actors, a strong story line, and consistently good scripts. While Lucy was undoubtedly the star of the show, her real-life husband Desi Arnez, as her TV husband Ricky Ricardo, and their next-door neighbors the Mertzes, Ethel and Fred, played by Vivian Vance and William Frawley, were critical to its huge success. The setting and the situations fit neatly into cultural expectations about women's lives. The scene is the living room in the home, the domestic world, where women presumably live all the time. The crises are tied to the woman's role as wife and homemaker. And the resolutions are cheerfully provided by the good-natured husband. These ingredients were shared with many other successful situation comedies—the "Dick Van Dyke Show" comes immediately to mind. Though many enjoyed great success, none equalled the spectacular success of the "I Love Lucy Show." Within six months of the show's premiere, it was viewed in ten million homes, in a period when there were fifteen million television sets in the whole country. Though Lucy returned to television comedy with two other shows ("The Lucy Show," 1962–1967, and "Here's Lucy," 1968–1974), neither would reach the success of the first series.

Its very novelty, combined with the novelty of television itself, surely contributed to the show's popularity. But its unique combination of physical and verbal humor, its slapstick and screwball elements, made it an excellent example of comedy, especially of women's comedic skills. Lucy was not above wearing baggy clown's clothes, dressing like Chaplin in a Little Tramp skit, having a pie thrown in her face, imitating a seal, and breaking down and bawling at the drop of a hat. She delivered clever lines to her Latin husband, made fun of his malapropisms, imitated his accent (still acceptable behavior in the early 1950s and reminiscent of ethnic humor of an earlier era), sang out-of-tune songs, schemed with Ethel, and concocted elaborate plots to accomplish her purpose. But always—and this surely assured conforming audiences—Ricky had the last word; Lucy was tamed, ashamed, and contained within the home. The big world of show business, the allure of the nightclub, Ricky's domain which Lucy yearned for, remained beyond her grasp.

The genius of "I Love Lucy" was its ability to march off into new directions for women comedians while upholding the status quo.[2] Audiences were treated to Lucy's mobile face and body performing routines reminiscent of Chaplin and Keaton, while uttering lines that sounded right out of a Carole Lombard screwball movie or a Gracie Allen radio routine. She showed the boundless capacity for comic women to express themselves while playing a housewife-mother whose frustrations were always defined humorously. Everyone left happy, presumably, because laughter resounded around the room and no one was seriously challenged. Women could look silly and unattractive, empty-headed and scatterbrained, and bring roars of laughter to the viewers. Lucy made physical comedy acceptable comedic material for women while continuing in the screwball comedy genre. She showed a stubborn insistence on a career in show business, while making fun of the foibles of domesticity. In so doing, she was both subversive and supportive of cultural values. Her threat to domesticity was always expressed good-naturedly; it was gentle fun with no serious challenge to the power balance in the home.

The plot of each episode of "I Love Lucy" also reveals a repetitive theme: Lucy's neglect of the home in pursuit of her own ambition. Because her rebellious behavior, her wish to become a performer with an identity and career outside the home, was always presented as funny, audiences were reassured of the stability of the separate spheres and the continued authority of the man in the household. The very predictability of the story, week after week, was part of the strength of the show. Audiences were treated to tensions resolved, their expectations were always fulfilled, and there were not surprise endings to upset them. Their heroine amused them, showed her frustration and weakness, but ended up happily reconciled to her fate, safe in her husband's arms. The crisis, the chaos, and the happy ending—parts one, two, and three of every situation comedy—provided the knowing structure for audiences. Throughout all 179 episodes, Lucy showed her indifference to domesticity and her ardent wish to become a performer in Ricky's club.

Lucy is constantly botching up the household budget, failing to pay bills, and spending more than she has. She also has problems keeping the house neat and clean—in one episode, the Ricardos hire a maid who takes very good care of herself but not of them. Lucy, in another episode, accuses Ricky of being a slob and spends the rest of the half-hour messing up his belongings. She constantly wishes for fabulous clothes and glamorous activities but appears as the naive child who, impressionably, wants everything lovely but has no sense of responsibility to manage what she does have. Audiences never questioned Ricky's insistence that Lucy stay home, and this was in the early years before they had children, but always assumed that Lucy, arrested at an early stage of human development, could do no more than end up crying in frustration after she had created another mess. Interestingly, situation-comedy husbands, as late as "The Jeffersons" in the 1970s, continued to demand that their wives stay home and concern themselves exclusively with hubby's well-being.

While Lucy wreaked havoc in the home, she schemed to launch her show-business career. If a ballet dancer was needed, Lucy claimed she qualified; if a Shakespearean actress was called for, she could do it. Elaborate deceits were engaged in by Lucy, often with the help of Ethel. However carefully she planned, Lucy failed to convince Ricky to audition her; if she succeeded in fooling him and gained an audition, as she did in one 1951 episode, her success and the contract offered by the TV bigwigs were turned down to preserve domestic harmony. Lucy always backed down, surrendering her will to the inevitable role of homemaker and wife. Preserving her happy marriage was paramount, a value surely shared by most members of the TV audience in the 1950s. But during the show, while she was creating tumult and chaos, she challenged cultural expectations for women and acted as a subverter of established patterns.

But the frequent repetition of this theme—and its obverse (after all, if you are concentrating your energies on a show-business career, why would you bother dusting every day?)—suggests a real conflict which was then seen as, not an irreconcilable one, but rather one in which women suborned their wishes for the good of the family. Women could not have both a happy marriage and a public career. Their sole adult occupation had to be in the domestic arena. "I Love Lucy" reflected America's ideal cultural values, an ideal that was clearly in danger of being overturned. Methinks the writers protested too much. If the problem was not a problem, why did it keep recurring? The solution did not satisfy all of the parties, especially Lucy. Her yearning to perform remained an active and constant part of her comic persona throughout the show. Her unsatisfied ambition, like an out-of-control jack-in-the-box, kept reappearing.

Lucille Ball's great talent in both physical and verbal comedy was always on full display. Her willingness to stamp on grapes, engage in a fight with another grape crusher, and end up the color blue endeared her to audiences who also had weaknesses and often felt foolish, though they never had had the nerve to display their silliness so publicly. Lucy's sharp tongue, clever wit, fiery eyes, and sweet demeanor added to her rich personality. She was shrewd yet could appear simple; she was a planner yet could seem scatter-brained; and she was sensible, though she often appeared nonsensical. She had ambition and talent that she wanted to express, but she contained it within expected boundaries. Lucille Ball ventured into comedic territory never explored before by women and paved the way for Carol Burnett and other worthy imitators.

Lucy was a very attractive woman who downplayed her good looks and her great legs. She dressed in baggy clothes, made grotesque facial expressions and silly noises, and emphasized awkwardness rather than her natural gracefulness. Before her, women physical comedians, like Marie Dressler and Martha Raye, were physically unattractive by society's standards, and they simply built on that stereotypical bias. They conformed to society's view that ugly women could be physical comics. Pretty women were only supposed to be dimwits or nitwits. A naturally attractive woman, Lucille Ball went against type, made herself look unappealing, and combined physical comedy with verbal wit. She saw both types as available to women, indeed to any one woman. This was her genius.

Without verbalizing it, however, she also provided a devastating commentary on traditional role expectations for women in this society. Lucy's stubborn and persistent wish to become a public person and to receive social approval for her talent was a powerful, though unspoken, critique of a culture that denied women public recognition. Everyone agreed that the domestic realm was trivial, its concerns undemanding, and yet when Lucy showed an understandable lack of interest in that very realm, she was ridiculed, and she accepted the ridicule. The lack of satisfactory resolutions, from a feminist-hindsight perspective, demonstrates the failure of the cultural imagination. The boundaries of human possibility seemed clearly drawn. Career women were mannish, homemakers were feminine, and the two shall never meet. "I Love Lucy" showed the cracks in that vision and the crossing of the two paths.

Both slapstick and screwball comics break out of established patterns. Both types of humor challenge accepted limits. In this sense, both are anarchic, threatening, and rebellious. Women are not supposed to look undignified with a cream pie smeared all over their faces. Women are not supposed to make fun of housecleaning. Revolutionary possibilities abound when humor is taken seriously. And as many comics declare, comedy is a very serious business. How far is it, then, to move to bawdy humor, humor that deals with another kind of forbidden material for women? Though dirty jokes, male braggadocio tales, and bathroom humor have always been expected from men, told usually in male-only settings, none of these themes has been expected, or accepted, from women comics. If physical, slapstick comedy is not ladylike, imagine what the comment is for women who talk dirty, boldy discuss their sexual needs, and deign to criticize men's sexual equipment?

As slapstick comedy breaks down barriers, so does screwball comedy. Though seemingly based on stereotypical views of women, it allows women comics to create their own universe with its own rules. Gracie Allen's thinking had an inner logic and a quirky sense of justice that was not only funny but appealing. Bawdy women's humor is not far behind (or below). The crazy and funny angle of vision exhibited by the screwball comic creates opportunities for the bawdy woman comic. Surely she may have coexisted throughout time in the confines of her home, amid her female friends, relatives, and neighbors. But it is only in this century, with the advent of the intimate nightclub, the gay bathhouse, and the pop concert stage, that women bawds have found new, and approving, audiences of men and women—in the case of the concert stage, big audiences. The other vehicle for bawdy women entertainers in this century, of course, has been the record. Sophie Tucker recorded many of her off-color songs and stories from the 1920s through the 1950s, while she performed regularly in America's nightclubs. Rusty Warren's material is available on record, as is that of Totie Fields and numerous others.

Bette Midler, half Jewish, growing up in Honolulu amid Hawaiian and Chinese children, always felt different. As she later recalled, "I was not a hip color. I was white in an all Oriental school. Forget the fact that I was Jewish. They didn't know what that was. Neither did I. I thought it had something to do with boys."[3] In the late 1960s, she began working in New York at the Continental Baths, a gay spot that also had entertainment. It was here that she developed the persona that made her famous. Surely the enthusiastic encouragement and support of her audience egged her on to become more and more outrageous in her material and style. She dressed in black lace corsets with gold lamé pedal pushers, strutted around the stage in an exaggerated manner reminiscent of Bette Davis imitators, winked, leered, smiled broadly, and sang old Sophie Tucker songs. She always insisted on her extreme good looks. "I am a living work of art," she told her audiences, and they roared their approval.

Both women's sexual needs and men's sexual inadequacies were fair game for Midler's active intelligence. Just as Sophie Tucker sang red-hot-mama songs that proclaimed her need to see her papa every night, so Midler sang of her sexual needs and of the vanities of her lovers. Her sketches—and she parodied old movies, old movie stars, and other personalities of popular culture—were situation and screwball comedic forms carried to the *n*th degree. She entered into her own dimension with the material, but it was a natural extension of mocking the human/woman's condition exhibited in the other forms of women's humor. Now, instead of the woes of housework, Midler joked about the woes of having too few lovers, and inconstant ones at that. One major advance, however, in style and image was Midler's brash intelligence which could never be mistaken for nitwit status. The bawdy comic was never scatterbrained.

While bawds shared their audacity with slapstick comics, they also displayed a sharper intelligence, indeed a willingness to be recognized as intelligent. This trait surely distinguished them from the screwball comics as well. Bette Midler's quick wit, her sharp analyses of gender roles, and her ribald interest in life crossed the border into male comic territory. Before the popular bawds, America had never heard women talk, sing, gesture, and wiggle with such obvious success. Burlesque queens and stripteasers were imprisoned in male-determined formats, and they rarely could, or did, exhibit any individuality, satiric self-awareness, or intelligence. Their routines followed male audiences' expectations and were often deadly serious, if not dull, actions. They rarely, if ever, showed the women in control of their material; rather, they were the implementers of preestablished forms.

Bawdy women comics—and Midler is surely one of the most talented of the group—were satirists, both self and social mockers of society's role expectations about women. They openly challenged the rules of politeness, the sex role divisions, and the willingness to discuss publicly forbidden subjects. But women bawds could be victims, too. In this sense, they failed to rise above cultural traditions. After all, what could they do? Midler sang the blues while proclaiming her sexual freedom. As free as Midler was in her language ("Fuck them if they can't take a joke," she declared on stage) and in her subject matter, she, too, wanted a man, a good, steady man, and was willing to do most anything to keep him. So, while Lucy tearfully and/or joyously embraced Ricky at the end of an "I Love Lucy" episode, so Midler affirmed the power and need for love and companionship during the course of her show. Midler's material and her style were bold and accepting in the more sexually free age of the late 1960s and the 1970s. But ultimately, the bottom line, as business America says, is that women still want love and marriage, even bawdy women entertainers.

Midler's performance style, both at the baths and later on the stage, resembled both Mable Normand and Lucille Ball. She was in constant motion; she walked, danced, stood on her head, and fell to the floor with great regularity. Her comedy was both physical and verbal. While gyrating, she also sang the blues or told a joke: "What happens when you cross a donkey with an onion? Occasionally, you get a piece of ass that is so wonderful you want to cry." While Normand looked like an attractive young athlete and Ball emphasized her awkwardness, Midler dressed in sexy costumes, always reminding her audiences how incredibly attractive she was and how desirable everyone in the audience thought she was. She asked them if they agreed and received a resounding cheer.

Midler's style also contained elements of the screwball genre. Her angle of vision was uniquely her own, her logic as sensible as Gracie Allen's. While Carole Lombard pursued the object of her romantic desire with steadfastness in *My Man Godfrey,* Midler never wavered from her subject matter. Her occupation, or preoccupation, with sex never left her onstage, but she discussed and sang about the subject with such obvious good humor and self-deprecation that audiences identified with her, not against her. Fanny Brice once said that a successful comic identifies with the humorous weakness described and not as a judge or critic of it; Midler understood this requirement and performed accordingly.

Bette Middler allowed her audiences to enter into the joke. After all, don't we all take sex, and ourselves, entirely too seriously? Don't screwballs have a better view of the world than conventional folk? In the liberation seventies, when many established ideas and conventions came under attack, Midler joined the chorus of critics, but she did so with a twinkle in her eye and a laugh in her throat. She never took herself or anyone else seriously, and the result was enormous success. Her concert tours, her records, and her appearances on the "Tonight Show" were great celebrations of her boisterous, aggressive-but-sweet style.

The interaction, indeed the close connection, among cultural expectation, acceptance, and possibility produced an exciting and powerful mixture in the career of Bette Midler. While Janis Joplin, with whom she shared some traits, was too desperate and self-destructive in her aggressive proclamations of sexual freedom and dependence, Midler never lost her sense of humor, her ability to mock herself as well as the foibles of her audience. In the 1980s, she made the transition to the movies; she had come in from the cold. Though she had a rocky start (her 1981 *Jinxed* was just that), she hit her stride in the late 1980s with *Down and Out in Beverly Hills, Ruthless People,* and *Outrageous Fortune.* Women joking about sex was no longer such a big deal. Comedy clubs sprang up all over America, and women stand-up comics became part of the regular bill. They had finally arrived. Their subject matter, also in light of the postfeminist era in which we live, covered the waterfront. There was no taboo subject or a traditionally expected one. Women comics could, and did, talk about anything and everything that interested them.

In the movie *Punchline* (1988), Sally Field played a housewife who yearned to become a stand-up comic. Her material is based on her life: her husband's foibles, her kids, and domestic frustrations. Rosanne Barr plays a working housewife and mother in a TV situation comedy. The women stand-up comics, too many to list, talk about sex, politics, domesticity, and personal neuroses. The subject matter and the style are based on the unique talent and interest of the performer. The genres are all mixed up. Screwball and bawd mingle congenially. Political satire, previously forbidden territory for women, receives attention from women comics today. Current events become the stuff of women's comedy as well. In the more tolerant and eclectic 1980s and 1990s, the old comic conventions have been replaced with a more egalitarian acceptance of women comics. The performers are judged by their wit and effectiveness, not by their close conformity to preconceived categories of gender-determined humor.

It has been a long time on the highway of American humor to reach our current destination. Lucy and Bette were important and exciting stops on that road. Indeed, they lit the way. And in so doing they have become permanent parts of the landscape, places always to stop and remember, both for their unique contributions to women and comedy and to remind us where we have been and where we are today. There are no longer separate spheres; the private is discussed, often in great detail, in the public sphere, and women move freely in both areas. Women's performing is now visible for all to see, no longer whispered in the kitchen or forgotten by subsequent generations, thanks to the new media, the new and improved circumstances of women's lives, and the profitable possibilities in discovering new talent. Many current practitioners may be unaware of their predecessors in slapstick, screwball, and bawdy forms of humor, but they are indebted to them nonetheless.

Notes

1. Bart Andrews, *Lucy & Ricky & Fred & Ethel: The Story of "I Love Lucy"* (New York: E. P. Dutton, 1976), contains a summary of all of the episodes.
2. One of the few scholarly sources to explore some of the issues I raise in this essay is Patricia Mellencamp's "Situation Comedy, Feminism, and Freud: Discourses of Gracie and Lucy," in *Studies in Entertainment: Critical Approaches to Mass Culture,* ed. Tania Modleski (Bloomington: Indiana University Press, 1986), 80–95.
3. Clair Safran, "Who Is Bette Midler and Why Are They Saying Those Terrible Things about Her?" *Redbook,* August 1975, 57.

Moms Mabley and the Afro-American Comic Performance

Elsie A. Williams

momma
teach me how to hold a new life
momma
help me
turn the face of history
to your face.[1]

In eulogizing Jackie Moms Mabley, Billy Rowe of the *Amsterdam News* wrote, "Though none is aware where in death Moms Mabley is going, it is unforgivable not to know where she came from and what she came through."[2] She was born Loretta Mary Aiken in 1894 in Brevard, North Carolina. Mabley was raped twice before reaching her thirteenth birthday and ran away from home at fourteen to find work in black vaudeville.[3]

Mabley's first role in black vaudeville (known formally as the Theatre Owners Booking Association—TOBA,[4] and less formally as the chitlin' circuit) was a skit in which she combined comedy with singing and dancing to portray the Rich Aunt from Utah. Taking her cue from 1920s headliners Buck and Bubbles,[5] Mabley's comedy act rarely came to a close without a song and a dance.

In the 1920s, Mabley began performing at nightclubs such as the Cotton Club and Connie's Inn and shared billings with such greats as Louis Armstrong, Duke Ellington, Bennie Goodman, Count

Basie, and Cab Calloway. Before the day of the stand-up comedians, she teamed up with such comics as Tim "Kingfish" Moore, Dusty "Open the Door" Fletcher, "Spider Bruce" John Mason, and Dewey "Pigmeat" Markham. In the revues *Look Who's Here* (1927) and *The Joy Boat* (1930),[6] Mabley performed in burnt cork, the traditional makeup of the black clown before the early 1950s.[7]

Mabley collaborated with Zora Neale Hurston on the Broadway play *Fast and Furious: A Colored Review in 37 Scenes* (1931),[8] in which she both wrote and acted. Listed in *The Best Plays of 1931–32* and *1939–40,*[9] respectively, are the Broadway plays *Blackberries* (1932) and *Swingin' the Dream* (1939), in which Mabley also acted. In *Swingin' the Dream*—a parody of Shakespeare's *A Midsummer Night's Dream*—Mabley played the role of Quince in the opera *Pyramus and Thisby.* Satirizing the opera was to become a standard theme in Mabley's comedy act.

In 1933, she appeared in Paul Robeson's *The Emperor Jones.* From the 1930s until the 1960s, Mabley was a standby at the Apollo Theatre, where she was "a strong act to close the show."[10] In 1942, Mabley added film credits to her name with *Boarding House Blues* and *Killer Diller,* and the radio show *Swing Time at the Savoy: National Minstrel Audition* had her billed as the "Female Bert Williams." In the 1950s and 1960s, Mabley took her laughing, singing, and dancing act throughout the segregated circuits of the South, playing at such theaters as Washington's Howard, Baltimore's Royal, and Philadelphia's Uptown.

Through the popular medium of television, the vaudeville performer of nearly a half-century, whose career had spanned the eras of Jim Crow and Negro, was discovered in the 1960s by white audiences and reacclaimed by her ethnic community. Mabley appeared on the Smothers Brothers, Bill Cosby, Merv Griffin, Mike Douglas, Ed Sullivan, Gary Moore, and Flip Wilson shows and in the ABC special *A Time for Laughter* (1968), produced by Harry Belafonte. Carnegie Hall, the Kennedy Center, and the Copacabana invited her to perform, and college campuses—both white and black—sought her. Mabley's popularity reached an all-time high in the late 1960s, and from her many performances she produced more than twenty-five recordings. The first, on the Chess label, *Moms Mabley: The Funniest Woman in the World,* went Gold. Of her late-arrived success, Mabley commented, "Wouldn't you know it? By the time I finally arrived at the big money, I'm too old and sick to really enjoy it."[11] In a more philosophical mood, Mabley said, "I try not to be bitter; I would like to have gotten my chance earlier but that's the way things were in those days . . . better times are coming."[12]

The era of the 1960s did deliver Mabley better times. In 1961, Moms earned $1,000 for one engagement at the Apollo, and as Mabley became the headliner in 1962 and 1963, her salary climbed to $5,000 per week.[13] After Joe Glaser booked her on Merv Griffin's show, Mabley's rates often exceeded $5,000 a week—a rate far from the $350 weekly she had previously received.[14] With a ten-day stint with B. B. King at the Regal in Chicago in 1968, Mabley grossed $91,000.[15] Moms's explanation of how she made her money differed, yet may not be any less apocryphal of what really happened: "I made most of my money at the Club Harlem in Atlantic City. . . . I made it from a horse race room into one of the finest clubs in the East. I made money because I had a gimmick."[16]

Her gimmick, she explained, involved her audience throwing money at her. She had a young helper, Moms relates, "About the size of a midget; he picked up the coins and I picked up the bills."[17] When asked by the interviewer, specifically, "What kind of money did you make?" Moms replied in character: "I can't tell you that. . . . Or that devil Nixon'll make me pay him another $1,000 in taxes and then he'll take it out there and stash it in Fort Clemente."[18]

In 1974, even more financial success came to Moms when she made her first full-length motion picture, *Amazing Grace*. The movie—a longtime career goal—was barely completed before her illness and subsequent death on May 23, 1975. As Moms explained, "I wanted to do something to make my children and great-grandchildren proud of me, like all mothers do."[19]

Mabley's reference to her children and her great-grandchildren includes, of course, not only her biological family but her ethnic community and Moms's "other children"[20] as well. In adopting the title "Moms" for professional use, Mabley claimed her community and the world as her family and craftily orchestrated a comic performance stitched together from the cultural shreds of the Afro-American people. What shreds these were, and what a fabric these shreds were to become! Humor—laughter—competes for top bill-ing as the most quintessential of these cultural fabrics in understanding Afro-American culture. Lawrence Levine states, "No inquiry into the consciousness and inner resources of black Americans can ignore the content and structure of Afro-American humor."[21] Writing also of the significance of laughter and humor, Jessie Fauset, during the Harlem Renaissance, characterized laughter as "our greatest gift, our emotional salvation which arose from the very woes which beset us."[22]

W. E. B. DuBois, in his 1940 *Dusk of Dawn: An Essay toward an Autobiography of a Race Concept,* reiterated, describing laughter's greatness as a dancing, singing gift, loving men and women behaving deliciously human and challenging: "if you will hear men laugh go to Guinea, 'Black Bottom,' 'Niggertown,' Harlem; if you want to feel humor too exquisite and subtle for translation sit invisibly by a gang of Negro workers."[23] Langston Hughes, in *The Book of Negro Folklore,* extensively records historical memories in which slaves discovered a functional use of humor and started "grinnin' and skinnin'," pulling tricks to keep their masters laughing and appeased, to cut down on their work."[24] In fact, Afro-Americans used this gift so surreptitiously that they "put on ole Massa,"[25] and ole Massa's response (as folklore has it) was a laughing barrel,[26] a receptacle regulated by status quo laws which required Blacks when provoked to laughter to place their heads into a barrrel so as to control, silence, and segregate their "exquisite" gift. In Atlanta, Sterling Brown's Slim Greer (1932) held his sides in pain—in front of a telephone booth, waiting behind a hundred blacks in double lines, holding their sides and their jaws "to keep from breakin' De Georgia laws":

Hope to Gawd I may die
If I ain't speakin' truth
Make de niggers do deir laughin'
In a telefoam booth.[27]

From the chitlin' circuit, Mabley's laughing barrel burst open. Yielding to the pressure for laughter's liberation, the slats and constricting tin bands of the barrel collapsed, transforming into a comic arena where Mabley claimed center stage as her community's *griot,*[28] the storyteller. As the group's storyteller, in a dialectic through laughter, Mabley renders audible the frustrations, aspirations, and realities of her community's uniqueness and its relationship vis-à-vis the larger culture. Like the "hipsters," "blockmen," and "cool people" Mabley impersonates, she emerges as a "dynamic transmitter" of her culture and easily subsumes Abraham's categorization as the "[wo]man of words."[29] To quote Baker quoting Abrahams: "This ability of a person to use active and copious verbal performance to achieve recognition within his group is observable throughout Afro-American communities in the New World. It has given rise to an observable social type which I have elsewhere called the 'man of words.' His performances are typified by his willingness to entertain and instruct anywhere and anytime, to make his own occasions."[30]

Any conversation with Mabley offstage as well as with her audience onstage was likely to produce a unique image or phrase which articulated the unique position of black Americans in the larger society. From Mabley's perspective, her words were a "talent from God," and she was quick to add that "when I get up there, what comes up, comes out."[31] She once contested onstage with her drummer, declaring that her thoughts could "bust" his head wide open and that she had more sense accidentally than he had on purpose.[32]

Central to understanding Mabley's comic performance is perceiving the intricacy and complexity that operate behind the mask, the persona "Moms." In his 1953 "Change the Joke and Slip the Yoke," Ralph Ellison reminds us of our legacy in masking, describing "America [as] a land of masking jokers [where] we wear the mask for purposes of aggression as well as for defense . . . the motives hidden behind the mask [being] as numerous as the ambiguities the mask conceals."[33] Like the peel of an onion, Mabley's mask unfolds what seems to be a never-ending layer of motives.

By Mabley's account, the character "Moms," which she started to develop in her twenties, was motivated by her feelings of love and respect for her grandmother: "I had in mind a woman about 60 or 65 years. She's a good woman with an eye for shady dealings. . . . She was like my granny, the most beautiful woman I had ever known. She was the one who convinced me to go make something of myself. . . . She was so gentle, but she kept her children in line, best believe that.[34] On another occasion, to a Philadelphia audience, Moms related her granny's influence on her outlook:

> I never will forget my granny. You know who hipped me? My great grandmother. Her name was Harriet Smith. She lived in Brevard, North Carolina. This is the truth. She lived to be 118 years old. You wonder why Moms is hipped today. Granny! Granny hipped me. She said they lied to the rest of them but I am not going to let you be dumb. I tell you the truth. . . . One day she was sitting on the porch and I said, "Granny, how old does a woman get before she don't want no more boyfriends?" (She was around 106 then.) She said, "I don't know, Honey. You have to ask somebody older than me." She said, "A woman is a woman as long as she lives; there's a certain time in a man's life when he has to go to a place called over the hill."

Applying Granny's philosophy (and authority), Mabley then talks directly to the men: "And when you got to go, Son, go like a man. Ain't no use to say I ain't going. Yes, you are. You going. You don't have to be old 'cause her head's bald or 'cause you hair is gray. But when you mind starts to make them dates that your body can't fill—OVER THE HILL!"[35]

While appropriating her granny's philosophy to cross the threshold into the off-limits territory of the male sexual ego (where few female comics have dared to tread), Mabley adapts for performing purposes the folk poem "Over the Hill," which her audience undoubtedly recognized:

> It's not the gray hair that makes a man old,
> Nor that faraway stare in his eyes, I am told.
> But when his mind makes a contract that his body can't fill,
> He is—over the hill, over the hill.
>
> Now, life is a conflict, and the battle is keen.
> There are just so many shots in the old magazine.
> When he has fired the last shot, and he just can't refill,
> Then he is—over the hill, over the hill.
>
> He should salvage his energy while he can,
> Because Lydia Pinkham can't help a man.
> You can't get a new gland from the little pink pill,
> So you're over the hill, over the hill.
>
> He can fool the dear wife with the tenderest of lies,
> He can shear that poor lamb and pull the wool over her eyes.
> But when she calls for an encore, and he pretends that he's ill,
> Then he's—over the hill, over the hill.

Now his sporting days are over, and his tail light is out,
And what used to be his sex appeal now is just his water spout.
So that's the story, alas and alack,
When he's squeezed out the toothpaste, he just can't squeeze it back.

So if we want to make whoopie, don't wait until—
We get—over the hill, over the hill.[36]

Mabley's performance makes extensive use of folk themes, sayings, jokes that were commonly known by the Afro-American community, a body of lore that points to the perpetuation of a cultural tradition from the "woman of words" to the community and, equally, from the community to the "woman of words."[37] As a result, Mabley's comedy was often a laughter of recognition which established bonds of identity and friendship with her audience.[38] There was a participatory basis for humor as Mabley performed and mediated scenes from black life.

In an interview with Larry Wilde, the late Jack Benny said that the condition for the audience's laughter is directly tied to the comedian's ability to make his audience like him: "They [the audience] must have a feeling like 'Gee, I like this fella—I wish he was a very good friend of mine'—'I wish he was a relative.' "[39] Mabley's savoir-faire in performing matters rivals Benny's.[40] By dubbing herself "Moms," she connected with her audience intimately and played to the veneration and authority generally given the elderly in the Afro-American community, virtually guaranteeing her success as an entertainer.

In addition to bonding with her audience, assuming the maternal pose provided Mabley with a vehicle for boundary setting, for controlling the relationship between herself (the performer) and the audience. To stake out territory brought both protection and freedom, since early female vaudeville entertainers were often looked upon with suspicion and as loose women crossing the threshold of a man's world.[41] Ma Rainey (Gertrude Pridgett), Sweet Mama Stringbean (Ethel Waters), and the Last of the Red Hot Mamas (Sophie Tucker) had made functional use of the sobriquet. Phyllis Diller, too, created a similar sanctuary (and fort) through her housewife character with the funny stoles, glasses, wigs, and so on.[42]

In addition, the adoption of the position "Moms" gave Mabley a natural platform for expounding folk wisdom, leveling world leaders and bigots, and instructing a society on what to teach its young. Mabley used the "Moms" stance to teach through mother wit such irrefutable observations as "It ain't the depths of the river that drowns a man; it's the water,"[43] or, in warning children to watch the traffic lights when crossing the street, "Damn the lights; watch the cars; the lights ain't never hit nobody."[44] In *Moms Mabley at the "UN,"* she addressed Nikita Khrushchev as "Mr. Clean,"[45] after the all-purpose cleaner, appropriating and stripping the description of its complimentary function in the black community to ridicule a common enemy whom Mabley, too, described as she did the FBI ("fat, bald and impossible").[46] In *Moms Mabley: Live at Sing Sing,* Moms called the warden to the stage: "Come out here a minute; Son, come on out, Baby!"[47] To the uproarious laughter of the inmates, the warden heeded Moms's call with a penal propriety and obeisance straining to maintain control. The persona of Moms dictates the rules: the audience is her children; world leaders and heads of state are boys, Mamie Eisenhower is "Mame," and Moms to America's first lady is "Mrs. Mabley."[48]

Moms constantly talked about the book she was writing, a rewriting of the Mother Goose stories for her young people and her teenagers who had been told "a bunch of lies":

> You teach 'em Mother Hubbard went to the cupboard to get her poor dog a bone. I say Mother Hubbard had gin in that cupboard. You tell 'em Jack and Jill went up the hill after some water. I tell 'em water don't run uphill. You tell 'em Mary had a little lamb. I tell 'em wasn't the doctor surprised. Sure the cow jumped over the moon; that's the only truth in there. The cow did jump over the moon. . . . You would have jumped, too; that man's hand was cold! You tell 'em the wolf ate up Red Riding Hood's grandmother. I tell 'em if he did, then he must have used tenderizer. As tough as Grandmother was, that wolf had a hard time![49]

Mabley lamented angrily to another audience: "My brother is dead because of one of those fairy tales they kept telling him . . . 'Ding Dong Bell/Pussy's in the Well." . . . And he got drowned like a fool!"[50] The decision to call herself Moms would pay off even more in the 1960s when Mabley, like other ethnic comedians facing mass audiences, turned her humor loose on such topics as racism, integration, and Vietnam.[51]

On an even more profound and ambiguous level, the persona of Moms confronted the ambiguities often experienced by the Afro-American regarding the myth of the matriarchy and the stereotype of the mammy.[52] By choosing the guise of Granny—the grandmother—Mabley honors the matriarchate, described by E. Franklin Frazier's 1939 *The Negro Family in the United States* as "the guardian of the generation": "The grandmother's prestige and importance were as great among the slaves on the plantation as the whites in the master's house. She was the repository of the accumulated lore and superstition of the slaves, and was on hand at the birth of black children as well as white. She took under her care the orphaned and abandoned children."[53] Frazier further credits the grandmother's importance to the fact that she was the oldest head in the maternal family and that she functioned as midwife among a simple peasant folk.[54] In *Life among the Lowbrows,* as cited by Frazier, we have a description of the grandmother from real life:

> Great-grandmother hobbles in on crutches, her garments pinned across her chest with a safety pin, and her cap tied on with a black ribbon. But it takes more than crutches and discarded ribbons to abash a colored grandmother. In fact, they are the only grandmothers whom I have ever known to come into their own. They are still persons. They never quail before a stylish granddaughter by so much as a fraction of an inch. *If they look like scarecrows, it embarrasses neither the one nor the other. Let the girl be saucy, and one look from her grandmother's dark heavy-lidded eyes hits its mark. . . . Of all people these old women represent the eternal feminine.*[55]

Frazier's citation continues: "They have drunk of the fount of youth and have never lost its flavor. Nothing, one feels, but rheumatism keeps them from joining in the dance of life with their great-grandchildren."[56]

The resemblance of Mabley's artistically constructed granny to Frazier's historical portrait constitutes a tour de force. Introduced as the "Clown Princess of Comedy," Mabley would appear onstage without her teeth and wearing a floppy hat, an oversized floral-print dress that resembled a housecoat, knee-length wool socks, shoes two sizes too big, and she'd greet her audiences as "children," apologize for not coming earlier, and relate a few funny things that happened to her on her way to the forum. Getting in character and reading her audience's mind, Mabley once cautioned, "Don't let my looks deceive you; I've been where the wild goose went."[57] Hirshey's recent article in *Vanity Fair* describes Mabley as "one mean visual lebensbild!"[58] In caricaturing herself for performing purposes, Mabley satirized the legitimacy of class and social distinctions as defined by the proper look. Moms's entrance onstage was often accompanied by a desperate plea to the cameramen: "Make me look like Lena Horne—*not* Beulah! Lena!"[59]

Whereas the name "Beulah" suggests the Aunt Jemima mammy figure who was essentially the loyal servant and nurturer caring for the needs of whites and having no physical or emotional needs herself, the name "Moms" involves perspectival shifts. To begin, the *s* Mabley attached to the standard American Mom suggests a more eclectic character than the baker and server of apple pies. In addition, in the Afro-American community, the *s* added to a person's name commonly suggests a relationship of endearment. Mabley's fellow performers called her Moms, for example, because of her pizzazz in caring, sharing, and behaving maternally.[60] In performances and interviews, Mabley instructed "her children" to read her name upside down to get "Wows" and summed up her position as "I'm just Moms; that's all—M-O-M forward and M-O-M backwards."[61]

Mabley often began performances by facing up to her reputation and the gossip about her love life: "Moms been accused of liking young men and I'm guilty. Can't no old men do nothing for me (*laughter*), but bring me a message from a young man (*laughter*). Let me tell you girls something! George took me home last night and kissed me (*laughter*). My big toe shot up in the air just like that (*laughter*). He's a nice boy, though. Goes to bed every night at nine o'clock and gets up at four and goes home." George, Moms explains further, makes her so mad because when they were out west and he was going on vacation, George wanted to "do the paper doll" ("cut out") without her. Moms questioned him, "Baby, are you going to take me?" This exchange followed: "He said, 'Naw! Have gun will travel.' " And Moms said, "Yeah, have knack will shack 'til gun gets back."[62]

To borrow Michael Jackson's label, Moms is "B-A-A-D"—downright awesome, lascivious, bold, and she speaks openly of her need for sexual fulfillment.[63] Unlike Michael, Moms doesn't grab her crotch while performing, but when sitting down talking (performing), she does take special care to turn her chair a certain way, "to keep [the young men in the audience] honest."[64]

By Alice Walker's definition, Mabley's take-charge "outrageous, audacious, courageous [and] willful behavior" would earn her the title "womanist," a black feminist acting with strength.[65] Despite Mabley's successful career in comedy, however, Redd Foxx and Norma Miller suggest that so few black women made it in comedy because they "never got over the stereotype of playing servants and housekeepers [and as such] black women never get the Lucille Ball or Carol Burnett–type roles."[66] Mabley's comic response to Redd Foxx might have been, "Vote for me for President! If Elizabeth can run England, I can run America. What is she got that I don't have? And where can I get more of it?"[67] Toni Morrison suggests a less threatening and offensive stance regarding the traditional stereotypes of black women:

> When you really look at [it] . . . the worst you can say about them, that is, after you disregard the vocabulary and the dirty words and deal with the substance of what is being said, is quite complimentary. Think about it. What is being said is that black women are wonderful mothers and nurturers (mammies), that we are sexually at home in our bodies (oversexed), and that we are self-sufficient and tough (henpecking and overbearing). And isn't that exactly what *every* woman wants to be: loving and nurturing, sexually at home in her body, competent and strong?[68]

Whoopi Goldberg's performance in the film *Clara's Heart* renders rather sensitively Morrison's viewpoint. Much of Moms's humor is enjoyed by women because it provides sexual catharsis, celebrating the notion that women can be at home sexually in their bodies and that they can cast off male domination.

One of Moms's most popular routines is the ridicule of the old man her father made her marry:

> . . . This *old*—d-e-a-d, p-u-n-y, m-o-l-d-y man. I mean an OLD man. Santa Claus looked like his son (*laughter*). He was older than his mother (*laughter*). He was so old that his sister died, and we went to

> the funeral and after the funeral the minister walked over and tapped him on the back and said, "How old are you, Pops?" He said, "Ninety-one." He said, "Ain't no use of you going home (*laughter*)." . . . My daddy liked him so I had to marry that old man. My daddy should have married him; he the one liked him (*laughter*). The nearest thing to death you ever seen in your life. His shadow weighed more than he did. He got out of breath threading a needle. And UGLY! He was so ugly he hurt my feelings. . . . He was so ugly he had to tip up on a glass to get a drink of water. . . . I thought he never would die. . . . I shouldn't talk like that about him though. He's dead. They say you shouldn't say nothing about the dead unless you can say something good. He's dead, GOOD! (*laughter*). I know he's dead 'cause I had him cremated; I burnt him up—I was determined he was gonna get hot one time. . . .[69]

The insults Mabley levels at the old man reflect the ritual technique of "playing the dozens," traditionally a game played by black male adolescents and historically directed at the mother.[70] Moms, the mother figure, attacks the male, reversing the ritual insults and redirecting them toward the father figure and away from the mother. Employing a womanist perspective, Mabley renders topsy-turvy the folk aphorisms to suggest that "I would rather be a young man's fool than an old man's darling," and "What's good for the goose is good for the gander."

Yet Moms's comic mask characteristically contorted, springing the performer beyond dichotomies of black and white, rich and poor, age and youth, or male and female. Like her spiritual protégé Richard Pryor,[71] Mabley slipped on the truthsayer's mask (which she claimed she always wore) and poked fun at real-life conditions wherever she found them. Among women, men, whites, blacks, Chinese, Jews, husbands, wives, gays, drug addicts, winos, psychotics, diplomats, the KKK, the NAACP, the USSR, and the USA, none was exempt.

As Mabley notices, "Everybody's crazy. Do you know if you see anybody acting normal nowadays, they're probably just not well."[72] Admitting, then, to her audience that she has never seen so many people go "insinity"[73] in all her life, Mabley continues: "Man walked into the psychiatrist office. He said, '*Phoo, phoo, phoo, phoo, phoo.* Oh my goodness!' The psychiatrist said, 'What's the matter?' He said, '*Phoo, phoo, phoo,* butterflies *phoo, phoo* flying all over me, *phoo, phoo. . . .*' The psychiatrist said, 'What the h-e-l-l, *phoo, phoo;* don't blow 'em on me.' " The panorama of characters Mabley assembles on the White House lawn to discuss the spending crisis suggests further the breadth of Moms's comic perspective:

> I was standing on the White House lawn talking to Ike the other day (*laughter*), me and him, and Adam Clayton Powell, Governor Faubus (*laughter*) and Bo Diddley (*laughter*) and Big Maybelle.[74] (*laughter*) My goodness! Big Maybelle! We were standing out there talking about different things, about them spending so much money, you know. . . . Do you realize how much money they spend a week at Pokodembaka, Florida? One billion dollars, a week. Trying to get a bomb in the air; I know some bums 'round there you can get up there for a quarter. Give them a drink of Thunderbird and they're go anywhere![75]

Mabley pulled from an eclectic bag of tricks jokes which she acted out using a combination of double entendres, metaphors, insults, gaps, malaprops, misinterpretations, and parodies. Unlike the "new wave" stand-up comics[76] Mabley relied largely on double entendres in approaching risqué themes, since the Moms persona as well as Mabley's gender and time restricted her use of explicit four-letter words with the probable exceptions of *damn, hell,* and *fool.*

One of Mabley's most creative routines was parodying the opera. As a debunker of high culture, Mabley's name fits easily between Charlie Chaplin and the Marx Brothers, who, as Levine observes, "built parodies . . . into the very heart of their humor" and stood with their audience "against the pretensions and patrons of high culture."[77] Mabley would begin her opera routine by calling out in a prestigious accent to her piano player Luther, challenging him to play like "you play it for a big opera star—like Big Maybelle"[78] or "Little Stevie Wonder."[79] As Luther shifts to what he thought Moms wanted—ostentatious and intricate classical chords—Moms would stop him and "signify" on him. Mabley would then sing her aria—the content of which reflected such concerns as ghetto life, segregation, and racism—to a medly of popular tunes.

Quite popular with college students was Mabley's song inspired by James Meredith's battle to enter the University of Mississippi:

Now I ain't go'n sit in back of no bus.
And I'm goin' to the white folks' school.
I'm go'n praise the Lord in the white folks' church.
And I'm goin' to swim in the white folks' pool!
I'm go'n vote and vote for whoever I please.
And I'll thumb my nose at the Klan.

And I'll double-dare 'em to come out from behind them sheets
 and face me like a man.
They don't scare me with their bomb threats.
I'll say what I wanna say!
And ain't a damn thing they can do about it.
'Cause I ain't goin' down there no way!

And you know why?
Because it took a marshall, the army too,
JFK, and I don't know who!
Every law, and every rule
To try to get one boy in the Mississippi school.

School days, school days
Barnett said, "To hell with the congressional-rule days!"
Lead pipes, and black jacks and pistols, too!
Those are the books that they take to school!
They don't study science or history.
They study hate and bigotry.
They been scaring the heck out of you and me.
Since we was a couple of kids.

What kind of school is this? (What kind of fool am I?)
The school they call "ole miss"?
I know that sticks and stones may break my bones
But this is ridiculous.
How can we pretend
We love our foreign friends
When they can plainly see
What kind of fools they've been.

So, take me out to the ballgame (to the campus)
And if we don't win
It's a shame
But with our trust in the Lord
And the National Guard
We'll get in just the same.[80]

Much of Mabley's material she wrote herself,[81] and many of her most ingenious and memorable repartee originated in the spontaneous interaction with her audience. In an appearance at Sing Sing prison, for example, Moms declared, to the delight of inmates: "Children, I feel safer than I felt in a long time. 'Cause BABY, it's ROUGH OUT THERE! (*laughter*) A little boy ten years old walked up to Moms and said, 'Stick 'em up.' I said, 'You too little, Son, to be carrying on like that.' He said, 'Moms, I don't want that damn jive! Give me some money!' It's ROUGH out there!"[82]

As generally recognized, the style of the Afro-American performer goes beyond that of a mere storyteller; she or he acts out the tale. Mabley, of course, is no exception. Because of her impersonations, nuances, and gestures, a written analysis can hardly render justice to how she made her humor work aesthetically. Keil's analysis of soul ideology in *Urban Blues,* however, offers a "mechanic" which is particularly insightful in understanding why Mabley's style was so successful: "*It don't mean a thing if it ain't got that swing.*" As Keil describes the Afro-American style, "Timing is a variable that runs through walking, talking, singing, dancing, preaching, joking—the whole gamut of social behaviors. Without a well-developed sense of timing, of how to phrase or place notes vis-à-vis the pulse, a sure knowledge of when to pause, where to accent, how to hold and bend a note, a word, or a limb and so forth . . . there is no soul worth mentioning."[83]

Mabley's comedy routines and performances had that swing. Her jokes, her songs, and her dance coalesced into a ritual of communication that went to the roots of the Afro-American cultural experience. Her humor transmitted the group's mores, attitudes, and values. Keil's likening his blues lyric to "a naming-and-curing ceremony, a grand synecdoche (a receiving together),"[84] is more than applicable to Mabley's comic arena. The audience was her children, and she their "woman of words," their Moms, and their *griot*—stitching back together their cultural history. From her face they witnessed the face of history, and they feasted. They had "*real* food: collard greens, hog maws, cracklin' bread and buttermilk—the works!"[85] They laughed; they bonded;[86] they grew strong.

Notes

1. June Jordan, "Gettin Down to Get Over," in *Things That I Do in the Dark* (New York: Beacon Press, 1981), 37.
2. Billy Rowe, *Amsterdam News,* May 25, 1975.
3. Leslie Bennetts, "The Pain behind the Laughter of Moms Mabley," *New York Times,* Aug. 8, 1987, sec. 2. Clarice Taylor—who starred in the play *Moms*—through ethnographic interviews with Mabley's family learned that Mabley was raped at the age of eleven by an older black man and that she was raped again two years later by the white town sheriff. "Both rapes resulted in pregnancies; both babies were given away," Taylor's research reported.
4. Robert C. Toll, *On with the Show* (New York: New York University Press, 1977), 138. Dewey "Pigmeat" Markham suggested that TOBA stood for "Tough on Black Asses," alluding to the precarious working conditions black entertainers experienced on the segregated circuit.
5. Jack Schiffman, *Harlem Heyday* (New York: Prometheus Books, 1984), 21–22.
6. Henry T. Sampson, *Blacks in Blackface* (Metuchen, N.J.: Scarecrow Press, 1980), 496, 507.
7. Schiffman, *Harlem Heyday,* 216.
8. The revue ran for ten days at the New Yorker Theatre, opening September 15, 1931. Forbes Randolph is credited as the "presenter" of the revue with sketches by Randolph, John Wells, Hurston, Lottie Meany, Tim Moore, Dusty Fletcher, Mabley, Leighton Brill, and Sigmund Herzig. Music and lyrics were done by Mack Gordon and Harry Revel, with additional numbers by Rosamond Johnson, Porter Grainger, Joe Jordan, and Allie Wrubel. See Burns Mantle, ed., *The Best Plays of 1931–32* (New York: Dodd, Mead, 1932), 392.
9. Burns Mantle, ed., *The Best Plays of 1931–32* (New York: Dodd, Mead, 1932), 502; idem, *The Best Plays of 1939–1940* (New York: Dodd, Mead, 1940), 417–18.
10. Schiffman, *Harlem Heyday,* 121.
11. Ibid.
12. Mark Jacobson, *New York Times,* Oct. 14, 1974.

13. Schiffman, *Harlem Heyday,* 121.
14. *Sepia,* August 1968, 35.
15. "Behind the Laughter of Jackie (Moms) Mabley," *Ebony,* August 1968, 90.
16. *Atlanta Constitution,* July 30, 1974.
17. Ibid.
18. Ibid.
19. "Moms Mabley, 75, Comedienne of TV, Stage and Radio, Dead," *New York Times,* May 24, 1975.
20. Mabley had a most natural way of making whites in her audience feel comfortable. At the end of a Playboy Club performance, for example, Mabley added this comment: "Half of this record was made for my other children. 'Cause Moms is color blind. Thank God!" Of course, making such a disclaimer could not hurt record sales! Again, to a mixed audience at Sing Sing prison (recorded on *Moms Mabley: Live at Sing Sing,* SR61263 Mercury), Mabley announced that she was "going with Tom Jones." When the inmates laughed nervously, Mabley added aggressively, "I know he's white; I ain't got time to look for no damn color." The audience clapped approvingly, and Moms then responded with self-deprecation, "When you get as old as Moms is, you glad to get youth as you can," shifting the issue from the battle of the races to the desperation of old age.
21. Lawrence Levine, *Black Culture and Black Consciousness* (New York: Oxford University Press, 1977), 300.
22. Jessie Fauset, "The Gift of Laughter," in *The New Negro,* ed. Alain Locke (New York: Albert and Charles Boni, 1925), 161.
23. W. E. B. Du Bois, *Dusk of Dawn: An Essay toward an Autobiography of a Race Concept* (New York: Schocken Books, 1968), 148.
24. Langston Hughes and Arna Bontemps, eds., *The Book of Negro Folklore* (New York: Dodd, Mead, 1958); see especially "A Laugh That Meant Freedom," 67.
25. Gilbert Osofsky, ed., *Puttin' on Ole Massa* (New York: Harper and Row, 1969). Osofsky quotes Henry Bibb's *Narrative:* "The only weapon of self-defense I could use successfully was that of deception," 9.
26. Alan Dundes, ed., *Mother Wit from the Laughing Barrel* (En-

glewood Cliffs, N.J.: Prentice-Hall, 1973). See also Ralph Ellison, "An Extravagance of Laughter," in *Going to the Territory* (New York, Random House, 1986), 145–97.

27. Sterling Brown, "Slim in Atlanta," in *Southern Road* (Boston: Beacon Press, 1974), 88–89.

28. *Griot* was originally a translation of the Fulani *Gaoulo* (wandering poet or praiser) or Wolof *gewel* (poet and musician). See Ruth Finnegan, *Oral Literature in Africa* (Oxford: Clarendon Press, 1970), 96–97. The term, in general, describes the oral historian whose knowledge of the group's preliterate tradition allows him to tell the group's story. The *griot*'s position in a low-status, special caste, Finnegan explains, gives him the power to insult or verbally abuse without impunity other members of his society. Mabley as comedian had a similar kind of *griot* status and function. On the comedian's role and function, see further Lawrence Mintz, "Standup Comedy as Social and Cultural Mediation," *American Quarterly* 37 (Spring 1985), 71–80; Stephanie Koziski, "The Standup Comedian as Anthropologist," *Journal of Popular Culture* 18 (Fall 1984), 57–76.

29. Houston A. Baker, *Long Black Song: Essays in Black American Literature and Culture* (Charlottesville: University Press of Virginia, 1972), 112.

30. Ibid.

31. F. X. R. Giles, "Moms Mabley: 'Routines from God,' " *Washington Post,* Aug. 21, 1972, B4.

32. *Moms Mabley: Young Men Si, Old Men No!* [recording], LP1477 Chess.

33. Ralph Ellison, "Change the Joke and Slip the Yoke," in *Shadow and Act* (New York: Vintage Books, 1964), 55.

34. Linda Martin and Kerry Segrave, "Jackie 'Moms' Mabley," in *Women in Comedy* (Secaucus, N.J.: Citadel Press, 1986), 289.

35. *The Funny Sides of Moms Mabley* [recording], LP1482 Chess.

36. Daryl C. Dance, *Shuckin' and Jivin'* (Bloomington: Indiana University Press, 1978), 266–67.

37. Other jokes from Mabley's repertoire which Dance collected include "That's Why I Poisoned Ya, Honey" (148), "I'll Take Hymn" (273), "Peeled It, Cored It, Diced It" (217), "Fried Egg" (129), and "He Ate the Whole Thing" (301).

38. Levine, *Black Culture and Black Consciousness,* 363.
39. Larry Wilde, *The Great Comedians Talk about Comedy* (New York: Citadel Press, 1968), 41.
40. Mabley once commented that every comedian had stolen from her except Jack Benny, saying that Benny was "an original." See "Moms Mabley," *New York Times.* Jack Benny and Mabley share the same birth year, 1894.
41. Donald Bogle, *Bubbling Brown Sugar* (New York: Harmony Books, 1980), 21.
42. Wilde, *The Great Comedians,* 213.
43. *Moms Mabley at the "UN"* [recording], LP1452.
44. *The Best of Moms and Pigmeat* [recording], LP1487 Chess.
45. *Moms Mabley at the "UN."*
46. *Moms Mabley at the Geneva Conference* [recording], LB1463 Chess.
47. *Live at Sing Sing.*
48. *Moms Mabley: The Funniest Woman in the World* [recording], CHC91556 Chess.
49. *The Best of Moms and Pigmeat.*
50. Ibid.
51. See *Ebony,* April 21, 1966, for a list of "Comedy Row's Top Ten": Dick Gregory, Bill Cosby, Godfrey Cambridge, Redd Foxx, Slappy White, George Kirby, Timmy Rogers, Nipsey Russell, Richard Pryor, and Moms Mabley (the sole female).
52. See John H. Bracey, August Meier, and Elliot Rudwick, eds., *Black Matriarchy: Myth or Reality* (Belmont, Calif.: Wadsworth Publishing, 1971).
53. E. Franklin Frazier, *The Negro Family in the United States* (New York: Dryden Press, 1951), 115.
54. Ibid., 119.
55. My italics. Frazier's citation suggests Goethe's earlier statement that "the eternal feminine draws us onward." Zora Neale Hurston, in "How It Feels to Be Colored Me," describes herself as the "cosmic Zora" emerging beyond race and time into the "eternal feminine"; see *I Love Myself When I Am Laughing,* ed. Alice Walker (New York: Feminist Press, 1979), 152–55. For further discussion of the terms *feminine* and *femininity,* see Lisa Appignanes, *Femininity and the Creative Imagination* (New York: Barnes and Noble, 1973), 2–19.

56. Frazier, *The Negro Family,* 125.
57. *I Like 'Em Young* [recording], PBS2402 Partee-Stax.
58. Gerri Hirshey, "The Black Pack," *Vanity Fair,* July 1988, 120. *Lebensbilder,* Hirshey explains, translates as "the pictures of life" and was the term Apollo Theatre owner Frank Schiffman reserved for the "bawdy black comics."
59. *Moms Mabley Breaks It Up* [recording], LP1472 Chess. Writer Sidney Skolsky wrote in 1944 that Lena Horne is "unique . . . because she is the only colored actress who has sustained a career in Hollywood without being a comedy character or portraying servants." See Gail Lumet Buckley, *The Hornes: An American Family* (New York: Signet, 1988), 221.
60. Jacqueline Trescott, "Moms Keeping God in Front," *Washington Star-News,* Oct. 4, 1974, F-3.
61. " 'I'm Hip,' Says Moms Mabley," *Journal and Guide,* May 5, 1966; *I Like 'Em Young.*
62. *Moms Mabley Breaks It Up.*
63. Used especially in the emphatic form, *bad* means very good, powerful. See David Dalby, "The African Element in American English," in *Rappin' and Stylin' Out,* ed. Thomas Kochman (Urbana: University of Illinois Press, 1972), 177; Geneva Smitherman, *Talkin and Testifyin* (Boston: Houghton Mifflin, 1977), 59–60.
64. *Moms Mabley On Stage* [recording], CHC91556 Chess-MCA.
65. Alice Walker, *In Search of Our Mothers' Gardens* (New York: Harcourt Brace Jovanovich, 1983), xi.
66. Redd Foxx and Norma Miller, *The Redd Foxx Encyclopedia of Black Humor* (Pasadena: W. Ritchie, 1977), 220.
67. *Moms Mabley: Live at the Greek Theater* [recording], SR1360 Mercury.
68. Laura B. Randolph, "The Magic of Toni Morrison," *Ebony,* July 1988, 106.
69. *Moms Mabley On Stage.* Mabley's talent as an ad-libber is most evident in her handling of the old-man theme; from one performance to another—depending on Mabley's mood and audience—different images are added and expanded.
70. Smitherman, *Talkin and Testifyin,* 128–34; Levine, *Black Culture and Black Consciousness,* 344–58.
71. See Elsie Griffin Williams, "The Comedy of Richard Pryor as

Social Satire," *American Humor: An Interdisciplinary Newsletter* 4, no. 2 (Fall 1977), 15–19.

72. *The Funniest Woman in the World.*
73. Ibid. "Insinity" is one of Mabley's infamous malaprops.
74. Schiffman describes Big Maybelle, the blues singer, as being of "King-Kong size" and as having a "voice as large"—*Harlem Heyday,* 209, 247.
75. *The Funniest Woman in the World.*
76. See Lawrence E. Mintz, "The 'New Wave' of Standup Comedians," *American Humor: An Interdisciplinary Newsletter,* 4, no. 2 (Fall 1977), 1–3.
77. Lawrence W. Levine, *Highbrow and Lowbrow: The Emergence of Cultural Hierarchy in America* (Cambridge: Harvard University Press, 1988), 235.
78. *Young Men Si, Old Men No!*
79. *Moms Mabley Breaks It Up.*
89. *Young Men Si, Old Men No!*
81. Mabley's brother, Eddie Parton, assisted Mabley with the writing and production of some of her best materials.
82. *Live at Sing Sing.*
83. Charles Keil, *Urban Blues* (Chicago: University of Chicago Press, 1966), 173.
84. Ibid., 181.
85. *The Best of Moms Mabley* [recording], SR 63119 Mercury.
86. Through evoking common traditional foods in the black community, Mabley further reinforced the bonds of identity and solidarity for an oppressed people.

Whoopi Goldberg and Lily Tomlin: Black and White Women's Humor

Zita Z. Dresner

In the fall of 1984, one of the hottest tickets on Broadway was for a one-woman show by a little-known black comedian who called herself Whoopi Goldberg. A monologist who created character sketches of misfits and outcasts, Goldberg was compared in reviews to Richard Pryor and to Lily Tomlin, whose own one-woman show, *The Search for Signs of Intelligent Life in the Universe,* opened the following fall and immediately became the Broadway sensation of the season. The success of *Search for Signs* (which continued to play to sold-out audiences in its post-Broadway tour) did not come as a surprise to the large following of Tomlin fans and cultists that had developed over the years. After all, Tomlin's previous work on television (in "Laugh-In" and in her own Emmy-award-winning television specials), in films (like *The Late Show, Nashville,* and *Nine to Five*), and onstage (in concerts and in her 1977 one-woman Broadway show, *Appearing Nitely*) had all been highly acclaimed.

Goldberg, on the other hand, was pretty much an unknown quantity until Mike Nichols attended her New York debut in early 1984; he was so impressed by her talent in *The Spook Show* at Dance Theater Workshop that he helped prepare her show and produced it on Broadway less than a year later. From opening night to the present, Goldberg's success has been startling, the popularity of the show leading to television appearances, the starring role in the film version of *The Color Purple,* and title roles in subsequent movies (*Burglar, Jumping Jack Flash, Fatal Beauty,* and *Clara's Heart*) created especially for her. Since both these humorists have caught the public's interest and imagination so profoundly, looking at their work in relationship to theories and analyses of women's and ethnic's humor that have developed since the early 1970s can provide some insight into the nature of women's humor, the differences between white women's and black women's humor, and the ways in which the work of these humorists challenges or reinforces the culture's values and goals.

Ideas about what differentiates the nature of men's and women's humor have focused on both style and content. The greater overt expression of hostility and aggression in male than in female humor has been the major stylistic difference noted by humor analysts. Nihilistic humor, humor of cruelty, scatological and sexual jokes, and racial slurs have been considered male rather than female modes of comic expression. In contrast, the humor of women has traditionally been defined as more gentle, compassionate, and sentimental than the male variety. As for the content of women's humor, as anthologists of women's humor from Bruere and Beard in 1934 to Walker and myself in 1989[1] have stated, the topics of women's humor reflect their lives as women, their interests as women, their positions as women in male-dominated cultures, and, consequently, their world as women—a world always a little apart from that of men.

To a significant degree, the humor of Tomlin and Goldberg supports these generalizations about the style of women's humor. For example, in reviews of Goldberg's show, critics commented on the humane quality of her humor. "She never, not once, makes us laugh at anyone's expense—save perhaps our own," wrote Susan Dworkin in *Ms.;* and Audrey Edwards emphasized in *Essence* that Whoopi made her characters "believable and at times oddly heroic," weaving a "fine line" between "humor and pathos."[2] Similarly, New York theater critic Mel Gussow asserted that Goldberg's "aim is ameliorative. She wants theatre-goers to see the humanity in the characters she creates on stage."[3] Similar remarks have been made about Tomlin's characters throughout her career and were repeated in reviews of *Search for Signs*. Typical of these were Jennifer Allen's comment that Tomlin portrayed her characters "with great sentiment but not with condescension"; Jack Kroll's view that the show was permeated by "a tough innocence that embraces as it lampoons, that empathizes as it satirizes"; William A. Henry III's belief that each character was presented "with humor as well as sympathy"; and Frank Rich's recognition that "for all the anger that underlies the piece, it is more seductive than abrasive in the watching," because "Tomlin makes us care."[4]

To a large degree, the "humanity" of the humor ascribed to these two performers derives from the form and content of their work. For one thing, both women insist on defining themselves as actresses rather than comedians, because neither is interested in simply standing up and telling jokes or performing a comic routine as herself or in the persona of herself as jokester. In other words, neither sees herself in the traditional role of the male clown, simply knocking someone down, verbally and/or physically, with mockery and ridicule. Rather, each depends on monologues, on narrative, to create characters who have their own individual identities and personalities and who, to a smaller or greater degree, are outside the social mainstream or the majority culture—people who, because of race, gender, age, economic status, political beliefs, physical or mental handicaps—are disenfranchised from or disillusioned with the social establishment.

In Goldberg's show, for example, the cast of characters includes a black male junkie who is moved by a visit to the Anne Frank house in Amsterdam; a white middle-class "Valley Girl" who gives herself an abortion; a crippled young woman who finds love; a young black girl who longs for blond hair; and a female Jamaican souvenir vendor who inherits a fortune from an old man she takes care of. In *Search for Signs,* Tomlin portrayed a large cast of interacting characters, including a fifteen-year-old suicidal punk rocker, a disillusioned 1960s feminist, two prostitutes, a lesbian, a counterculture male, and a "bag lady," the "narrator" of the show. In earlier shows, Tomlin created characters who have become almost trademarks for her, as well as possible influences on Goldberg: Ernestine, a telephone operator who enjoys threatening people with the power of Ma Bell; Edith Ann, a precociously obnoxious five-year-old; Rick, a self-styled singles bar Romeo who fails to score; Crystal, a quadriplegic seeking to hang-glide over the Pacific; and Suzie, a quintessential sorority girl, supercilious and insecure.

While most of these characters may fit the categories into which reviewers have placed them—outcasts, misfits, and eccentrics—neither performer has used them simply to poke fun at their "otherness." Rather, what both performers seem to zero in on are the strengths and weaknesses that, despite the characters' differences or deformities, make them human. As developed by their creators, the characters evoke both our laughter *at* them for their follies and our laughter *with* them at the foibles and flaws within ourselves that they embody. As Tomlin stated in a 1977 interview, "It's so easy in comedy to ridicule the characters you do. Too easy. And low. What do my characters have in common? I think, a humanity. A human vulnerability. A dignity, even when they're in a ridiculous situation."[5] Since Goldberg's view of her characters is similar, Jack Kroll's description of *Search for Signs* as "a human comedy that strikes home so sharply it brings gasps of recognition as well as outbursts of laughter"[6] is applicable as well to Goldberg's show.

As these comments suggest, neither performer uses derogatory or self-deprecating humor to depict her mostly female characters, as women comedians have traditionally been accused of doing. In fact, although the focus on marginal characters may not mirror precisely the "different world" of the average American woman today, it does reflect Goldberg's and Tomlin's sympathy, as women, with those who, for whatever reasons, have been victims of society's prejudices against individuals, behaviors, and/or ideas considered out of the mainstream. Both women's shows, then, illustrate the views that Lorne Michaels, creator of "Saturday Night Live," expressed in 1977 about Tomlin's work. Calling her "the progenitor of 'comedian's lib' " for creating "a place where comedy is given more than one dimension, where jokes per se are abandoned," and where a "female aesthetic" in humor style can emerge, Michaels explains her style as follows: "Male comedy is punchy, broad, aggressive; it assaults you. Men shy away from the 'moment' and go for the joke. They get nervous if they don't get a laugh immediately. Except in the most mawkish and sentimental ways, they're not able to touch you. Lily, by refusing to be hostile, by making herself vulnerable, is breaking the mold."[7]

Echoing Michaels, Marilyn French, in an article on *Search for Signs,* describes Tomlin's work as "feminist art." According to French's definition (which would also fit Goldberg's show), feminist art serves as a counter to the "traditional masculinist perspective" of both popular culture and "high art" by assuming four major attitudes that challenge those taken for granted by the dominant culture: "that everything that exists is interconnected, that dominance is factitious, that body and emotion are as important as mind, and that these three are more important than domination."[8] In contrast, then, to comics who create a hostile or aggressive persona, both Tomlin and Goldberg want their characters to make the audience leave the theater feeling that, as crazy and cruel as life can be, each of us has some potential, some power, to make ourselves and the world a little saner and more benign.

While this feminist perspective connects Goldberg's and Tomlin's work to the tradition of female humor in America, their individual ethnic and economic backgrounds and experiences make the specific content and style of their work unique to each of them. Goldberg grew up in a Manhattan housing project, the daughter of a Head Start teacher who had to struggle to raise two children as a single parent. After dropping out of high school and into the East Village hippie community in the late 1960s, marrying briefly, and giving birth to a daughter, she moved to San Diego in 1975. There she entered the local theater scene and supported herself and her daughter through welfare and odd jobs, such as bank teller and morgue beautician. In the early 1980s, she teamed up with an actor to perform improvisational skits in comedy clubs around the Bay Area before developing the solo act she eventually took to New York as *The Spook Show.*[9]

As a black performer, more influenced perhaps by Moms Mabley (whose life she depicted in a play she cowrote) than Richard Pryor (whose similarities with her she has tended to downplay), Goldberg does reflect, through some of her characters, the experiences and concerns of blacks in America. In addition, some of the qualities that have been seen as intrinsic to ethnic humor are evident in Goldberg's work. These include using the patterns and idioms of ethnic speech for comic entertainment as well as covert rebellion against the white establishment; also, role reversal and ironic incongruity are utilized, to undermine, by exposing the absurdity, the logic of the values and institutions that promote a system that discriminates against minorities.

For example, the show opens with the character Fontaine, a streetwise dope dealer and thief, whose jive patter and physical mannerisms signal black male hip. The character evokes laughter with his rap, his use of obscenities, as well as his bravado—his differences from white, middle-class Americans. At the same time, in his attacks on the airline industry, he establishes a solidarity with the members of the audience who, whatever their color or nationality or gender, have been victims of the same bad food, lying stewardesses, and overbooked flights that he targets. This sense of solidarity enables the audience to accept the incongruity inherent in the idea that a black hustler, made cynical by his own experiences of racism, could visit the Anne Frank House in Amsterdam, could feel moved by the words written by the young Anne Frank on the walls of her family's hideout—"In spite of everything, I still believe that people are really good at heart"—and could assume the role, however briefly, of an instructor in compassion for the audience.

At the same time, Goldberg doesn't sentimentalize Fontaine by having him suddenly become a new man. Rather, recognizing that Anne's words reflect the innocence and naïveté of a child, he continues to find that the world in which he has to function disproves the validity of Anne's belief. For Goldberg never lets us forget that Fontaine is black and that the world that abuses him is not going to treat him any more decently because he can empathize with another's misery. (For example, at one point he tells the audience, "Yeah, I have a Ph.D., but I don't like to brag about it because I can't do Jack with it.") Nevertheless, his response to the Anne Frank House establishes unmistakable connections for the audience between the victims of oppression, whether Jewish or black, whether in Europe or America, and reveals the common humanity of those who can sympathize with the sufferings of others. In making the incongruous seem congruous, Goldberg confronts the audience (and, possibly, encourages them to question and alter) their own negative attitudes and behavior toward black ghetto males in particular, and blacks and other minorities in general.

Less potentially threatening to audiences than a black adult male criminal like Fontaine is Goldberg's characterization of a nine-year-old black girl who wears a a white shirt on her head both to hide her own hair and to simulate the "flowing blond tresses" that white society has made the hallmark of beauty for American females. While the audience can laugh at the child's efforts to be white and her reasons for wanting to be white (so she can appear on the television show "Love Boat"), it also is forced to look not just at the racism of a culture that equates whiteness with beauty and goodness but also at the self-hatred bred in those who are oppressed by such an equation. By having the child look around at the audience members and notice how many of them do *not* have long blond hair, blue eyes, and perfect bodies, Goldberg makes the audience identify with the child—not just as a black but as a victim of the models prescribed by the culture for all of us to emulate. As the child begins to realize that the majority of people do not meet the golden ideal but nevertheless appear to have friends and fun, she begins to discard her self-hatred. As her identification with the audience enables her to question the validity of the model, so does the audience identify with her. At the same time, as with Fontaine, Goldberg underscores the power of cultural images to maintain their emotional hold over us, even as we intellectually reject them, by having the child decide to keep the shirt she finally removes from her head. As she tells the audience, she's not going to throw away the shirt, "just in case you're wrong."

Goldberg's other characters—a white "Valley Girl," a young woman with crippling deformities, and an older, wiser Jamaican woman—are similar to Fontaine and the child in their basic powerlessness in society, their potential victimization by those in authority, and the double-edged nature of their characterizations. In addition, all three illustrate the importance for Goldberg of language and voice in creating her characters and her use of incongruity to make her points. For example, we laugh at the Valley Girl for her ditziness and linguistic vacuity almost until the end of the piece when she matter-of-factly dismisses as unimportant the horrifying consequences of her self-afflicted abortion. "Like I'm not freaked out about not having kids, you know," she says with obviously false bravado. "Like, you know, there's so much I really want to do, . . . like it's totally OK, you know, 'cause, like, I really love my life. . . ." In so doing, she reveals the incongruity between the claims and the actual behaviors of the middle-class family and the church, both of which are depicted in this sketch as having failed to minister to the needs of their own children.

In a similar way, we may laugh at the Jamaican woman (a kind of Moms Mabley clone) for her "funny" way of speaking and for her naïveté about the intentions of the old man who hires her as his housekeeper. However, we mostly laugh with her at those who seek to use or abuse her, because, despite her vulnerability as a woman, a foreigner, a black, and a domestic, she stands her ground against the old man's sexual advances, the lawyer's implications that she is a liar and a thief, and the old man's family's contempt. In the end, she triumphs over them all when she is named the old man's beneficiary, a kind of poetic justice, and we both exult with her and feel badly with her that we don't appreciate the good points of people even like "the old raisin," as she refers to the old man, when they are alive.

Finally, Goldberg's portrayal of a crippled woman is compassionate without being maudlin and funny without being cruel. We can laugh with the woman when she pokes fun at herself and her handicaps and about the incongruities that she experiences as an "abnormal" person in the "normal" world—for example, when she tells us she lives in a nursing home as a kind of antidote for the old people who don't feel so bad about their lives when they look at her. However, as she begins to see herself, through the eyes of a man who loves her, as not so different from anyone else, the audience begins to see her similarly. Again, Goldberg does not minimize the realities of the woman's disabilities—they do not disappear as they do in her dreams—but Goldberg's portrayal suggests that the quality of the woman's life depends less on the restrictions imposed by her disabilities than on the extent to which she can accept herself, and society can accept her, as having the same human needs and aspirations as the rest of us for love, for respect, for understanding, and for happiness.

While Goldberg does use ethnicity, or race, to create vivid and specific characters, her black characters are presented not simply as blacks but as representations, along with her other characters, of all individuals in American culture who lack power and prestige, who are viewed as aberrant or abnormal, and who are denied compassion and respect because of their otherness. By emphasizing the sameness in our otherness, Goldberg strikes a blow against racism and other forms of oppression that diminish the oppressor as well as the oppressed. Consequently, what Jill Robinson wrote of Tomlin's work is also applicable to Goldberg: "Lily's messages come from Inner Space and catch us on that perfect edge where laughter topples into self-recognition, pulling us back just before we might plunge into despair."[10]

Although Tomlin does not address racism per se in her work and does not try to impersonate black characters, she does focus on depicting cultural types who, despite their quirks or oddities, have a basic integrity that compels our sympathy through our laughter. Robinson believes that Tomlin's humor comes from her own background as a "street kid survivor" in the blue-collar area of Detroit where her parents, Kentucky farm people, transplanted themselves. Her father, a machinist, was a man's man who spent most of his nonworking time in bars and at the track and who died of alcoholism at the age of fifty-seven; her mother was a traditional working-class housewife. Tomlin studied acting and mime at Wayne State University in Detroit before going to New York, where she performed in the new comedy clubs of the late 1960s and wrote for Joan Rivers before being hired as a regular on television's "Laugh-In."[11]

A strong feminist by admission and a lesbian by rumor, Tomlin, with her longtime companion and collaborator, Jane Wagner (author of *Search for Signs*), created in the play a story about American society and its discontents in which Tomlin, on a bare stage and with only a few props, played a wide variety of representative characters of the past two decades whose lives and paths intersect. Although few of Tomlin's staple characters from her earlier shows and concerts (e.g., Ernestine, Edith Ann, and Bobbi Jeanine) appeared in the new show, Tomlin's motivations and methods were consistent with her previous work.

Like ethnic humor, Tomlin's humor (and much of women's humor) depends on role reversal, the exposure of incongruity (from the perspective of the other), and verbal devices (especially the playing with cultural clichés) to reveal the absurdities and injustices of life, as well as the attributes that enable us to survive them. The main narrator, the "framing device" of the play, is Trudy, a "certified crazy" Manhattan bag lady, who opens the show by explaining to us that she is serving as host and guide to a group of extraterrestrials who have come to investigate life on earth. A dropout from the rational world, Trudy, as Marilyn French points out, sets the point of view of the show "from the lowest stratum in American society," functioning as a kind of wise-fool figure who illustrates the old adage about the greater sanity of the mad.

There is much that is comical about Trudy to evoke our laughter, but she is never dismissed as a freak—partly because she is aware of her peculiarities and revels in the freedom from conventions that they enable her to enjoy; partly because the audience can laugh with her at the absurdities she exposes in society's embrace of things as diverse as gene splicing and pop art; and partly because we recognize the sanity of many of her statements. "You people look at my shopping bags, call me crazy 'cause I save this junk," she tells the audience. "What should we call the ones who *buy* it?" Or, speaking of her last job in the "straight" world, as a creative consultant for Nabisco, and of her proposal "to sell the concept of munching to the Third World . . . to millions and millions of people [who] don't even know where their next *meal* is *coming* from," she explains, "I heard myself sayin' *this!* Must've been when I went off the deep end."[12] Through the reversal of having the "madwoman" lead the "rational" audience to a "saner" worldview, Tomlin succeeds in making the audience acknowledge, by the time Trudy closes the play, that the apparent incongruity of Trudy's guiding the aliens' search for signs of intelligent life is not incongruous but infinitely logical.

Trudy's voice and face reappear throughout the play, dissolving into and interacting with other characters: Chrissy, a young woman who can't seem to find any direction in her life and who spends hours in self-improvement programs (like her "yuppie" male counterparts) trying to create an image of herself; Kate, a wealthy woman suffering from "affluenza" (ennui and apathy); and an assortment of other American types, the most developed of whom are Agnes Angst, a fifteen-year-old punk rocker suffering from anomie, and Lynn, an early convert to feminism, whose story (and that of her counterculture husband and feminist friends) comprises most of Act II.

Through Agnes, Tomlin and Wagner are able to target not only the adolescent angst and unfocused rage of the punk rock generation but also the world that has produced Agnes—a world Agnes describes as "a tampered-with-Tylenol, pins-in-girl-scout-cookies, grond zero kind of place," in which air pollution makes breathing "a bio-hazard," friends die from drugs and suicide and anorexia, and the only "deep" conversations that take place between parents and children are between their T-shirts. To survive in such a world, Agnes believes that she has to train herself not to mind rejection and pain, just as Gordon Liddy trained himself to hold his hand over a flame without flinching. The price the audience pays for laughing initially at Agnes's narcissistic and antisocial attitudes and behavior is being forced to face its own complicity in creating a world that seems to offer little of value or substance to the younger generation—that appears bereft of hope, of vitality, of altruism, of integrity, of human caring. And so, in a way, the last laugh is on us.

It also seems to be on Lynn, a California cultist whose life and that of her feminist friends is reviewed from the birth of *Ms.* magazine to the nomination of Geraldine Ferraro as vice-presidential candidate. Using Lynn's story to poke fun at the men and women, artists, and activists of the 1960s and 1970s, Tomlin and Wagner make great sport of the fads and fashions of the counterculture movements, the contradictions of the upwardly mobile liberal establishment, and the dilemmas produced by feminism. While the audience may identify with Lynn and her husband, Bob, who live in a geodesic dome and eat only natural foods, they are also made comic in their tireless attempts to combine and live out all the clichés of New Age consciousness and feminism. While Lynn strives to be all things to all people—Earth Mother to her kids, emotionally supportive and sensual wife, career professional, political activist, spiritually growing person, and caring friend—Bob tries to be a humanistic entrepreneur and nonsexist husband and father, getting so far "in touch with his feminine nature," Lynn believes, as to fake an orgasm.

Through Lynn, Tomlin and Wagner also have an opportunity to follow the lives of Lynn's closest friends from her consciousness-raising group and to use them both to poke fun at the clichés of lesbian feminist politics and to show us the ironic contradictions between the women's hopes and the circumstances of their lives, between who they are and the labels society hangs on them. Because Wagner and Tomlin use these characters, especially Lynn, to mirror society's failure to realize their dreams, as well as to make us laugh at the excesses of the movements and cults of the '60s and '70s, Lynn does emerge, as her story progresses, as a person who evokes our respect because she is not crushed by the fact that her obsessive efforts to always be and do what is "correct" do not bring her the happiness or personal fulfillment she expected.

Despite the irony of her ending up as any nonfeminist, non-liberal, non-growth-oriented American woman might end up—being left by her husband for a younger woman, losing her home, being passed over for promotion, having friends die or move away—she does not indulge in laying blame and self-pity. She is a survivor, not because of the "human potential movement" but because of her personal courage to continue, in the face of dashed dreams, to care about the world and the quality of life. Thus, she saves from the sale of her possessions the autographed copy of *Ms.* that initially changed her consciousness and the T-shirt saying "Whales Save Us" that her ex-husband was wearing the first time she met him. Both of these items symbolize for her what Agnes lacks: faith in the possibility of human connection and of positive change.

In both shows, the performers seem to have offered to their audiences an antidote to the values and goals associated with the Reagan presidency and its patriarchal, conservative tone. For audiences of their own generation—those in their twenties and thirties during the heady years of the 1960s—as well as for the yuppies disillusioned or dissatisfied with the promises of consumerism and for the younger generation seeking meaning and direction in their lives, both Tomlin and Goldberg affirm the validity of the basic human ideals that fueled the movements of the 1960s and early 1970s for social justice, equal rights, world peace, and a healthy environment.

At the same time, both performers implicitly criticize the self-indulgence and self-absorption that replaced the commitment to political activism with a commitment to personal "growth," leading to the apathy and cynicism about social change that, in the 1980s, allowed racism, sexism, militarism, and material greed to be sold to the public under the guise of a conservative platform called "Making America Great Again." As female humorists, both emphasize qualities that Carol Gilligan, in *A Different Voice* (1982), cited as distinguishing male and female moral development: women's preference for cooperation rather than competition, for communal rather than hierarchical systems. By implying that the "majority" is really a "minority," because most of us are actually "outsiders" in different ways, both shows not only emphasize the common humanity of the distinct individuals who make up the world but also empower the audience by suggesting that, in tapping into what connects rather than divides us, as the song "We Are the World" proclaims, we can both save our own lives and create a better world for everyone.

Notes

1. See Martha Bensley Bruere and Mary Ritter Beard, eds., *Laughing Their Way: Women's Humor in America* (New York: Macmillan, 1934); Deanna Stillman and Anne Beatts, eds., *Titters: The First Collection of Humor by Women* (New York: Collier, 1976); Gloria Kaufman and Mary Kay Blakely, eds., *Pulling Our Own Strings: Feminist Humor and Satire* (Bloomington: Indiana University Press, 1980); and Nancy Walker and Zita Dresner, eds., *Redressing the Balance: American Women's Literary Humor from Colonial Times to the 1980s* (Jackson: University Press of Mississippi, 1988).
2. Susan Dworkin, "Whoopi Goldberg—In Performance," *Ms.,* May 1984, 20; Audrey Edwards, "So, Whoopi, Can We Talk?" *Essence,* March 1985, 84–85.
3. Mel Gussow, "Whoopi as Actress, Clown and Social Critic," *New York Times,* October 28, 1984, H5.
4. Jennifer Allen, "Lily Tomlin," *Life,* November 1985, 17–22; Jack Kroll, "Divinely Human Comedy," *Newsweek,* September 23, 1985, 66; William A. Henry III; "Let a Hundred Lilys Bloom," *Time,* October 7, 1985, 68; Frank Rich, "The Stage: Lily Tomlin in 'Search for Signs,' " *New York Times,* September 27, 1985, C20.
5. Tim Burke, "Lily Tomlin Brings Her Gallery of Zanies to Broadway," *New York Times,* March 20, 1977, B1.
6. Kroll, "Divinely Human Comedy," 66.
7. Ellen Kohn, "Lily Tomlin: Not Just a Funny Girl," *New York Times Magazine,* June 6, 1976, 90.

8. Marilyn French, "Lily Tomlin," *Ms,* Janaury 1986, 32–34.
9. Biographical material from Pamela Noel, "Who Is Whoopi Goldberg and What Is She Doing on Broadway," *Ebony,* March 1985, 27; and "Whoopi Goldberg," *People,* December 23–30, 1985, 99–105.
10. Jill Robinson, "A Bunch of Lily Tomlin," *Vogue,* June 1977, 149, 186–87.
11. Biographical material from Jill Robinson, Tim Burke, Ellen Kohn; and from Letitia Kent, "Lily Tomlin," *Vogue,* June 1971, 102–3; Amy Gross, "Lily Tomlin on Lily Tomlin," *Mademoiselle,* November 1975, 141; and Jack Kroll, "Funny Lady," *Newsweek,* March 28, 1977, 63–66 (cover story).
12. All quotes are from Jane Wagner, *The Search for Signs of Intelligent Life in the Universe* (New York: Harper and Row, 1986).

There's a Joker in the Menstrual Hut: A Performance Analysis of Comedian Kate Clinton

Linda Pershing

The world is always humor-poor. There is never enough of it. Yet, without humor we cannot survive. Our world is too relentlessly cruel, too callous, too uncivilized, and feminists who contemplate it will die of depression or lapse into cynicism and inaction without our humor. By joking, we rehumanize, recivilize ourselves. By joking, we remake ourselves so that after each disappointment we become once again capable of living and loving.[1]

February 20, 1985. It is after 8:00 P.M., the time Kate Clinton's performance is scheduled to begin, when the doors are opened to the Ritz Theater in downtown Austin, Texas. Streams of women rush in to find seats. Within minutes the theater is full downstairs, and there are people sitting in the balcony, making a total crowd of between two and three hundred. The audience is comprised almost entirely of women, with the exception of about a half-dozen men scattered throughout the crowd. A range of signifying haircuts, jewelry, and clothing suggests that the audience is largely lesbian. Although there are a few women of color, most of the audience is white. Many women have come together in groups; many know one another and greet friends with hugs and affection. The theater is buzzing with the voices of women who sound happy, excited, and expectant. There is an atmosphere of celebration. As we wait for the show to begin, I am aware of the exhilarating sensation of being in a large public gathering of women. Only upon later reflection do I come to realize that the menstrual hut Clinton jokes about during her performance is a metaphor for this theater full of women:

> Now, we have this new album out. . . . But the new album—we had some problems with the titles, okay?—some "artistic differences" about the title, also known as big fights. . . . See, I tried to call the album "There's a Joker in the Menstrual Hut." And can you see the video? Alright, the menstrual hut is where tribesmen sent their menstruating women because they were "unclean," for God's sakes, and they'd go in these little huts, and there'd be a lot of women in there, and they'd talk, you know, sing a few songs, tell a little gossip, give a low back message now and again. I say: BRING BACK THE HUT! I think the Astrodome would be just fine! Now, can't you just see some guy outside going, "Honey, you've been in there for twenty-three days! We're practically out of casseroles. When are you coming out?" And she'd say: "Hey, I can't come out now. There's a joker in the menstrual hut!" (1985).[2]

Kate Clinton is a contemporary stand-up comic, originally from upstate New York, who is attracting widespread attention for her distinctive brand of humor. She describes herself as a "feminist humorist" or "fumerist"; celebration of women's experiences and using comedy to encourage feminist awareness are characteristic of her approach. This article is an exploration and analysis of Kate Clinton's February 20, 1985, and April 4, 1987, Austin appearances using concepts that have been central to performance theory as it has developed in folklore studies, most clearly articulated by Richard Bauman.[3] My analysis is also informed by the somewhat limited but growing body of research that is available concerning women's humor.

Performance theory, as it emerged in the 1970s study of American folklore, is built on an organizing principle that includes within a single conceptual framework the artistic act, expressive form, and aesthetic response, all within its own locally defined, culture-specific context.[4] This approach is predicated on the belief that it is essential to understand not only the content but also the context of the humorous event or joke and its relation to particular patterns of social reality in which it occurs.[5] The concept of performance has enabled folklorists and other scholars to shift their focus from concentration on texts or products to verbal art as action or process. I use the term *performance* in its dual sense to mean not just the event but also the act of communication: "the term 'performance' has been used to convey a dual sense of artistic *action*—the doing of folklore—and artistic *event*—the performance situation, involving performer, art form, audience, and setting—both of which are basic to the developing performance approach."[6]

I treat the verbal art form that Clinton uses—stand-up comedy—as a genre in its own right. Although this is a commercial and formalized performance form that would not conventionally be studied by folklorists, I have found that performance theory offers valuable insights into the study of verbal artists on and off stage.[7] My discussion will include analysis of the context, performer-audience relationship, subject matter, and functions of Clinton's comedy. I suggest that analysis of Clinton's humor within a performance theory orientation reveals that her work is shaped by her self-definition in the public and private spheres as a lesbian feminist, and that this distinguishes the style, content, and rendering of her humor. Constraints of time and space make it impossible for me to compare Clinton's performances with those of particular male stand-up comedians, although that would make an interesting and useful study.[8] However, I will discuss the ways in which she operates within what has traditionally been a male-dominated genre.

Finally, I make no attempt here to conceal my own bias. I think Kate Clinton is enormously funny. There were times during her performances that I was gasping for air from laughing so much. This was only compounded by friends who were sitting next to me holding their sides and hooting with laughter (one moaned, "I've got a headache from laughing so hard!"). I am hungry for the comic relief Clinton offers. As a feminist who often goes through the day feeling like a stranger on an alien planet, I was moved by Clinton's worldview and enamored of her ability to use wit as a tool for survival. In attempting to write a summary about feminist humor for the book *Pulling Our Own Strings: Feminist Humor and Satire,* Mary Kay Blakely eloquently describes the difficulty I share in removing myself from my subject:

> I couldn't write because I kept hearing the voices, the fascinating intonations, the fluctuating moods, and yes, yes, yes, I listened to the tremors of revolution that our humor inspires. I lost interest in diagramming the sentences, explicating the themes. . . . I wanted to listen. I heard the faint voice of self-consciousness in our humor, the nervous laugh of the messenger who doesn't want her head cut off for reporting damaging news: The natives are restless. We use our humor to deliver our complaints about the status quo. We tend to be a bit edgy at times because we know from experience just how many potential toes we are stepping on.[9]

The Setting

Popular notions about Austin as a politically progressive city with a visible feminist community, a sizable lesbian and gay community, and a strong intellectual faction (Austin is a university town) play an important role in providing a framework for Clinton's performance.[10] The overtly sexual and political content of much of her humor is specifically designed for an audience who will be receptive and, moreover, will share her viewpoint. Clinton suggests this in a 1985 parody of the television show "Bloops, Blunders and Practical Jokes": "[In an overly enunciated emcee-type voice.] Hello, welcome to 'Heterosexual Bloops, Blunders and Practical Jokes.' My name is Dyke Clark. Tonight we're going to play a practical joke on comedian Kate Clinton. Now, Clinton thinks tonight that she's going to go out and face an audience of radical lesbian separatists. In fact, the entire audience is filled with born-again, fundamentalist women from Little Rock, Arkansas. And they've been told that Clinton will be preaching in tongues!" (1985).

As with most touring performers, Clinton's actual contact with her audience is limited. Her shows are usually one- or two-night engagements. She mentions often that she is on tour, and during the introduction to her act the announcer tells the audience that Clinton "travels extensively throughout the country," thus conveying her mobility and lack of geographical affiliation with any one audience. One-time interaction with her audience is significant in light of Clinton's attempts to do more than simply entertain. Her closing exhortation to act upon the newly shaerd experience of her performance is bounded by the fact that she will be elsewhere, doing another show for a different group of people. Even though she mentioned that she would like to return to Austin—and I believe she makes this comment as a way of expressing her desire for continuity with the audience—they know that this is an indefinite commitment. Clinton performs in Austin once every two years. The audience is left to return to their everyday lives without her, and to make their own decisions about how the experience of that evening will (or will not) be integrated into their daily existence.

Clinton's Performance as "Situated Behavior"

Comedy is a business that has traditionally been the domain of males, and their influence still dominates—in numbers, in attitude, and in determining the way things are done and who does them.[11]

And a lot of it has to do with being a woman. Why are they upset with what I'm doing when Richard Pryor is being deified and Eddie Murphy is being deified?[12]

Clinton is a verbal artist who practices her craft within clearly bounded parameters. She performs during a scheduled event that occurs in a restricted setting (a theater or club) and is open to the public (although I will argue that only a specific segment of the general public is meant to participate). Citing the work of Milton Singer, Bauman describes such performances as "cultural performances," those "involving the most highly formalized performance forms and accomplished performers in the community."[13] Clinton exhibits considerable skill as a verbal artist within this context, using the traditional performance to her advantage. Her routine includes memorized material and improvisation; both contribute to her success as a stand-up comedian. It is evident from her delivery that her routine and stage presence are the result of years of practice and the careful honing of her material. However, I contend that the particular significance of her performance lies not in the way she has mastered her craft in the traditional sense (although that in itself is formidable) but in how she manipulates it in original ways to go beyond the boundaries of "cultural performance" to a performance that calls those boundaries into question.

The idea of a feminist humorist is an intriguing one. Although historically there have been and continue to be notable exceptions (Gracie Allen, Phyllis Diller, Joan Rivers, and Whoopi Goldberg come to mind), the field of highly paid, mass media stand-up comedy has been dominated largely by men (Johnny Carson, Richard Pryor, George Carlin, Bill Cosby, Steve Martin, David Brenner, Don Rickles, Bob Newhart, Eddie Murphy—the list goes on). Much of the significance of Clinton's humor is dependent on its context and on the way she negotiates her performance against cultural and social expectations. Like all humor, it is useful to consider her performance as "situated behavior, situated within and rendered meaningful with reference to relevant contexts."[14]

In examining Clinton's work as "situated behavior," four aspects of her humor are striking: (1) she is a woman operating within a predominantly male domain; (2) she is a self-defined and outspoken feminist; (3) she is a lesbian; and (4) she uses the first three personal characteristics in a public way as the basis of her humor.

First, as a woman performing in a male domain, Clinton faces comparison by her audience, the media, and herself against societal expectations about male stand-up comedians. It is somewhat unusual for women to go into this line of work, although their numbers are increasing.[15] Some people have even suggested that humor itself is alien to "woman's nature." In a 1966 analysis of the interrelationship of gender and humor, for example, David Zippin wrote: "Comediennes[16] are numerically rare compared with male comics. This suggests that humor is somehow alien to femininity. When the woman is a comedienne, she takes on the male role."[17] Rose Laub Coser's data support this notion about women's lack of participation in joking behavior. Among women and men in the workplace,

Coser attributed the lack of humor she observed among women to their passive social enculturation: "In this culture women are expected to be passive and receptive, rather than active and initiating. A woman who has a good sense of humor is one who laughs (but not too loudly!) when a man makes a witticism or tells a good joke. A man who has a good sense of humor is one who is witty in his remarks and tells good jokes. The man provides; the woman receives. Thus at the meetings, men made by far the more frequent witticisms—99 out of 103—but women often laughed harder."[18] The fact that so many authors support the contention that there is no long-standing tradition of American women's humor is testimony not to the veracity of this belief but rather to the way in which women's humor, like so many other expressive forms used by women, has been overlooked or ignored in our cultural history. Even some feminist writers seem to feel that there is no history of American women's humor, or that they are discovering women's humor for the first time. Other scholars acknowledge the existence of women's humor, while simultaneously suggesting that it has been confined primarily to the private domain: "Although women are no less capable of developing and appreciating humor than men, women have been denied similar opportunities for publicly engaging in humor. Because modesty, passivity, and virtue are associated with ideal womanhood, women have been confined to the private domain, with many contraints imposed upon them. Only marriage, old age, and the greater freedom of behavior granted to women in groups to some extent alleviate this inequality of the sexes."[19] However, contemporary feminist scholars, such as Alice Sheppard and Nancy A. Walker have begun to identify the long-standing historical tradition of American women's humor. Sheppard, for example, argues that there *is* a tradition of women's humor, which she has partially reconstructed by digging through archival materials, and that scholars ought to be asking not "why didn't women develop a humor tradition?" but "why has the humor which was created and appreciated by women been ignored?"[20]

The popular conception that women are not funny presents particular obstacles to comedians like Clinton. Not unlike women in other traditionally male-dominated occupations (e.g., business executives, clergy, academicians), she has had to learn how to function successfully in a "man's world." Clinton has done this by learning the traditional tools of her trade well enough so that the public, who may be more accustomed to watching male performers, will recognize and affirm her as a legitimate stand-up comic. This negotiation against a male model is both implicit and explicit. Implicitly, Clinton uses elements of style that seem to be a compromise between stereotypical patterns of expression among women and men.[21] For example, her voice pitch is in middle range, neither extremely high (conventionally associated with the female) nor extremely low (conventionally associated with the male). Onstage her body language is fluid yet controlled, expressive (she uses occasional gestures and mimicry) without being too "flowery." Although she uses her hands to gesture while she talks, she does not flail them about. When she gestures, her fingers usually remain closed, thus creating an impression of strength and control of her immediate environment.

Explicitly, some of Clinton's material deals with the ways in which the experiences of women and men substantially differ in white, middle-class American culture and, moreover, how men often look foolish in the eyes of women. In so doing, she legitimizes her female identity and uses the contrast to strengthen her performance before an audience that is almost entirely composed of women: "How many of you think that if you were a guy . . . and you were going bald, that you probably *would* part your hair right here [gestures to the far right side of her head just above the ear]—and drag pieces of hair over your head? I know I would. Have you ever seen those guys come out of swimming? [She mimics long strands of hair hanging down the right side of her face down to her shoulder] Wow, lookin' good!" (1985). Similarly, in her 1987 performance, Clinton commented on the stifling conservatism and conformity that is endemic to the male-dominated business world, thereby ridiculing male standards of status: "Doesn't it feel like you live on the Planet of the Guys? I travel a lot, and when I'm in airports, I look around, and it's all guys. And they're all wearing those three-piece suits. What imaginative dressers! Whenever I'm at an airport, I always feel like going up to a guy and saying, 'Ooh, I love your outfit! Especially what you're doing with the pinstripes. It's just so—up and down!' " (1987).

Secondly, Clinton publicly describes herself as a feminist and is unusual in this way, even among women comedians. Her explicit identification with feminism is noteworthy since traditionally so much of both men's and women's humor has used women as its target. Although other, less-known women comics seem to be focusing less on humor that deprecates women, they often describe their approach not as feminist but as "enlightened, but still looking for a man" or as "gender-neutral."[22] In contrast, Clinton's jokes are decidedly profemale, often revolving around the shared experiences of women, which she articulates, laughs about, and enjoins her audience to celebrate with their laughter:

> The thing that bugs me about the condom ads is, did you notice that when the problem with sex was just pregnancy, one million teenagers a year—mostly girls—when the problems with sex were just pregnancy or just some gay men with AIDS, there were no condom ads. But I'm telling you, when a couple of straight white guys get AIDS, then we've got ourselves some condom ads on TV. The other thing is, they're targeting women. Once again, we're in charge. What's the deal here? . . . See, I think that if we're supposed to carry condoms around for guys, that we should be able to go up to a guy in the street and say, "Oh, I just got my period. I'm kind of out of luck. May I borrow a tampon?" (1987)

Thirdly, Clinton introduces her act by making a reference to lesbianism: "Thank you all for *coming out.*" Much of her humor, particularly her bawdy and sexual jokes, involves her experiences as a lesbian. Like her feminism, she talks about her lesbianism proudly, without apologies.[23] On the contrary, by poking fun at "straight" women, she offers a feminist critique of their compulsory heterosexual orientation: "Now, I went to a party once . . . and I was talking to this woman. And she was kinda neat. She came up to me and she said, 'You know, I really liked your show. Uh, I'm straight, but I liked your show.' I don't know, that tickles me, ya know? When I can get—its's powerful when you can make somebody, before you can start out, give you a heterosexual disclaimer: 'Loved your show, I'm heterosexual.' I say, 'Okay, but don't let it happen again!' " (1985). Sometimes Clinton becomes an advocate for lesbianism by using her humor to target public figures, wildly disrupting any conventional sense of propriety:

> I said I would go to this school in San Bernadino, I do all of these Gay Awareness weeks. I said, but do me a favor . . . I'm sick of the

> word *awareness. Gay awareness,* it's too passive: "I'm aware. I'm gay. It's okay." I said, "I want it to be more active, something like, oh, Gay Conversion Month." And its an easy thing. What you do is you select a heterosexual . . . you plan your strategy, and then you just go for it. Okay? I think that for me—I'm aiming high—I think that pound for pound Elizabeth Dole is the cutest Secretary of Transportation we've ever had, and I'm goin' for it! Can't you hear me say it: "Uh, Liz, come up to my room; I want to show you my underpass!" (1987)

Clinton performs in relationship to what Bauman calls "ground rules," either by conforming to them or by purposely disregarding them: "As a kind of speaking, performance will be subject to a range of community ground rules that regulate speaking in general."[24] In negotiating her performance, Clinton often chooses to use her skills as a stand-up comic to set herself over against traditional expectations.[25] While she observes certain conventions (e.g., standing on stage telling jokes, integrating material about the location in which she is performing, commenting on current events), Clinton purposely disregards others (by telling many bawdy jokes, being openly critical of men, and refusing to use disclaimers, apologies, or self-deprecation to legitimize her "intrusion" into a traditionally male-dominated arena of activity).[26] There is also "a set of ground rules specific to [the] performance itself."[27] Having attracted a female audience, predominantly feminist and lesbian, Clinton conforms to a particular set of expectations, addressing the experiences of women living within an androcentric and homophobic society. Accordingly, she avoids a style of communication that might be perceived as being too "male," stereotypically characterized by authoritarianism or emotional detachment. As a lesbian feminist performing in the public sphere, she is also under pressure to be "politically correct." One could hardly imagine, for example, that she would be accepted by her audience if she were to use humor to support anti–gay rights legislation, the policies of the Reagan and Bush administrations, or the antiabortion movement.

Fourthly, Clinton's limited access to a particular form of verbal art is essential to the understanding of her humor as situated behavior. In Clinton's case, as a woman, and particularly as a lesbian feminist, her access to the public role of stand-up comedian is restricted and negotiated by cultural norms. Hence, within this traditionally male-dominated domain, she has to work very hard to find a forum for validation and public recognition. This affects her performance by putting increased pressure on her, as a woman performer, to measure up to conventional male-identified standards while simultaneously attempting to call them into question. Abby Stein, another female stand-up comedian, comments on the problems this poses for women: "What you're really trying to do is be imitative of a male comic because that's the only role model you have. What happened to me is what happens to all of us: we get into the business because we were naturally funny, because for years all our friends said we were the life of the party. Then we systematically try to destroy everything that made us funny to begin with."[28]

Clinton's performance also produces a feeling of incredulity for her audience. My reaction the first time I watched her was "I can't believe she's really up on stage doing this stuff!" Because of its lesbian feminist orientation, her performance was like nothing I had seen before from a stand-up comic. Clinton is able to create a sensation of increased and intensified enjoyment for her audience because she negotiates her unusual role successfully and offers them an unexpected surprise: humor resonant with their own life experiences. Because of her particular worldview, her audience is limited by each individual's ability to share, or at least sympathize with, her ideology. Restricted access to an expressive art form has encouraged Clinton to distill her material for a particular, nonmainstream audience that can accept and enjoy her art. This means that men and nonfeminist or politically conservative women are not a large or visible segment of her audience.[29]

The Performer

As part of her style dependent on self-disclosure, Clinton offers a considerable amount of personal information about herself during her performance. In so doing, she intimates that she plays social roles other than that of the entertainer.[30] Some of these roles are as follows: a member of a family (with parents, one sister and three brothers, aunts and uncles), ex–high school teacher, "recovering Catholic," lesbian lover, feminist critic in the community ("I keep up on these things"), political activist (working against the La-Rouche Initiative), and everyday ordinary woman (who watches television, likes to eat, goes to a gynecologist, attends parties, and survived adolescence). The audience hears about these but does not see them. During the 1987 show, the audience was told her age (in November 1987, she turned forty) and that she is from upstate New York but recently moved to Los Angeles.

Since the audience does not actually see her in these capacities, her primary identity for them is still as a stand-up comedian. According to Bauman's theory, much of the verbal artist's success is determined on her ability to convince the audience of her eligibility as a legitimate performer.[31] As a performer, Clinton assumes responsibility to the audience for a display of communicative competence. Given the social setting, "this competence rests on the knowledge and ability to speak in socially appropriate ways."[32] For a stand-up comedian, establishing one's legitimacy usually entails special talent and training (practice, appearances in clubs, booking tours) and an arduous period of apprenticeship. I have already noted how Clinton is required to negotiate her performance against social expectations and how she uses that framework in her favor. Nonetheless, as a woman, feminist, and lesbian working in a traditionally male-dominated framework, the obstacles facing Clinton are formidable:

> Of all the avenues in humor women can pursue, stand-up comedy has got to be the toughest. The proving grounds are dingy clubs, often filled with audiences of persistent hecklers. The hours are long and late and require anxiously awating the nod to go on, which usually comes after the busboy has been given his chance. The pay is low or nonexistent, and the peer group of other women to turn to for support is minuscule. A look around at the number of women who have made successful careers in stand-up comedy confirms the grim prospects.
>
> Tremendous mettle is required for a woman to stand alone on a stage and attempt to capture the attention and amuse an assortment of skeptics who have paid hard cash for a good time. Most women don't consider the possibility. Many become discouraged and give up. A few make it.[33]

How does Clinton's humor compare with that of other contemporary women comedians? One similarity is the use of women's shared experiences as one of the primary subjects of her humor. As with Clinton, jokes about relationships, personal insights, adolescence, and women's appearance are common among comedians such as Joan Rivers, Phyllis Diller, Gilda Radner, and the new women comedians making their way into the comedy business on the East Coast (e.g., Abby Stein, Carole Montgomery, Carol Suskind, Phyllis Stickney). In a 1984 interview for *Ms.* magazine, for example, Joan Rivers mentions several personal experiences that Clinton also uses as a springboard for her humor, including learning to cope with the difficulties of being a woman comedian, having to pay the consequences for risk taking, and acknowledging the ways in which humor can be used as a mechanism to remind audiences about oppressive and painful situations. There are, however, aspects of Clinton's performance that, when taken collectively, distinguish her from other women comedians, or at least from those I have encountered. These include her attitude toward (1) self-deprecatory humor, (2) humor that demeans other women, (3) the use of comic characters or personas, and (4) public self-identification as a feminist.

First, although she satirizes difficult stages in her life (e.g., "coming out" to her family, teenage growing pains, being overweight as a kid), Clinton's humor is decidedly not self-deprecatory. Instead, she conveys self-confidence and celebrates her experiences through laughter. Recent interviews with younger, less-known women comedians suggest that self-deprecatory humor also plays a minimal role in their routines.[34] However, for older and well-known women comics, the tendency to make the audience laugh at the comedian's expense (usually at her stupidity, homeliness, or sexual inadequacy) was and is a common humor technique.[35] For example, journalist Lee Israel describes Joan Rivers's humor as "a comedy of tension and surprise, suspended uneasily between physical observation and vulgarity, between that which is about self-deprecation and that which is apologetic."[36] It is easy in hindsight to fault women comedians who first "made it" in show business for their self-denigrating style. Given the social climate of the day, however, these women may have had little choice if they wanted to succeed in a traditionally male-dominated profession.

Phyllis Diller noted: "People back then were not ready for a lady comic. They had no basis for acceptance. 'It's a *woman!* What's she trying to do?' 'she's got to be an ugly person.' 'She's got to be a butch person.' 'She's got to be a nasty woman.' Not true at all. No one is more feminine than I. I'm basically a mother and a wife and a grandmother and all those good things. But to make it on stage, I had to make fun of myself first . . . of course, I was accused of being self-deprecatory. I've got to be."[37]

In her discussion of women's consciousness-raising groups, Susan Kalcik cites the use of humor among group members as a support mechanism for group solidarity. Moreover, she notes the tendency of those women to turn "the humor in on themselves rather than on supposed oppressors."[38] Similarly, Rose Laub Coser, in her study of the uses of humor among hospital employees of varying rank and seniority, found that "a junior member can safely take the initiative to decrease social distance through humor if [s]he uses [herself/]himself as a target."[39] Given this trend of women's self-disparaging humor, it is noteworthy that Clinton makes a strong effort not to publicly devalue herself for the sake of a laugh.

There has also been a historical tendency among stand-up comedians—male and female—to use women as the targets of their humor.[40] In her article about the bawdy humor of Southern women, Rayna Green notes that "the media comediennes stand alone in their presentation of women as inventors and perpetuators of humor, but even there, few—beyond Moms Mabley and Lily Tomlin . . . have gone outside the boundaries of portraying women as humorous objects rather than as humorists."[41] This is not particularly surprising, since women in American society are frequently devalued and encouraged to compete with one another for favor and prestige. Among contemporary women media comedians, Joan Rivers has been particularly singled out for telling jokes that attack or degrade individual women:

> Increasingly, however, she is using real people in the comedy dynamic. I am bothered by that tendency. I can't help thinking that Elizabeth Taylor and Christina Onassis, in spite of their position and power, are still vulnerable human beings. It's one thing to say that the Emperor has no clothes, it's quite another to point to his double chin. That's not audacious, it's mean. While Joan may argue that it is necessary to shock in order to amuse, I'm sometimes hearing a

> different kind of laughter coming from her audiences—the kind that derives not from what is being said but from the fact that it is being said at all. The laughter follows as a collective gasp and it is as much horrified as jollified.[42]

In fairness, it should be noted that Rivers degrades both women and men in her routines, and she contends that she drops out material if she believes (or is told by the "target" or the "target's" family) that it is hurting anyone. When asked why she does this kind of comedy, she replied, "I found myself saying to people: Don't you understand? It's *all* in fun. *All* in fun."[43]

Clinton is unusual because she publicly acknowledges her ideology about satirizing women: "Ali McGraw does something to me. It's not a good something. Ali McGraw, like, arouses my gag reflex. I mean, she is something. She is a woman who makes me regret that I ever vowed that I, as a feminist comedian, I would not make fun of other women. Because with Ali McGraw we are talking a major, major temptation!" (1985). In actuality, however, she does poke fun at a selected number of women, including (in her 1985 performance) women who speak to her after her shows and say silly things, Mary Lou Retton, Nancy Reagan ("she seems so lifelike"), her old Aunt Marjorie, her mother, and Ali McGraw. In 1987, she satirized the rock star Madonna ("a radical heterosexual separatist"), Mother Theresa ("she looks like the movie creature E.T. dressed up for Halloween"), Nancy Reagan, Fawn Hall, Vanna White, and Tammy Bakker ("I think about the days before the Lord appeared unto Tammy and told her about waterproof mascara"). Although Clinton contends that her humor does not make fun of women, in actuality she hedges somewhat on this principle. While her jokes about these women could rarely be considered cruel, they do represent a small portion of her material. Hence, there is a discrepancy between Clinton's ideology and her practice as a performer, one that goes unreconciled. It may be that Clinton's satiric characterization of certain women is a device for promoting group solidarity among members of her audience by defining them in opposition to other women of whom they disapprove (particularly those who are very rich, conxservative, or naive).

In comparing Clinton with a range of other women stand-up comedians, I noticed that she makes little use of comedic characters or personas. In contrast, characters are central to the comedy of Lily Tomlin (e.g., Ernestine, the telephone operator; Edith Ann, the impertinent five-year-old girl: and Trudy, the bag lady), Gilda Radner (Roseanne Roseannadanna, the coarse East Coast woman; Judy Miller, the exuberant little girl with a vivid imagination; and Candy Slice, the punk rock star), and Whoopi Goldberg (who plays a crippled woman who loves to go disco dancing and wear a bikini; a poor Jamaican woman who is courted by a rich old man; and a junkie thief who has a Ph.D. in literature) come to mind as contemporary examples. These comedians seem to use personas to say things they cannot effectively communicate when they are "themselves." This technique was very common among women comedians of an earlier time (e.g., Elaine May, Phyllis Diller, Totie Fields) and may have been popular because through personas "they [the comedians] were all protected in some way by the kind of comedy they were doing, by their outside comedic *personas*. They were camouflaged, or, at least, accompanied."[44]

Finally, Clinton is unusual among women stand-up comedians because she publicly identifies herself as a feminist and talks about feminism, explicitly using that term in her routines. Other women comics, such as Joan Rivers, also consider themselves feminists: "Everyone forgets that I was the first lady ever to come on television and laugh about being single, laugh about all the nonsense and the first lady to bring Betty Friedan on television, on 'The Mike Douglas Show,' and deal with those issues. I always tell feminists that my life is a feminist life—just turn around, you idiots. I have done a movie—I cast it, got my own money, did my own editing—what do you want from me?"[45]

Lily Tomlin, in fact, is very articulate about her views on feminism, aptly describing gender inequalities by noting that "this whole society is like slow dancing—the men get to lead and the women get stepped on!"[46] In a 1981 interview, Tomlin spoke with conviction about her ideology:

> *Q*. Has the woman's movement had an impact on your career?
> *A*. If it hadn't been for the women's movement people would call it my hobby.

Q. Why does it seem that the women's movement needs to be revived every fifty years or so?

A. Maybe because the women's movement is, in some way, a metaphor for women's accomplishments. And there seems to be a pattern in the culture by which women's accomplishments always disappear. It's like doing the dishes—no matter how many times you do them, they're always there to be done again.

Women have always accommodated to the values of men. Men need to accommodate to the values of women. Instead of talking about drafting women, we should question the futility of war. The entire culture is built as a support system for men and men's values. One of those values is that women are providers and accommodate to the system. We really should be developing a system that values men and women equally. Not to mention children and other living things, as that famous nun Sister Mary Corita once said.[47]

Rosanne Barr is another popular comedian—"the symbol of the disgruntled American housewife, hanging in but perpetually pissed"[48]—whose humor is also avowedly feminist. Calling herself a "gynarchist," Barr sarcastically rejects the cultural value conventionally assigned to women's role in mothering, housekeeping, cooking, and maintaining her personal appearance. Although she differs from Kate Clinton in that her humor is decidedly blue-collar and heterosexual, she, too, lambasts the devaluation of women, homophobia, and male sexual prowess: "My husband walks in the door one night, he says to me: 'Roseanne, don't you think it's time we sat down and had a serious talk about our sex life?' I say to him: 'You want me to turn off "Wheel of Fortune" for that?!' "[49]

Like Barr and Tomlin, Clinton's feminist stance is central to her presentation. In contrast, however, she attracts audiences composed almost entirely of women.[50] In part, this may be attributed to differing understandings of whether or not women can claim a shared experience that is distinct from that of men: "Women now have much more access than before. The only sad thing about lady stand-up comics now is they think they have to do 'women's humor.' There is no women's humor. I have fights all the time about this. If something is funny, it's funny."[51] I suspect that another reason for the infrequent mention of feminism in women's comedy routines is a concern about alienating men and "nonfeminist" women in mixed audiences. Most women stand-up comedians perform in mixed-gender settings and must tailor their performances accordingly. To reach a general audience, a feminist comedian may have to address experiences that are uniquely women's that that also partake of qualities of human experience that all people can understand. Within a context of an almost all-female audience sympathetic with her political stance, Clinton has access to a "safe" environment in which to experiment with explicitly feminist material. Not surprisingly, it is here that she can play with the humorous treatment of extremely controversial issues that might not be well received by mixed-gender audiences, such as abortion, menstruation taboos, protection and care for AIDS victims, and surrogate motherhood:

> Now, I'm having problems with this Baby M thing. Is anybody scared about this? Didn't we have the Civil War pretty much about this issue of buying and selling people? And didn't we pretty much decide it with the Thirteenth Amendment that you really shouldn't buy and sell people, thank you very much? Maybe you say, "But Kate, he had a contract!" These are the same people who tell you that pit bulls have a sweet disposition! And I worked this out, and it's $1.57 an hour. For $10,000 for nine months, those women are getting $1.57 an hour! I mean that the stretch marks and $10,000 would not begin to cover it! (1987)

The Audience

> *Kate Clinton causes fun. Being in her audience reminds me of the wild pleasure of being with slap-happy girlfriends.*[52]

In that Kate Clinton's humor is directed to a particular audience of women who can share, or at least sympathize with, her worldview without being alienated or offended, her jokes are gender-specific. Carol Mitchell, in her studies of differences in joke telling between the sexes, confirms that the gender of both the performer and the audience are crucial factors in how they are appreciated: "In determining the degree of appreciation of jokes, the sex of the performer and the audience is probably as important as the content of the joke itself. For instance, a joke that is primarily derogatory to men is more likely to be appreciated by men when it is told one man to other men, but it seems less funny to men if it is told to them by a woman, and the reverse holds true of jokes that are primarily derogatory to women."[53] The women in the audience would not be amused upon hearing Clinton's material delivered by a man. If this occurred, humor that she now uses as celebratory of the female experience might be taken as derogatory, alienating, or presumptuous.

Similarly, Clinton's performance would be affected if the audience were composed of a substantial number of men, attending either as individuals or as members of heterosexual couples. The men who were a part of the audiences in Austin were so few in number as to be virtually invisible, and Clinton made no attempt to draw them in as participants in her performances. In studying the differences between women's and men's speech, Thorne and Henley have noted how "the speech used in situations where both sexes are present may be quite different from the speech of the single-sex occasions."[54] This is evident both in the way Clinton speaks as though men are "out there somewhere," not present in the audience, and in the way she uses openly hostile jokes about men to create cohesion among women. As a member of the audience, I got the impression that Clinton's attempts focused not on demeaning or embarrassing specific men in the audience but rather on disregarding their presence altogether. This would correspond to Mitchell's findings that "women are still less likely than men to use jokes for the purpose of embarrassing the listener. And most of their openly hostile jokes will be saved for the all-female audience."[55]

Clinton's interaction with the audience is one of the keys to her success. Her approach is one of camaraderie between women, sisterhood in the feminist sense. She wants to convey the impression that she is "just one of the girls," confiding about her personal experiences, daily frustrations, and political views as though she were a close friend with the audience as a whole. This is not unlike Joan Rivers's hallmark phrase "Can we talk?" By creating the impression that she and the audience share a friendship, Rivers tries to win their sympathy and trust: "If you come on with a superior attitude, they [the audience] cannot relate to you. And you must relate in comedy, you must be friends or you have no chance at all."[56] But it is more than camaraderie that Clinton wants to engender. Since much of her material focuses on her experiences as a lesbian and a feminist living in a hostile society, she assumes that her audience has shared her experiences of alienation and marginalization. Clinton intentionally uses humor as a support mechanism for herself and the women she addresses.[57] In her study of the effects of humor on group dynamics, Coser observes that "by inviting the listeners to indicate through laughter that they share the awareness of the conflict, humor is both a means of self-protection and a means of providing the support of the collectivity. In both instances, the humorist may be said to play the informal role of an agent of socialization."[58] The following excerpt from Clinton's 1985 routine illustrates this dynamic:

> What you've gotta do is, whenever Reagan or any of his henchmen appear in your town—and I guess there is one living, isn't there? [George Bush comes from Texas.] What you've gotta do: you go by the house, maybe go by George's house, you know? And what you've gotta do is, you've gotta get all of your wildest lesbian-looking clothes out again, okay? Get 'em out. Some of you have been "femming" it up a little bit. I rolled a woman at the Inaugural Ball for this very outfit. . . . But what you've got to do is: you've got to get out your oldest lesbian-looking clothes, okay? You've got to get out your white painter pants again. You've gotta get out your flannel shirts again. You know, your rainbow suspenders out again; your purple tie-died underwear out again. You've gotta get your Birkenstocks out again, okay . . . ? And then your ten-pound, three-inch labyrises out again, okay, with blades so sharp as to make a Cuisinart seem dull, do you know what I'm saying? Get it all together now, and you take your wildest lesbian-looking friends out, okay? Amazonians at their very best. And then, whenever Reagan appears or any of his little buddies appear, you be there, okay? And you carry signs, and smile, that say: "LESBIANS FOR REAGAN!" (1985)

Clinton makes it a point to continuously interact with her audience. She does so by using set phrases ("You know?", "How many of you. . . . ?"; "And did you notice . . . ?"; "Have you ever . . . ?"), asking for audience response ("I am interested in finding out more about my audiences"), and ending her act by walking offstage and up the theater aisle to the lobby, where she is available to autograph albums and talk with people who want to meet her. Several times during her routine, she tells the audience that an individual's requests and comments have later been incorporated into her routine ("I love it when people tell me stuff"). All of these devices work to strengthen her bond with the audience and to create an atmosphere of group participation.

Primary Subjects in Clinton's Humor

Clinton's routines address a range of topics. I have chosen four that are particularly characteristic of her worldview: (1) the Catholic church, (2) hostility toward men, (3) bawdy sexual humor, and (4) controversial political issues.[59]

Clinton calls herself "a recovering Catholic," often referring to her Catholic schooling (at "Our Lady of Psychological Warfare") and upbringing.[60] She sees herself as an iconoclast, making fun of the church and spurning the piety that seems to have caused her so much pain as a girl growing up under its influence. Through one-liners, run-on commentary, and wordplays, she lays waste all that is sacred (e.g., at one point in her 1985 performance she referred to the eucharistic wafer as "the deodorant pad of Christ"). Although they are couched in humor, one has the feeling that Clinton's criticisms of the church are deadly serious: "Now, you've probably read about the pope. The pope is very upset about these condom things. But just look what he's wearing on his head!" (1987). During her 1985 performance, Clinton asked four women from the audience who attended Catholic school when they were younger to come onstage to be her "backup band," which she named the "Vessels of Sin." In order to "qualify" for the band, they each had to answer one question about Catholic religious practice or doctrine. The questions she asks the first two women are "Are Gregorian notes square or round?" and "When you buy a pagan baby, do you buy it by the pound?" She turns to the last two women, who have attended Catholic school for a combined total of eight years, and instructs them: "Now, you two are going to work together on this one, okay? So, just get close now. [They wrap arms.] What you're going to do . . . I'm going to sing a song for you, and you have to tell me if this *is* an actual Catholic song—or the new Gay National S&M Anthem. All right, actual Catholic song or the new Gay National S&M Anthem? We've got eight years of experience on the line here. Are you ready? [Clinton begins to sing a litany.] 'Eat His body, drink His blood. Hallelu, hallelu, hallelu, hallelu . . . jah' " (1985).[61]

Clinton makes no apologies about her disgust concerning church dogma and church officials. She challenges what she sees as the superficiality of penance, hypocritical moral norms, and the pope himself:

> There's a guy who's been driving me crazy lately. I mean nuts . . . : the pope. Pope John Paul George Ringo. Can you believe him? A grown man going all over the world kissing airports. [She motions towards the floor.] Get up! Get up! What are you looking at down there? He went to Canada. You know what he did in Canada? He made people up there nuts before he even got there. Women in Canada were crazed because before he went, he said, "I'm not going to go there. I will not perform any liturgical rituals there, because you use altar *girls.*" And he said he only wanted altar *boys.* [Clinton hisses and encourages the audience to hiss.] I'll bet! And so what did he do for Canada? What he does to make it up to the women in Canada that he's offended, I guess: he raises to the level of sainthood a woman whose claim to fame is that she formed an order of housekeeping nuns! Don't do me any favors, Pops! Now, can't you see his new Encyclical on the Status of Women? [It will be called] "Spic-em and Span-em. Born to Clean." . . .
>
> I would like to talk to the pope, just for sec. . . . I would say, "Your Largeness," or you could, "Your Extreme Roundheadness," [or] "Your Extreme Narrow-Mindedness." I would say to him, "Listen, if abortion is murder, why isn't fucking a felony?" I think it'd make a dynamite bumper sticker, don't you? And the trick of this bumper sticker is: you put it on *other* people's cars. (1985)

Clinton also uses her humor to criticize men. In fact, I was unable to detect a single instance in either the 1985 or the 1987 routine of her speaking positively about a man. Men are, at best, disregarded and, at worst, the targets for hostility and aggression. Clinton's humor about this subject is oppositional, satirizing men who are in positions of authority (such as governmental officials or the pope) or who simply appear ridiculous to her in trying to live up to a macho image.[62] The following is an assortment of her one-liners describing men:

On having a boyfriend as a teenager: "We're driving home in the car, and my mother says to me, 'You'll never have a boyfriend if you're this heavy!' [Clinton's response was:] 'Hey, there's a Kentucky Fried Chicken right over there!" 1985).

On women who have never "done it with a guy": "Pure and proud" (1985).

On the first and only time she had intercourse with a man: "He was about the size of a cocktail frank" (1985).

On men's valuation of large women: "Guys don't like big women because they take up too much space" (1985).

On Ed McMahon: "Doesn't it look like Ed McMahon probably ate his own children?" (1985).

On Phil Donahue: "I can't really trust a man who has gray meringue for hair" (1987).

On various men in the Reagan administration: "Have you noticed, too, that since Reagan has been in office there have been a lot more bran commercials?" *Donald Regan:* "The man has had a charisma bypass!"; *Caspar Weinberger:* "What a slime!"; *Oliver North:* "Based on a GI Joe Doll" (1987).

Clinton's jokes go beyond ridiculing the foolishness of men to the suggestion of open hostility and aggression against them.[63] In her survey of college students, Carol Mitchell detected two types of jokes about men that women particularly liked: (1) jokes whose theme is related to the female experiences, specifically jokes in which male sexual aggressiveness is ridiculed; and (2) jokes in which violence is done to a male by a female.[64] Clinton tells both kinds of jokes, making little attempt to disguise her intentions. In the following sequence of menstruation jokes, she comments on the "unspoken rule" that men are never supposed to actually see a sanitary napkin. She holds one up, waving it around, and notes: "They are *never* supposed to see these things, you know . . . ? And so, one of the fun things that I say to do at work, you know, they were never supposed to see these. You would think that if a guy saw one of these, it would kill him. So I say get 'em out! Having trouble with somebody at work? [She waves it around as if directed toward some particular man.] And it's so cheap, okay?" (1985).

Clinton delights in telling "bawdy" jokes, particularly those that make graphic reference to sexual activity. She excels in this area, breaking all the conventional rules about the "proper" topics of conversation for women in a public setting.[65] Clinton is not unique in including sexual humor in her comedy routines. Increasingly, mainstream women comedians such as Phyllis Diller and Joan Rivers use sex as a permissible humor topic. Rivers commented:

> sex is a good topic for everybody. Comedy is changing radically, thank goodness. We're all here because of Lenny Bruce—he broke the barrier. That means for the men as well as the women. Bruce said, "This is what I'm talking about and it's really true." So, obviously, sex comes out of that. But it has nothing to do with women and men. I talk about sex in my act about as far as I would talk about it in private with my friends. I don't know what the barriers are because I just pretend I'm in a livingroom. I guess you could talk more freely in the livingroom than you did ten years ago, but I'm not aware of it.[66]

In contrast to Joan Rivers, Clinton is unusual in that she uses sexual humor, although she does not make women the butt of her jokes. Folklorist Gershon Legman, well known for his work on sexual humor, apparently had not encountered material like Clinton's when he wrote that "one fact strikingly evident in any collection of modern sexual folklore . . . is that this material has all been created by men, and that there is no place in it for women except as the butt . . . the situations presented almost completely lack a protagonist position in which a woman can identify herself, *as a woman,* with any human gratification or pride."[67] Some of Clinton's bawdy sexual humor concerns the shared experiences of both lesbian and straight women, particularly menstruation rituals and taboos: "You think that's fun? One great thing to do . . . now, a woman told me about this. She said another great thing to do is to get out one of your tampons and just put it behind your ear. [She pauses and gestures as if she's doing so.] It is a riot! Put it behind your ear, and just walk around. Walk around. And then when somebody comes up to you and says, 'Uh, you've got a tampon behind your ear,' then you say, 'Oh my God, where *is* my pencil?' " (1985). Moreover, Clinton's use of bawdy humor is iconoclastic in that she also celebrates the lesbian sexual experience:

> The reason I gained thirty pounds the summer before my senior year was because that summer was the first summer I spent away from home—at summer camp. Do you hear what I'm saying? And I was a waitress, okay? And in about two days [I] immediately fell in love with another one of the waitresses I was working with, okay? And we wanted each other. It was "hot," you know? I mean it was "hot." But unfortunately, we were both good little Catholic girls. . . . So, instead of each other—we ate peach cobbler and chocolate pies, *whole* chocolate pies. Uh-huh. And we ate Schnecken. Do you know what Schnecken is? I'll tell you. It's this hot, sticky, swirly, caramel, cinnamony bun. [She pauses and then carefully enunciates with more sexual inference given to each word progressively.] Hot . . . sticky . . . swirly . . . cinnamon . . . buns. HOT . . . STICKY . . . SWIRLY . . . CINNAMON . . . BUNS. Do you hear where thirty pounds is happenin'? It was so beautiful and so delicious that you would want to kiss them before you even take a bite out of them, okay? Just like my girlfriend, yum! (1985)

Clinton also tackles controversial political issues with her incisive satirical commentary. Politics and current events are common subject matter for stand-up comedians; Clinton approaches these topics with feminist fervor.[68] In comparing the material in her two Austin performances, I noted a greater emphasis on overtly political issues in 1987. Clinton performs at political rallies and fund-raisers for the causes she supports. In her comedy routines, she is vehement in assailing right-wing legislators who work to restrict the rights of women or gays: "One of the things I did in the fall that was great was to do a benefit against the La Rouche Initiative. Now, the La Rouche Initiative—this was a guy, American Neanderthal—his idea, his idea was to quarantine people who had any kind of relation to the AIDS virus, alright? I mean, this man is clearly suffering from CRI, which those of you, yes, those of you in the health professions know that CRI is cranial rectal inversion. You like that? Know people at work who have it? Not a pretty thing to have, is it?" (1987).

In each of these four subject areas—jokes about the Catholic church, men, bawdy sexual humor, and politics—Clinton breaks the rules. The audience is incited to laughter because of repeated and unexpected shifting between the permitted and the taboo, the playful and the serious, fantasy and reality.[69] Clinton jokes about taboo subjects—or about socially acceptable subjects, but in a profane manner—in order to call dominant social structures and mainstream values into question. As I will attempt to demonstrate, this calling into question, or reversal, is the key to Clinton's unusual approach to stand-up comedy and to the way in which she uses her performances to do more than just entertain her audience.

Functional Aspects of Clinton's Humor, Particularly Humor as Subversion

Feminist humor is based on the perception that societies have generally been organized as systems of oppression and exploitation, and that the largest (but not the only) oppressed group has been the female. It is also based on the conviction that such oppression is undesirable and unnecessary. It is a humor based on visions of change. The persistent attitude that underlies feminist humor is the attitude of social revolution—that is, we are ridiculing a social system that can be, that must be changed. Female *humor may ridicule a person or a system from an accepting point of view ("that's life"), while the* non-acceptance *of oppression characterizes feminist humor and satire.*[70]

In her study of colleagues in the workplace, Coser outlines five functions of humor, noting that humor can serve as (1) entertainment, (2) a means of escape or release from a difficult situation, (3) self-validation for the humorist, (4) a mechanism to support or induce cohesion for a group or community of people, and (5) an expression of the desire to subvert established social orders or power structures.[71] These functions are all operative in Clinton's performances, and I will comment briefly on each. However, I give particular attention to the fifth function, since it is, I believe the distinguishing mark of Clinton's humor.

First, certainly Clinton's routine is designed to entertain. There were times during both the 1985 and 1987 performances when the audiences were laughing so loudly and raucously that my tape recorder picked up little else. For a stand-up comedian, one of the nonnegotiable ground rules for a successful performance is the ability to amuse one's audience. I learned something from watching Clinton's performances, but most of all I had a great time.

Second, Clinton's humor also functions as a sort of pressure valve for herself and for her audience. As she puts it, "she who laughs, lasts" (1985). In performing against a mainstream societal background that stereotypes or devalues women in general, and is openly mhostile to lesbians specifically, Clinton uses her humor as a survival mechanism. Clinton notes that "women laughing is a survival reflex."[72] However, instead of encouraging dissipation of rebellion by laughing at oppression, Clinton incites her audience to "talk back good."

Third, Clinton negotiates her performance in such a way that she is validated by the audience for her verbal skills and for her ability to make them laugh. During the performances I attended, she accomplished this with commendable results; in both instances, Clinton left her audience roaring with laughter and calling for an encore. As a performer using traditional and nontraditional tools of her trade, she must convince her audience of her competence as a stand-up comedian worthy of their time, attention, and financial support and her legitimacy in that role as a woman, a feminist, and a lesbian.

Fourth, I have already noted how Clinton encourages a sense of common identity and group cohesion with and among the audience. As such, her humor is a means of socialization, "of affirmation of common values, of teaching and learning, of asking for and giving support, of bridging differences."[73] Since much of Clinton's humor is adversarial, that is, descriptive of how she sees her role *over-against* what she considers to be oppressive social forces (i.e., the church, men, heterosexual bias, repressive political policy), she calls on the audience to accept—if only temporarily within the performance frame—a shared identity in order to perceive themselves in this adversarial position. She uses a number of techniques for engendering the notion that "we're all in this together," including rhetorical linguistic devices (e.g., "Ya'know?" or "Now, I know you'll understand this"), jokes that focus on the shared experiences of women (menstruation and rite-of-passage jokes), and audience participation ("Let's have a show of hands," or "How many of you have . . . ?").

Finally, and most importantly to this analysis, Clinton uses humor as a tool for subversion and transformation. Kaufman and Pabis argue that feminist humor, by virtue of its critique of male dominance, is inherently transformational: "Feminist humor is based on the observation that most modern societies are organized as systems of exploitation, and that the largest, but not the only oppressed group, has been women. It is also based on the idea that such systems can and must be changed, but it envisions positive changes."[74] Much like the bawdy Southern women described by Rayna Green, Clinton defies the rules by ridiculing and satirizing that which is supposedly sacred. Green states that Southern women's obscene tales are a form of countersocialization, debunking and inverting social norms: "Women are not supposed to know or repeat such stuff. But they do and when they do, they speak ill of all that is sacred: men, the church, marriage, home, family, parents."[75]

In Clinton's performances, the tables are turned against those who would otherwise seek to victimize her. This stance of "nonacceptance" causes Clinton to use the frame of conventional performance (stand-up comedy) in an unconventional way. The setting, ground rules, audience, content, and style of Clinton's performance all contribute to its transformation into something more than an entertainment event. Through humor, Clinton confronts—and thereby calls into question—the status quo, to undermine authority, to exercise control, to refuse to play by the rules.[76] She encourages members of her audience to do likewise. This is the kind of threatening potential that Coser also noted in her study of humor, stating that women's humor "may be acceptable in some situations, but it is disapproved in those social situations in which there is danger of subverting implicit or explicit male authority. What is aggressive in humor is that it takes control temporarily out of the hands of those higher in the hierarchy."[77]

The transformation of a performance that is merely humorous into one that suggests subversion is potentially dangerous to those who support and maintain the social order. While still meeting some conventional expectations (e.g., the ability to make her audience laugh by standing before them telling jokes onstage), Clinton manipulates her craft in unexpected ways (by utilizing humor in exhorting the audience to take action against repressive social norms). Bauman describes phenomena such as this as the "emergent quality" of verbal performance:

> the participants are using the structured, conventional performance system itself as a resource for creative manipulation, as a base on which a range of communication transformations can be wrought. . . . The structured system stands available to them as a set of convenient expectations and associations, but these expectations and associations are further manipulated in innovative ways, by fashioning novel performances outside the conventional system, or working various transformational adaptations which turn performance into something else.[78]

Moreover, in deliberately violating cultural taboos, Clinton takes full advantage of the double-edged character of performance noted by Bauman: "[There is a] . . . documented tendency for performers to be both admired and feared—admired for their artistic skill and power and for their enhancement of experience they provide, feared because of the potential they represent for subverting and transforming the status quo. Here too may lie a reason for the equally persistent association between performers and marginality or deviance, for in the special emergent quality of performance the capacity for change may be highlighted and made manifest to the community."[79] Clinton sometimes uses her humor as a weapon, incorporating openly adversarial jokes about men, the church, and the social order. She contradicts two aspects of Mitchell's findings on gender differences in joke telling: (1) that women tell more jokes with women as the target of humor than men do, and (2) that "as a general rule, the aggressive and/or hostile jokes that women tell are less openly aggressive and hostile than the jokes men tell."[80]

Clinton's humor also provides a counterexample to Coser's findings about the way humor functions among people within societal contexts where power and prestige are distributed hierarchically.[81] Coser concludes that among hospital staff members humor functions in socially acceptable structures so as to *relax the distances between people, without seriously attempting to overturn the hierarchy.* In this way, the aggression of those lower in the hierarchy "is safely used only within the limits of social approval."[82] She notes, for example, that women staff members who told jokes in informal situations "hardly ever used their wit and their sense of humor" in more formal settings such as staff meetings.[83] When humor is used by "the less powerful" (in Coser's study, by junior members of the staff), it is socially acceptable only when presented "in the guise of an aggression upon a specifically mentioned and legitimate target."[84] Traditionally, in women's humor the "legitimate target" or scapegoat has often been themselves. Noting that in the majority of cases humor is used aggressively by the more powerful against the less powerful (she calls this "downward humor"), Coser states that "those who are 'on top' have more right to be aggressors; those who are low in the hierarchy are not as freely permitted this outlet, even if it appears under the disguise of humor."[85]

Clinton's performance differs with these conclusions in several aspects. First, while she works to establish a feeling of camaradie with the audience, she also uses comedy to heighten the tensions, rather than relax the distances, between herself and other types of people. Her routines are full of examples of this, particularly in relationship to men. Second, in general Clinton uses neither herself nor other women as "primary targets" in her material. That is, her humor is neither self-denigrating nor misogynist, traits often found in the materials of popular women standing comedians in the past. Third, rather than functioning as a support mechanism for the social order, Clinton's humor works to subvert it. Using Coser's terminology, it is "upward humor," turning against the "more powerful" in an attempt to call them into question.

As I have suggested throughout this essay, Clinton intends to do more than entertain. She intimates this, for example, in one of the phrases she used several times in her 1987 performance: "You create the world; you invite the people in." By continually breaking the performance frame, she calls on the audience to participate in subversion. Clinton represents herself as a troublemaker, and, in asking the audience to identify with her, she implicates them in her rebellion:

> The gold glints in the hair are in honor of my new spirit guide for the '80s. Now, I know a lot of you have taken on a spirit guide. Do you have a spirit guide? No? Maybe you'd like mine. She's a multifac-

> eted gal and she could, she's yours too? Okay now, the gold glints in the hair are because I've taken as my spirit guide—you're going to love this—Cruella Deville from the movie *101 Dalmations*. Do you remember? Can you sing the theme song? [She gets someone in audience to sing it. The audience applauds.] But isn't that a perfect person to have as your spirit guide? A devil kind of gal! That's what we need. (1987)

Clinton moves beyond the confines of her performance by enjoining the audience to take their experience of the performance back into real-life situations.[86] In much the way that she uses a conventional genre—stand-up comedy—in an unconventional manner to call the status quo into question, she encourages her audience to reclaim their power to reject traditional social norms and create revolutionary ways of thinking and acting. Clinton makes little attempt to conceal her political purposes. Her description of feminist humor includes elements of critique, transcendence, and change:

> Feminist humor—as different from mainstream male and female humor—is active, based as it is on the possibility of change. . . . Feminist humor is not escapist. It is transformational. It transforms painful expression, and in transforming, it transcends them. It transcends the old dichotomy between serious and humorous—the one which says that serious is more real. Serious is truth. Humorous is less than real, trivial, trifling. Very often, I think, women try to "out-serious the boys." And we stay forever in painful, albeit comfortable, corners examining old wounds, old scars, old sufferings. Feminist humor moves us out of those corners. Here is the reclamation of making light. We make light, light enough to move through our heavy issues. The power of this making light is measured only by the power of that old insult: "the women's movement lacks a sense of humor." Feminist humor is not absurdist; it is thoughtful, frontal, I call it "fish jerky humor"—it's good for the brain, and it gives you something to chew on. Feminist humor is a reclamation of the practical joke. It is *good* practice, an antidote against absurdity. Humor demands a physical, visible response. Unlike music and poetry readings, where women can look like they're involved, but be thinking about what they're going to eat after, humor demands a certain response. It demands a presence. It demands that women laugh, and in that laughing that women put their bodies on the line. I think that's very good practice. The whole world hates the happy

> women, and it does its best to keep us apart. Times when women are laughing together are times which suggest and give intimations of how we can be together in community, and I think that's what we're all thinking about. They suggest another dimension, where separations and divisions are bridged. I don't mean to suggest some otherworldly kind of karmic zone, some transcendent leap into a world that is "oh, so beautiful." It's a very real place where, because we are present to ourselves, we are absent to the world of men—where we are thus present and absent at the same time. It is a utopic dimension in the here and now, and it is predicated on the sharing of joy. Feminist humor is not a compendium of jokes or reversal; it is a radical analysis of our being in the world, based on our commitment to our right to be joyful. In the context of male humor, our humor has too often been used for female binding. We have told jokes on ourselves, we have trivialized our actions, we have not taken ourselves seriously as we have tried to keep each other in place. The difference between the female binding of male humor and the feminist bonding of fumerists is that we are encouraging each other to be all that we can be. Male penile humor—the ultimate in stand-up comedy—is based on the hierarchical power structure of the put-down. Fumerists are more "stand-with" comedians. Each of us is equal to the task of making light, shedding light on our experiences, encouraging each other to change and move.[87]

Using her role as performer, Clinton exhorts the audience to use the "power of the old double reverse" and to subvert the established social order in the interests of a feminist vision. This is a trademark of her performance, one that she makes explicit at the conclusion of her comedy routines:

> But we call [my second album] "Making Waves." This is another one of those warnings that we always get, generally when we've really started to rock the boat. And I think it's time that women, feminists, lesbians, all of us learn to take the power of the old "double reverse." And that's why we watch football sometimes, we take those insults that we always get—"Oh, you castrating, ball-busting bitch!"—as *invitations;* and those warnings—"Don't make waves!"—as *welcomes.* So I encourage you to keep taking the slide down "the great turquoise waterslide called life" to make waves. Big waves! Tsunamis! *Whatever* it takes to turn the tide. (conclusion of 1985 performance)

> Somebody once said to me, "Kate, when you get up in the morning, each one of us has to decide if we're going to save or savor the world." And when I came out, I told a friend of mine that I was a lesbian, and she said to me, among other things—this is an ex-friend—she said to me very scornfully, "Well, you've certainly made a commitment to joy in your life!" And I almost denied it, but she's right. As a lesbian, as gay people in this world, we have made a commitment to joy in our lives, and Joy is not an easy woman to please! And we know we have to work at it, we really do. And we know it's not a question of either/or: either save or savor the world. We know we have to do both: save *and* savor the world. And it's a world that would like to gentrify the wildness of our souls, and just lock us up completely. And we know that we can't do that, we know that we have to do both, save and savor the world. So here in Austin, as always, keep it up. Keep up the good fight, and be bold! Be very bold! But most of all, be *bad!* (conclusion of 1987 performance)

In affirming and supporting women, Clinton exhorts audience members to validate their own experiences and to develop a stance of nonacceptance. Moreover, she incites women to action, encouraging them not to be afraid to laugh about—and thereby to be critical of—social norms that privilege men and male dominance. Here Clinton moves beyond her role as comedian to become a social critic who is at the same time a political activist, using humor as her tool for subversion and transformation.

Notes

M. Jane Young, Richard Bauman, Kay Turner, Laura Lein, and Jim Foley were kind enough to comment on earlier drafts of this essay. I thank them for their suggestions and insights. Most of all, I thank Kate Clinton for her wicked and inspiring humor. She makes us laugh, and these days a good laugh can be hard to find.

1. Gloria Kaufman, "Introduction," in *Pulling Our Own Strings: Feminist Humor and Satire,* ed. Gloria Kaufman and Mary Kay Blakely (Bloomington: Indiana University Press, 1980), 16.

2. Quotes from Clinton's routines are followed by the year of the performance in which they occurred. Clinton's April 4, 1987, shows took place in a very different setting, demonstrating elevation in her status as a performer. Her performances at Ellington's—a private club with the atmosphere and accoutrements of a nightclub—seemed classier and less "funky." Ellington's has a cash bar; the audience is seated around cocktail tables. Bamboo plants, reed mats, and pink plastic flamingos were used to decorate the stage, supplementing the dark walls of the club. Rather than appearing alone, Clinton was preceded by an opening act, Ann Reed, who was introduced as a feminist folk singer. Clinton performed in two consecutive shows, in contrast to the single performance of 1985. As in 1985, the shows were sold out. In her 1987 Austin performances, Clinton included a "channeling" routine in which she mystically assumed the persona of a "forty-thousand-year-old lesbian named Mona." Mona told the audience something about her own past experiences and then asked, "Is this a sort of tribal meeting right now?"
3. Richard Bauman, "Verbal Art as Performance," *American Anthropologist* 77 (1975), 290–312. All citations are taken from the book form of this essay by Richard Bauman: "Verbal Art as Performance," in *Verbal Art as Performance* (Prospect Heights, Ill.: Waveland Press, 1984), 3–58.
4. For an introduction to the performance approach, see Américo Paredes and Richard Bauman, eds., *Toward New Perspectives in Folklore* (Austin: University of Texas Press, 1972).
5. See Mary Douglas, "The Social Control of Cognition: Some Factors in Joke Perception," *Man* 3 (1968), 361–76.
6. Bauman, "Verbal Art as Performance," 4.
7. For an analysis of various approaches to the study of humor from an anthropological perspective, see Mahadev L. Apte, *Humor and Laughter: An Anthropological Approach* (Ithaca and London: Cornell University Press, 1985).
8. See Joan B. Levine, "The Feminine Routine," *Journal of Communication* 26, no. 3 (1976), 173–75, for a statistical analysis of the material used by well-known male and female comedians.
9. Mary Kay Blakely, "Dear Gloria," in *Pulling Our Own Strings:*

Feminist Humor and Satire, ed. Gloria Kaufman and Mary Kay Blakely (Bloomington: Indiana University Press, 1980), 10.

10. Clinton began her 1987 routine by commenting on her regret that the Lady Longhorns, the well-known women's basketball team at the University of Texas, lost the championship finals. She mentioned Austin's active lesbian community, and she satirized pseudo-spiritualism by soliciting audience response to her question "Do you like my aura? I just knew I could ask you that in Austin." These are devices for establishing rapport with the audience and creating a bond of similar interests that become a foundation for her humor.
11. Denise Collier and Kathleen Beckett, *Spare Ribs: Women in the Humor Biz* (New York: St. Martin's Press, 1980), xi–xii.
12. Joan Rivers, quoted in Lee Israel, "Joan Rivers and How She Got That Way," *Ms.,* October 1984, 110.
13. Bauman, "Verbal Art as Performance," 28.
14. Ibid., 27.
15. Some journalists have noted the recent increase in the number of women stand-up comics who are trying to establish themselves in the entertainment business. Suggesting that newer female comedians owe a debt of gratitude to Lily Tomlin, Joan Rivers, and Phyllis Diller for so visibly invading a male domain, McGuigan and Huck report that "today one hopeful in three is a woman. At the Comedy Store in Los Angeles . . . the ratio of female to male performers has jumped from 1 in 100 to 1 in 10." Cathleen McGuigan and Janel Huck, "The New Queens of Comedy: Women Comics Aren't Putting Themselves Down When They Do Stand-up," *Newsweek,* April 30, 1984, 58. See also Stewart Klein, "The Queens of Comedy," *Harper's Bazaar,* August 1983, 166.
16. I have intentionally chosen to use the word *comedian* to describe Clinton and all other women comics, since the term *comedienne* is itself a diminutive form.
17. David Zippin, "Sex Differences and the Sense of Humor," *Psychoanalytic Review* 53 (1966), 214. The notion that humor (particularly sexual humor) is alien to women has been popular with a range of authors. For other examples of male bias in this literature, see Gary Alan Fine, "Obscene Joking across Culture,"

Journal of Communication 26 (1976), 134–40; Sigmund Freud, *Jokes and Their Relation to the Unconscious,* trans. and ed. James Strachey, (New York: Norton, 1960), 99–101; Martin Grotjahn, *Beyond Laughter* (New York: McGraw-Hill, 1957), 37; Gershon Legman, *Rationale of the Dirty Joke, An Analysis of Sexual Humor* (New York: Castle Books, 1968), 10, 12, 319–25; Naomi Weisstein, "Why We Aren't Laughing . . . Anymore," *Ms.* November 1973, 49–51, 88–90. For a summary and analysis of this trend, see Mary Jo Neitz, "Humor, Hierarchy, and the Changing Status of Women, *Psychiatry* 42 (August 1980), 211–23.

18. Rose Laub Coser, "Laughter among Colleagues: A Study of the Social Functions of Humor among the Staff of a Mental Hospital," *Psychiatry* 23 (February 1960), 85. Unlike others (see above), Coser does not suggest that women have no sense of humor or do not tell jokes. Instead, she notes that in mixed-gender staff meetings women rarely made jokes, although some of them demonstrated excellent senses of humor and made witty remarks in other settings.
19. Apte, *Humor and Laughter,* 81. Although Apte acknowledges (p. 76) that women's humor is not totally constrained, that the social constraints that do delimit women's humor are not universal, and that not all women conform to them, he nonetheless makes a number of generalizations about women's humor that Kate Clinton contradicts. These include the contentions that women's humor generally lacks the aggressive quality of men's humor: that it does not attempt to belittle others (p. 70); that images of women as tricksters or clowns are not found in the narrative of any culture (pp. 70–71); and that women do not engage in slapstick humor or "horseplay" (p. 71). Apte observes that some types of humor usually absent from women's expressive behavior in the public domain are present in the private domain, where there are all-women audiences (p. 76). I contend that Clinton blurs the conceptual boundaries between the public and private domains, since humorous treatment of women's "private" or personal experiences are the essence of her public performances.
20. Alice Sheppard, "From Kate Sanborn to Feminist Psychology: The Social Context of Women's Humor, 1885–1985," *Psychology of Women Quarterly* 10 (1986), 167. Sheppard notes that

"although American history books and literary anthologies are generally silent on the topic of women's humor in the nineteenth century, popular women humorists existed, contributing to newspapers and magazines; writing short stories, children's books, and novels; and earning reputations as brilliant and witty conversationalists" (p. 159).

21. The differences, actual or imagined, between the expressive patterns of women and men have been the subject of some debate. Among scholars such as Lakoff, Phillips, O'Barr, and Thorne and Henley, there is disagreement about the degree to which women and men use distinctive forms of speech and gesture. Without going into the particulars in great detail, I am taken by O'Barr's argument that what had formerly been identified as "women's language" is, in fact, "powerless language." Relevant to my analysis is O'Barr's finding that "powerless language" is less convincing and less credible to the listener. My reference to "stereotypical patterns of expression among women and men" relies on just that: stereotypes rather than reality. Thorne and Henley enumerate these, and I have applied a few of them in my description of Clinton's performance style simply to illustrate the way in which she, as a woman, must negotiate her performance against a male standard. See Robin Lakoff, *Language and Women's Place* (New York: Octagon Books, 1976); William M. O'Barr, "Speech Styles in the Courtroom," in *Linguistic Evidence: Language, Power, and Strategy in the Courtroom* (New York: Academic Press), 61–91; Susan U. Phillips, "Sex Differences and Language," *Annual Review of Anthropology* 9 (1980), 523–44; Barrie Thorne and Nancy Henley, "Difference and Dominance: An Overview of Language, Gender and Society," in *Language and Sex* (Rowley, Mass.: Newbury Publishers), 5–42.

22. McGuigan and Huck, "The New Queens of Comedy," 58. Shelley Levitt notes, in interviewing "four of the funniest women in America" (Rita Rudner, Beverly Mickins, Carol Suskind, and Carol Leifer), that while all of these comedians tell jokes about the shortcomings of men and the strengths of women, much of their material still focuses on bemoaning the difficulties of finding a "good man." Shelley Levitt, "Take My Boyfriend—Please!" *Mademoiselle* 92, no. 5 (1986), 170–73, 256.

23. Adrienne Rich has noted that "lesbian existence comprises both the breaking of a taboo and the rejection of a compulsory way of life." "Compulsory Heterosexuality and Lesbian Existence," *SIGNS: Journal of Women in Culture and Society* 5, no. 4 (1980), 649. Certainly Clinton stresses both of these characteristics in her humor.
24. Bauman, "Verbal Art as Performance," 28.
25. There are several ways in which the characteristics of Clinton's humor are similar to those of a Texas "madam" described by Robbie Davis Johnson. Both women (1) use a tone of self-confidence that refuses to be self-denigrating, (2) tell profemale jokes that are triggered by men's antifemale sentiment, (3) enjoy bawdy sexual humor, and (4) take pride in their verbal skills. See Robbie Davis Johnson, "Folklore and Women: A Social Interactional Analysis of the Folklore of a Texas Madam," *Journal of American Folklore* 86 (1973), 215.
26. For a complete list of what have been termed "women's language" traits, see Lakoff, *Language and Women's Place.*
27. Bauman, "Verbal Art as Performance," 29.
28. Abby Stein, quoted in Julia Klein, "The New Stand-Up Comics: Can You Be a Funny Woman without Making Fun of Women?" *Ms.,* October 1984, 124.
29. I have recently heard that Clinton has begun to perform before more mainstream, mixed-gender audiences. Her material will undoubtedly reflect this change.
30. Bauman, "Verbal Art as Performance," 31.
31. Ibid., 30.
32. Ibid., 11.
33. Collier and Beckett, *Spare Ribs,* 1.
34. McGuigan and Huck note that, in contrast to the routines of those who are more established in the professional comedy circuit, the material of many up-and-coming women comedians no longer focuses on self-deprecation. "The New Queens of Comedy," 58.
35. In comparing the recordings of comedy routines by four popular male comics (George Carlin, Robert Klein, Bill Cosby, and David Steinberg) and four female comics (Totie Fields, Moms Mabley, Phyllis Diller, and Lily Tomlin), Levine found that the women used self-deprecatory humor 63 percent of the time,

while the male comics only did so in 12 percent of their material. See Levine, "The Feminine Routine," 174.

36. Israel, "Joan Rivers," 110.
37. Phyllis Diller, quoted in Collier and Beckett, *Spare Ribs,* 3.
38. Susan Kalcik, "Like Anne's Gynecologist or the Time I Was Almost Raped: Personal Narratives in Women's Rap Groups, *Journal of American Folklore* 88, no. 347 (1975), 5.
39. Coser, "Laughter among Colleagues," 87.
40. Cantor reported that controlled statistical studies in both 1970 and 1975 revealed it was still funnier to see a woman, rather than a man, as the butt of a joke. Her analysis provided evidence that in 1975 the antifemale bias still existed, and that it was the sex of the victim in the joke—rather than the sex of the dominator—that determined the effect. That is, more people believed it was funnier to watch a female be ridiculed than a male, whether the dominating agent was a male or a female and whether the subject (the reader of the joke) was a male or a female. For both males and females, the condition associated with the highest degree of humor was that of the male dominating the female. Joanne R. Cantor, "What Is Funny to Whom?: The Role of Gender," *Journal of Communication* 26, no. 3 (1976), 164–72. Neitz, however, argues that when a joke is a sexual joke, Cantor's generalizations appear to be less true. While several surveys reported that men enjoy sexual jokes more than women do, a study by Hassett and Houlihan qualified this. They found that men enjoyed sexual humor that was judged sexist by both men and women, but that they did not enjoy sexual humor when the status of men was threatened. In contrast, women did not enjoy misogynist sexual humor, but did enjoy sexual humor that was not sexist. Neitz, "Humor, Hierarchy," 219, citing J. Hassett and J. Houlihan, "Different Jokes for Different Folks," *Psychology Today* 12, no. 8 (1979), 64–71.
41. Rayna Green, "Magnolias Grow in Dirt," *Southern Folklore* 4, no. 4 (1977), 32–33.
42. Israel, "Joan Rivers and How She Got That Way," 114.
43. Joan Rivers, quoted in ibid., 110.
44. Ibid. in 1987, Clinton closed her act with a "channeling" routine in which she pretended to be going into a trance in order to become the mouthpiece for a forty-thousand-year-old lesbian

named Mona. Mona—a self-described activist, tether ball champion, and bull dyke—took impromptu questions from the audience. This was the only attempt Clinton made during her Austin performances to use humorous personas or characters, and, in my estimation, it was not terribly effective.

45. Joan Rivers, quoted in Collier and Beckett, *Spare Ribs,* 10–11.

46. Lily Tomlin, quoted in Gloria Kaufman and Mary Kay Blakely, "Clicking," in *Pulling Our Own String: Feminist Humor and Satire,* ed. Gloria Kaufman and Mary Kay Blakely (Bloomington: Indiana University Press, 1980), 66.

47. Lily Tomlin, quoted in Diane Judge, "Talking with Lily Tomlin," *Redbook,* January 1981, 16.

48. Susan Dworkin, "Roseanne Barr: The Disgruntled Housewife as Stand-up Comedian," *Ms.,* July–August 1987, 106.

49. Ibid. Like Clinton's, Barr's humor is often sarcastic and aggressive. Commenting on women's self-deprecating humor, she proclaimed, "Hey, I will not be insulted anymore. I will not hate myself anymore. There is no way to beat me, because I am so pissed."

50. In fact, in the fall of 1988, Roseanne Barr first appeared in the leading role of the ABC television sitcom "Roseanne." Apparently television executives believed that her humor would be palatable enough to a mixed-gender audience to risk putting the show in a prime-time slot.

51. Joan Rivers, quoted in Collier and Beckett, *Spare Ribs,* 7. McGuigan and Huck suggest that many of the up-and-coming women stand-up comedians joke not only about sex but also about such topics as parents, cars, and politics. The authors argue that there is no longer anything called "women's comedy," because women comics are not just joking about feminine hygiene and blind dates anymore. They cite the example of Sandra Bernhard, who played in comedy clubs for eight years before she was offered a costarring role in the film *The King of Comedy,* and who asserts: "Both men and women can relate to both the man and woman in me." McGuigan and Huck, "The New Queens of Comedy," 58–59.

52. Mary Kay Blakely, "Kate Clinton on the Feminist Comedy Circuit," *Ms.,* October 1984, 128.

53. Carol Mitchell, "The Sexual Perspective in the Appreciation and Interpretation of Jokes," *Western Folklore* 36 (1977), 305.
54. Thorne and Henley, "Difference and Dominance," 12.
55. Carol Mitchell, "Hostility and Aggression toward Males in Female Joke Telling," *Frontiers* 3, no. 3 (1978), 21.
56. Joan Rivers, quoted in Collier and Beckett, *Spare Ribs,* 10.
57. Neitz notes that "cohesion is also a result in situations in which a witty remark is ostensibly directed against a target but actually is intended to reaffirm the collectivity and the values held in common." Neitz, *Humor, Hierarchy,* 215). See also Stanley H. Brandes, *Metaphors of Masculinity: Sex and Status in Andalusian Folklore* (Philadelphia: University of Pennsylvania Press, 1980), 87–97; and Apte, *Humor and Laughter,* for insights on the use of humor in order to promote shared group identity.
58. Coser, "Laughter among Colleagues," 90.
59. In his comparative study of the anthropology of humor, Apte notes that common topics for humor in all-women gatherings include "men's physical appearance, their social behavior, their idiosyncrasies, their sexuality, their status-seeking activities, and their religious rites. These characteristics are generally presented in an exaggerated and mocking fashion." Apte, *Humor and Laughter,* 76. Certainly Clinton makes light of all of these topics, although a great deal of her material focuses on women's existence apart from men, especially with the lesbian community.
60. In her observations about joke telling among the women at a brothel, Johnson (in "Folklore and Women") notes that there are two types of jokes "the girls" especially like to tell: antimale jokes and antireligious jokes. Clinton shares this passion.
61. For an interesting comparison, see Apte, *Humor and Laughter,* 78, for a description of how Kwakiutl women mock the religious ceremonies of men in their tribe.
62. Mitchell notes that the female college students she surveyed expressed their appreciation for "gross jokes" in which men were made to appear disgusting. This parallels Clinton's attempts to denigrate men in her material. Mitchell, "Hostility and Aggression," 317.
63. Kaufman and Pabis contend that feminist humor is more "pick-up" than it is "put-down" humor, while mainstream or

nonfeminist humor is "attack humor," built on and continuing to build negative stereotypes. They argue that feminist humor does not attack people, although it may attack ideas. Gloria Kaufman and Madeleine Pabis, "The Politics of Humor: A Feminist View," videotape produced and directed by Gloria Kaufman. This simply does not hold true of Kate Clinton, who makes women laugh by pointing out the absurdity of particular men (often public figures) and of men in general.

64. Mitchell, "The Sexual Perspective," 306.
65. In much the same way, but in more private settings, the older Southern women in Green's study used "bawdy tales [to] debunk and defy rules." Green, "Magnolias Grow in Dirt," 33.
66. Joan Rivers, quoted in Collier and Beckett, *Spare Ribs,* 8.
67. Clinton, in performing her material as though she were close friends with the women in the audience, contradicts Legman's assertion that sexual jokes are actually "a disguised aggression or verbal assault directed against the listener, who is always really the butt." Gershon Legman, *Rationale of the Dirty Joke: An Analysis of Sexual Humor* (New York: Breaking Point, 1975), 20.
68. Kaufman and Pabis note that in her stand-up comedy Whoopi Goldberg also focuses on controversial political issues, including race relations and the exploitation of Third World Countries by the United States. Kaufman and Pablis, "The Politics of Humor".
69. See Maria Weigle, "Women as Verbal Artists," *Frontiers* 3, no. 3 (1978), 5–7, for her discussion of the prevalence of these tensions in women's verbal art.
70. Kaufman, "Introduction," 13.
71. Coser, "Laughter among Colleagues," 82.
72. Kate Clinton, "Making Waves!" recording, Wyscrack Records, 1984.
73. Coser, "Laughter among Colleagues," 83.
74. Kaufman and Pabis, "The Politics of Humor."
75. Green, "Magnolias Grow in Dirt," 33.
76. Emerson (1969) discusses the negotiation of humor usage as a means of providing a useful channel for covert communication on taboo topics. She argues that normal social rules about proper subjects for discussion can be suspended through negotia-

tion between the joke teller and the audience: "When parties succeed in negotiating such agreements, they establish a presumption of trust. Not only can they trust each other in routine matters, but they share complicity for rule violations which potentially can be extended. Thus, the cotnradictory pressures of social settings may encourage the formation of subgroups where an independent culture, subversive to the general culture, flourishes." John P. Emerson, "Negotiating the Serious Import of Humor," *Sociometry* 32, no. 2 (1969), 180.

77. Coser, "Laughter among Colleagues," 86.
78. Bauman, "Verbal Art as Performance," 34–35.
79. Ibid., 22.
80. Mitchell, "Hostility and Aggression," 20. Neitz, on the other hand, notes that the jokes told among a group of radical feminists were more overtly hostile, and the mention of castration more direct, than in the data reported by Mitchell. She found that these more radical women refused to participate in anti-woman jokes when told by outsiders. Neitz, "Humor, Hierarchy," 221. I recognize the problems inherent in trying to make generalizations about the functions of humor in different contexts. Mitchell's research only involved joke telling among college students in an academic setting, whereas Clinton's humor occurs in the formal setting of a professional stand-up comedy routine. I compare the two only in the hopes of identifying performance "ground rules" that appear to be operative for Clinton and may be unusual to the ways in which women conventionally use humor.
81. Coser's study involved both female and male staff of a mental hospital. Her findings about how those with prestige use humor differently from those without prestige have interesting correlations to O'Barr's theory of "powerful" and "powerless language."
82. Coser, "Laughter among Colleagues," 95. Structuralist-functionalist explanations of humor abound, although they do not adequately account for the subversive intent of Clinton's comedy. Douglas, for example, acknowledges the way that humor can point the arbitrary nature of social norms, but she believes that humor is ultimately "frivolous in that it produces no real alternative, only an exhilarating sense of freedom from form in general." Douglas, "The Social Control of Cognition," 365.

Similarly, Brandes argues that "political humor dissipates energy or deflects it away from direct political action." Stanley H. Brandes, "Peaceful Protest: Spanish Political Humor in a Time of Crisis," *Western Folklore* 346. However, Babcock-Abrahams notes that one of the pitfalls of the conventional structural-functionalist approach is that it tends toward teleological interpretations. Symbolic forms "are analyzed in terms of the function they play in maintaining the social system—as mechanisms of social control in the form of 'ritualized rebellion,' 'licensed aggression,' or some other steam valve." Barbara Babcock-Abrahams, "A Tolerated Margin of Mess: The Trickster and His Tales Reconsidered," *Journal of the Folklore Institute* 11, no. 3 (1975), 157. Apte observes that functional explanations focus on humor as the release of tension, avoidance of conflict, enforcement of social control, and thereby the reinforcement of social harmony and stability. This approach emphasizes the eventual reduction of hostility and the maintenance of social cohesion. Apte notes, however, that structural-functionalist assertions of this type are educated guesses at best. Because many functionalist explanations are merely hypotheses that cannot be tested, it is difficult to demonstrate that joking actually serves these functions. He concludes that humor can function either as a lubricant to smooth social interactions or as a way of expressing hostility and aggression. Apte, *Humor and Laughter,* 60–62, 261.

83. Coser, "Laughter among Colleagues," 84.
84. Ibid., 87.
85. Ibid., 85.
86. Compare this with Phyllis Diller's claim: "There's no reality whatsoever in my act. It's all for fun." Collier and Beckett, *Spare Ribs,* 4.
87. Kate Clinton, quoted in Kaufman and Pabis, "The Politics of Humor."

About the Contributors

Patricia Williams Alley is Professor and Chair of American Studies at Bellevue Community College in Seattle, where she teaches American studies and English and participates in learning communities throughout the state. She began work on women's humor with grants from the National Endowment for the Humanities and has several presentations and publications on the subject. Her current research project is early-twentieth century postcards.

Zita Z. Dresner is Associate Professor of English at the University of D.C., Washington, D.C., where she teaches courses in literature. She has contributed many articles on women and humor, the subject of her doctoral dissertation, to periodicals such as *Studies in American Humor* and *American Humor Newsletter.* She coedited, with Nancy Walker, *Redressing the Balance: American Women's Humor from the Colonies to the 1980s* (1988).

Judy Little is Professor of English at Southern Illinois University at Carbondale, where she teaches courses on women's fiction and feminist theory. Her published work includes *Comedy and The Woman Writer: Woolf, Spark, and Feminism* (1983).

Linda Pershing is a doctoral candidate in folklore/anthropology at the University of Texas at Austin. Her principle areas of interest are feminist folklore theory, gender studies, and material culture. A recipient of an AAUW dissertation fellowship and a Women's Studies Research Grant from the Woodrow Wilson National Fellowship Foundation, she is currently working on her dissertation on the Peace Ribbon that was tied around the Pentagon in 1985 and the ways in which women's needlework became a vehicle for social and political critique for particpants in the project.

Alice Sheppard is Assistant Professor of Psychology at Bloomsburg University, Bloomsburg, Pennsylvania, where she teaches courses on women's psychology. Her published essays on women and humor have appeared in the *Psychology of Women Quarterly* and the *Journal of American Culture.*

June Sochen is Professor of History and Women's Studies at Northeastern Illinois University in Chicago, where she teaches U.S. women's history and intellectual and cultural history. Among her publications are *Herstory: A Woman's Record of the Past* (1974, 1981), *Enduring Values: Women in Popular Culture* (1987), and *Cafeteria America: New Identities in Contemporary Life* (1988).

Nancy Walker is Professor of English at Vanderbilt University, Nashville, where she teaches courses on women and literature and humor. Among her publications are *Redressing the Balance: American Women's Humor from the Colonies to the 1980s* and *A Very Serious Thing: Women's Humor and American Culture.*

Elsie A. Williams is Assistant Professor of English at the University of D.C., where she teaches courses in literature and writing. She has published poetry in *Obsidian,* an essay on Richard Pryor in *The Interdisciplinary Newsletter of Satire and Humor,* and an essay on Richard Wright in *Papers in the Social Sciences.* She is currently writing her dissertation on Moms Mabley.

Books in the Humor in Life and Letters Series

The Contemporary American Comic Epic: The Novels of Barth, Pynchon, Gaddis, and Kesey, by Elaine B. Safer, 1988

The Mocking of the President: A History of Campaign Humor from Ike to Ronnie, by Gerald Gardner, 1988

Circus of the Mind in Motion: Postmodernism and the Comic Vision, by Lance Olsen, 1990

Horsing Around: Contemporary Cowboy Humor, edited by Lawrence Clayton and Kenneth Davis, 1991

Never Try to Teach a Pig to Sing: Still More Urban Folklore from the Paperwork Empire, by Alan Dundes and Carl R. Pagter, 1991

Women's Comic Visions, edited by June Sochen, 1991